Diverse Nations

U.S. History in International Perspective

Editors: Peter N. Stearns and Thomas W. Zeiler

NOW AVAILABLE

Revolutions in Sorrow: The American Experience of Death in Global Perspective, by Peter N. Stearns
From Alienation to Addiction: Modern American Work in Global Historical Perspective, by Peter N. Stearns
Diverse Nations: Explorations in the History of Racial and Ethnic Pluralism, by George M. Fredrickson

FORTHCOMING

Comparing American Slavery: The U.S. "Peculiar Institution" in International Perspective, by Enrico Dal Lago
A History of American Trade in International Perspective, 1890s to the Present, Francine McKenzie

Diverse Nations

Explorations in the History of
Racial and Ethnic Pluralism

George M. Fredrickson

Paradigm Publishers
Boulder • London

Contents

Series Preface

U.S. History in International Perspective

This series offers a new approach to key topics in American history by connecting them with developments in other parts of the world and with larger global processes. Its goal is to present national patterns in mutual interaction with wider trends.

The United States has functioned in an international context throughout its history. It was shaped by people who came from other countries. It drew political and cultural inspiration from other places as well. Soon, the nation began to contribute a variety of influences to other parts of the world, from new trade patterns to the impact of successful political institutions.

It is increasingly clear, however, that the field of U.S. history has not usually captured this perspective. National developments have been treated as significant but relatively isolated events. Distinctive American characteristics—sometimes systematized into a larger pattern called American exceptionalism—have been assumed but not tested through real comparison. Even the nation's growing role in world affairs has sometimes taken a backseat to domestic concerns. This kind of narrowness is inaccurate and unnecessary; it feeds a parochialism that is out of keeping with the global presence of the United States. A nation cannot be understood without placement in the perspective of other nations and transnational factors.

At a time when international developments play an increasing and incontestable role in any nation's affairs, the need for a new approach to national history becomes inescapable. This certainly applies to the United States. Calls for "internationalizing" the U.S. history survey reflect this realization. The calls are welcome, but we need to translate them into accessible treatments of key topics in U.S. history—from obvious diplomatic and military initiatives to less obvious themes that in fact involve global interactions as well, themes that go deeply into the nation's social and cultural experience.

The project of internationalizing American history involves drawing a variety of connections. This series will compare American developments to patterns elsewhere to see what is really distinctive, and why, and what is more widely shared. Influences from other places, from technological innovations to human rights standards, factor in as well. The U.S. impact on other parts of the world, whether in the form of new work systems, consumer culture, or outright military intervention, constitutes a third kind of interconnection.

The result—and the central goal of this series—is to see American history in a revealing new light, as part of a network of global interactions. Wider world history gains from this approach as well, as comparisons are sharpened by the active inclusion of the United States, and American influences and involvements are probed more carefully.

Overall, a global window on the domestic interiors of U.S. history complicates conventional understandings, challenges established analyses, and brings fresh insights. A nation inextricably bound up with developments in every part of the world, shaping much of contemporary world history as well, demands a global framework. This series, as it explores a variety of topics and vantage points, aims to fill this need.

Peter N. Stearns, George Mason University
Thomas W. Zeiler, University of Colorado, Boulder

INTRODUCTION

The fifteen essays in this volume were all written during the last ten years or so and published in scholarly journals, symposium books, and especially the *New York Review of Books*, in which seven of them first appeared. They have been very lightly revised or edited. My basic views have not changed during the past decade. In addition to correcting a small number of errors or clarifying a few imprecise statements, I have referred to relevant events or developments that occurred after the original text was written, thereby making an effort to update the discussion. Also, some bits of information came to my attention after an essay was published that I was able to use to strengthen or clarify one of my points.

The book is divided into three parts. The first—"Perspectives on Ethnoracial Diversity in the United States"—attempts to take a broad view of the subject. In the initial essay, presented originally as a paper to a conference of social scientists concerned with cultural differences and conflicts, I sought to establish a typology of American ethnic relations as they developed historically. The four models I identified were "ethnic hierarchy," "one-way assimilation," "cultural pluralism," and "group separatism." I was particularly interested in distinguishing between the last two types, which are often lumped together under the rubric of "multiculturalism." I have long argued that there is a "soft" and benign version of multiculturalism, which offers a right to be different but also unifies groups around common democratic and egalitarian values, and a "hard," potentially harmful type that puts up walls that prevent communities from interacting freely in ways that may lead to mutual enrichment or cross-fertilization.

Chapter 2 was originally my contribution to a symposium on "Racism and Public Policy" that was sponsored by the United Nations Research Institute for Social Development as part of the program at the World Conference Against Racism, Racial Discrimination and Related Intolerance that was held in Durban, South Africa, in September 2001. My paper and the subsequent essay were devoted mostly to tracing the history of the African-American struggle for equality and citizenship, with some attention devoted to denial of naturalization to Asians, leading ultimately to their total exclusion. But I end the piece by making some comparisons between the American case and the relationship between race and citizenship in the histories of France and Germany.

Chapter 3 was my presidential address to the annual meeting of the Organization of American Historians in 1998, as published later that same year in the *Journal of American History*. "America's Diversity in Comparative Perspective" attempts to shed new light on American pluralism by comparing it or contrasting it to the situation in several other countries—Canada, Great Britain, the Netherlands, Germany, and France. The cultural diversity created by immigration from outside the West has created some analogous debates between proponents of assimilation and those advocating some form of multiculturalism. But the United States, more than most other countries, is committed to a set of values that puts a premium on material success through individual effort. To the considerable extent that immigrants have been able to get ahead and realize a share of this "American dream," they have probably been less tempted than immigrants to more economically stratified societies to celebrate and accentuate their cultural differences from the national majority. What makes America's diversity unique when compared to the other industrialized nations adjusting to new immigrations and debating multiculturalism is the color line resulting from the involuntary immigration from Africa between the seventeenth and the early nineteenth century that entrenched slavery until the Civil War and left behind a readily identifiable minority that was the object of intense prejudice, disparagement, and discrimination. What I call "the caste-like character of black status," especially before 1965, has not been replicated by the situation of any group in the domestic societies of any of the countries I invoked for limited comparative purposes. Even today, despite the undeniable gain in black rights and legal status since the 1960s, blacks remain, by most measures, the most disadvantaged and isolated ethnoracial group in American society.

The last chapter in Part One is from *The New York Review of Books* and is a tribute to John Higham, the historian who was, until his death in 2003 (a little more than a year after this essay appeared), our foremost interpreter of anti-immigrant movements and sentiments. His 1955 book, *Strangers in the Land: Patterns of American Nativism, 1860–1925*, remains the classic study of its subject. In some of his last writings he subjected the concept of multiculturalism to a searching critique. Rejecting the implication of group solidarity and defensiveness that the term often conveys, he advanced instead the concept of "pluralistic integration." Ethnic groups in this view have a core of loyalists who devote themselves to preserving the group's cultural identity and distinctiveness. But they also have a periphery composed of people who, while still acknowledging an ethnic identity, are willing to interact with, learn from, and even intermarry with members of other ethnoracial groups. I end the essay with the observation that the interaction and self-identification of diverse students on California campuses might be seen as "pluralistic integration" in action.

Part Two is a series of review essays, all but one of which appeared originally in *The New York Review of Books*. They all concern the historiography of slavery and black-white relations in the United States, The first (Chapter 5—"The Skeleton in the Closet") is ostensibly concerned with three books published around the year 2000. But I use the occasion to put these books in context by summarizing and analyzing the historiography of slavery as it developed over the last half of the twentieth century. The issue that I found most intriguing is the question of the essential character of the master-slave relationship. To what extent was it a matter of brute force in the service of economic exploitation and to what extent was it a quasi-familial or "paternalistic" relationship? Were the claims of many masters that they treated their slaves as children to be protected, rather than work animals to be driven, merely propaganda directed at abolitionists and others who charged them with cruelty and inhumanity? Or did it reflect an ethic of responsibility for the health and welfare of their charges? In my view the physical reality of slave life was nasty and brutal, but the masters could not admit this to themselves without accepting an immense burden of guilt, and thus they had to devise the self-justifying ideology of paternalism as a defense mechanism.

The next essay juxtaposes recent books by the two most prominent living historians of slavery and gives me the license to summarize some of their earlier work and contrast their points of view. Eugene Genovese, coauthor with his wife Elizabeth Fox-Genovese of the 2005 book *The Mind of the Master Class*, has long been the principal exponent of the "paternalist" model of the master-slave relationship. He began as a Marxist contending that paternalism was the ideology of a ruling class seeking—and generally obtaining—"cultural hegemony" over a servile class. But his latest book shows that he has evolved into a cultural conservative who endorses paternalist hierarchy, if not in the specifically racist form that it took in the Old South, then as it has existed in some traditional premodern societies under strong religious influence. David Brion Davis, author of *Inhuman Bondage: The Rise and Fall of Slavery in the New World* (published in 2006), has long devoted himself to the history of thought about slavery in Great Britain as well as the United States. As he now looks more broadly at the economic, social, and political aspects of slavery, he emphasizes, much more than the Genoveses do, the racism that he sees as the principal justification for New World slavery and the main source of the cruelty and dehumanization that it entailed. Davis's humanitarian liberalism contrasts sharply with the backward-looking conservatism of the Genoveses.

Chapter 7—"America's Original Sin"—is a review essay on three important books about slavery that came out between 2000 and 2005. In one of them Ira Berlin shows how slaves made a life for themselves through their own efforts rather than because of the benevolence of the masters. In another, Don E. Fehrenbacher masterfully demonstrates "the full extent of the slaveholder's dominance over the federal government" between 1789 and 1860. Chapter 8—"The Long Trek to Freedom"—takes the story back to the eighteenth century and also discusses books that have a transatlantic dimension. More concerned with opposition to slavery than with the institution itself, they include an account of Lord Mansfield's legal decision of 1772 that in effect banned slavery in England, the biography of a Virginia planter who in 1791 made the extraordinary and unprecedented decision to free all 452 of his slaves, and a history of the "underground railroad" of the antebellum period that conducted slaves from captivity in the South to freedom in the North or Canada. On the basis of these three books one would have to conclude that it was not so much Enlightenment liberalism as religious piety and zealotry that sustained the most effective antislavery action. The prominent role of Quakers in the origins of British and American antislavery movements and in the Underground Railroad is evidence of the significance of religious commitments.

Chapter 9—"Redcoat Liberation"—is not another effort to grapple with the central issues in the history of slavery and antislavery. Rather it concerns a fascinating and little-known sidelight of the American Revolution that involved blacks. When the British left their former colonies after the Revolution, they took with them nine thousand escaped slaves who had come under their protection. Two of the books under review describe in some detail what happened to them. The third touches on this exodus as part of a broader study of the role of African Americans in the Revolution. To make a long story short, some went to Nova Scotia, some to England where they mingled with the urban poor, and most from both groups ended up in Sierra Leone in a colony established by British philanthropists as a haven for freed slaves. A few even turned up in Australia as part of the population of convicts transported there. One issue that especially interests me in this chapter is the question of whether, in the late eighteenth century, British attitudes toward slavery and blacks were more benevolent than those of the Americans. One might assume that they were, given the fact that the British freed some slaves during the conflict and the Americans did not. But after the Revolution, in the 1780s and 1790s, there was some serious questioning of slavery in the United States and hopeful expectations of its eventual abolition.

Chapter 10—"Black Hearts and Monsters of the Mind"—is a review essay from 2004 for a new scholarly journal, *Modern Intellectual History*, on the intellectual and cultural history of race in the antebellum period. The three books under consideration cover race theory, black protest thought, and the emergence toward the end of the period of a radical abolitionism that, unlike the hitherto dominant pacifist type, countenanced the use of force against the "peculiar institution." To quote the essay directly, "The three books under review, two of them especially, seek to obliterate the color line in the history of racial thought and attitudes [that has prevailed in previous studies] by presenting blacks and whites ... as engaged in a common interactive discourse." This strikes me as a great step forward.

The last chapter in Part Two brings the story of race in America up to the present. It is a review of a single book—Ira Katznelson's *When Affirmative Action Was White.* The author argues that affirmative action is justified not so much because of disadvantages passed down from the era of slavery and segregation, but because of the more recent record of ostensibly color-blind governmental policies that favored whites economically at the expense of blacks, such as the exclusion of farm laborers and domestic servants from coverage under the New Deal legislation establishing social security and the rights of organized labor. In other words, people who are still alive, or their immediate heirs, were cheated by a welfare state that was de facto racist, and they deserve to be compensated for what they have lost in a process that has increased the economic gap between the races. This is an ingenious argument and deserves to be taken seriously. But it struck me that Katznelson's version of affirmative action is not really race specific—some whites have been deprived of the same government benefits that were denied to larger numbers of blacks. Why not just advocate social policies aimed at the redistribution of wealth and the elimination of poverty regardless of the color of the disadvantaged? In addition to summarizing and evaluating Katznelson's thesis, this chapter provides me with an opportunity to look more generally at the history of affirmative action and the issues that it raises.

Part Three moves away from a preoccupation with race and ethnicity in the United States and goes beyond simply seeking comparative perspectives on the American experience. It moves into the realm of cross-national, two- or three-case comparative history, the kind of approach that characterized much of my earlier published work. Such an enterprise requires making a closer and more detailed examination of ethnoracial diversity in other countries. The ones in which I have developed the greatest interest are South Africa and France. For purposes of a three-way comparison with the United States and South Africa, I have also brought Brazil into the picture. The first essay in Part Three—Chapter 12 on "Race and Racism in Historical Perspective"—summarizes the comparative literature on race relations in the United States, South Africa, and Brazil. It first appeared as the introductory chapter of a volume produced under the auspices of the Comparative Human Relations Initiative. This organization, under the able directorship of Lynn Huntley of the Southern Education Fund, sponsored conferences in all three countries, bringing together Brazilian, South African, and American scholars and public intellectuals to compare notes on the relations between blacks and whites in the three societies. It went on to publish a number of reports and books in both English and Portuguese. My contribution to the final volume, *Beyond Racism: Race and Inequality in Brazil, South Africa, and the United States,* summarizes work in a range of disciplines—history, sociology, political science, anthropology, and economics—that compares or makes connections between at least two of the three cases. I pay particular attention to the first systematic comparison of the construction of racial orders in all three nations—political scientist Anthony Marx's *Making Race and Nation,* published in 1998. Marx explains the more rigid color lines that developed historically in the United States and South Africa as a function of efforts to overcome deep political divisions between white ethnic or regional groups. Brazil, lacking schisms comparable to those between North and South in the United States or between English and Afrikaners in South Africa, and therefore not needing to denigrate blacks as a way of mobilizing whites, could afford a more relaxed and fluid pattern of race relations. In my opinion this is part of the story but not all of it. A fuller and richer comparison would need to take into account "the interaction of the state, the economy, and the prevailing hierarchy of sociocultural identities without giving a priori primacy to any of them."

Chapter 13—"Beyond Race? Ideological Color-Blindness in the United States, Brazil, and South Africa"—is mainly concerned with recent efforts in the three countries to move beyond racism or white supremacy in an effort to remove color as a source of invidious distinctions. It was first given as a paper at a conference at Michigan State University in 1999 and then published two years later in a book entitled *Race in 21st Century America.* The main point I make in this essay is the futility of color-blindness as an ideology in instances where race or color continues to function surreptitiously as a source of inequality. The need for some kind of affirmative action or system of reparations, which explicitly acknowledges racial identities, will, in my opinion, be necessary for the foreseeable future in all three countries.

The last two essays demonstrate the recent shift of my main transnational comparative interests from black and white in the United States and South Africa to ethnoracial diversity in the United States and France. One of the reasons I have become so interested in France is that I have a French wife and have spent a good deal of time in that country. But in terms of my scholarly interests, comparison between France and the United States provided the opportunity to go beyond race—in the strict and narrow sense of innate biological capabilities as reflected in physical appearance (normally skin color) that can be socially constructed in a hierarchical fashion—and attempt to deal more directly with cultural ethnicity. France does not have a color line, but it does have diversity and group antagonism based on cultural more than biological differences. The distinction between physical race and cultural ethnicity is not absolute or categorical. Racialized groups have cultural attributes that are assigned to them or that they themselves find central to their identities. Ethnic groups are defined culturally—usually by a language, religion, and set of customs that differentiate them from the majority of the host society. (Ethnics are usually of immigrant origin.) But, like racialized groups, ethnic minorities may be subject to prejudice and discrimination that at times approach racism in their virulence. It might also be recalled that ethnic groups are normally characterized by common ancestry and kinship ties as well as by culture. One can readily join such a group only through intermarriage with one of its members. Ideologically speaking, however, the central difference between color-coded racism and the nativism directed at culturally disparaged minorities is that the latter offers the prospect of assimilation while the former does not. People can change their way of life but not the physical attributes that seem to mark them as permanently different and inferior.

The first of my two essays comparing race and ethnicity in the United States and France—"Diverse Republics: French and American Responses to Racial Pluralism"—was my contribution to a 2005 issue of *Daedalus*, the Journal of the American Academy of Arts and Sciences, that was devoted primarily to articles on race. I take a very broad view of the subject, looking at the racial and ethnic aspects of revolutionary republicanism, slavery in the American South and the French Caribbean colonies, the role of immigration in diversifying the societies, and the effects of geographical expansion and colonialism. I conclude with the special problem created for French republican identity by the large recent influx of North African Muslims. The United States has no precisely similar new immigrant minority. Latinos, especially Mexicans, are a matter of concern, partly because of their language retention. But evidence of English acquisition in the second and third generation is relieving some of this anxiety. Since 9/11 some American Muslims have been victims of harassment or discrimination. But America's history of religious diversity and tolerance, as well as the relatively small size of its domestic Muslim population, has prevented Islamophobia from becoming as intense and widespread as it is in France. But if the Muslims were to become culturally French, or so the argument goes, they would be assimilated and achieve full equality. Can the same be said of America's oldest and most disadvantaged ethnoracial minority—people of remote African descent? Color as such is not a major problem in France. It continues to be one in the United States.

The last chapter—"Mulattoes and *Métis*"—is an essay comparing the historical development of attitudes toward miscegenation in the United States and in France. It was first presented as a paper to a conference on intermarriage at the University of California, Davis, and was later published in the *International Social Science Journal*. In general it concludes that the United States through most of its history has been more consistently and rigorously opposed to race mixture—especially between blacks and whites and particularly in the form of legal intermarriage—than have the French.

The explanation takes us back once again to the centrality of black slavery and white supremacy in American history. If this entire collection of essays has a central preoccupation, it is to draw attention to that fact and increase our understanding of what it means by analyzing the historiography surrounding it, placing it in an international comparative perspective, and making systematic back-and-forth comparisons to race and ethnicity in other nations in search of similarities and differences.

George M. Fredrickson

PART ONE

Perspectives on Ethnoracial Diversity in the United States

CHAPTER 1

Models of American Ethnic Relations: A Historical Perspective

Throughout its history, the United States has been inhabited by a variety of interacting racial or ethnic groups. In addition to the obvious "color line" structuring relationships between dominant whites and lower-status blacks, Indians, and Asians, there have at times been important social distinctions among those of white or European ancestry. Today we think of the differences between white Anglo-Saxon Protestants and Irish, Italian, Polish, and Jewish Americans as purely cultural or religious, but in earlier times these groups were sometimes thought of as "races" or "subraces"—people possessing innate or inborn characteristics and capabilities that affected their fitness for American citizenship. Moreover, differences apparently defined as cultural have sometimes been so reified as to serve as the functional equivalent of physical distinctions. Indians, for example, were viewed by most nineteenth-century missionaries and humanitarians as potentially equal and similar to whites. Their status as noncitizens was not attributed to skin color or physical appearance; it was only their obdurate adherence to "savage ways" that allegedly stood in the way of their possessing equal rights and being fully assimilated. Analogously, conservative opponents of affirmative action and other antiracist policies in the 1990s may provide a "rational" basis for prejudice and discrimination by attributing the disadvantages and alleged shortcomings of African Americans to persistent cultural "pathology" rather than to genetic deficiencies.[1]

It can therefore be misleading to make a sharp distinction between race and ethnicity when considering intergroup relations in American history. As I have argued extensively elsewhere, ethnicity is "racialized" whenever distinctive group characteristics, however defined or explained, are used as the basis for a status hierarchy of groups who are thought to differ in ancestry or descent.[2]

Four basic conceptions of how ethnic or racial groups should relate to each other have been predominant in the history of American thought about group relations—ethnic hierarchy, one-way assimilation, cultural pluralism, and group separatism. This chapter provides a broad outline of the historical career of each of these models of intergroup relations, noting some of the changes in how various groups have defined themselves or been defined by others.

Ethnic Hierarchy

Looking at the entire span of American history, we find that the most influential and durable conception of the relations among those American racial or ethnic groups viewed as significantly dissimilar has been hierarchical. A dominant group—conceiving of itself as comprising society's charter members—has claimed rights and privileges not to be fully shared with outsiders or "others," who have been characterized as unfit or unready for equal rights and full citizenship. The hierarchical model has its deepest roots and most enduring consequences in the conquest of Indians and the enslavement of blacks during the colonial period.[3] But it was also applied in the nineteenth century to Asian immigrants and in a less severe and more open-ended way to European immigrants who differed in culture and religion from old-stock Americans of British origin.[4] The sharpest and most consequential distinction was always between "white" and "nonwhite." The first immigration law passed by Congress in 1790 specified that only white immigrants were eligible for naturalization. This provision would create a crucial difference in the mid-nineteenth century between Chinese "sojourners," who could not become citizens and voters, and Irish immigrants, who could.

Nevertheless, the Irish who fled the potato famine of the 1840s by emigrating to the United States also encountered discrimination. Besides being Catholic and poor, the refugees from the Emerald Isle were Celts rather than Anglo-Saxons, and a racialized discourse, drawing on British precedents, developed as an explanation for Irish inferiority to Americans of English ancestry.[5] The dominant group during the nineteenth and early twentieth centuries was not simply white but also Protestant and Anglo-Saxon. Nevertheless, the Irish were able to use their right to vote and the patronage they received from the Democratic Party to improve their status, an option not open to the Chinese. Hence, they gradually gained the leverage and respectability necessary to win admission to the dominant caste, a process that culminated in Al Smith's nomination for the presidency in 1928 and John F. Kennedy's election in 1960.

The mass immigration of Europeans from Eastern and Southern Europe in the late nineteenth and early twentieth centuries inspired new concerns about the quality of the American stock. In an age of eugenics, scientific racism, and social Darwinism, the notion that northwestern Europeans were innately superior to those from the southern and eastern parts of the continent—to say nothing of those light-skinned people of actual or presumed west Asian origin (such as Jews, Syrians, and Armenians)—gained wide currency. A determined group of nativists, encouraged by the latest racial "science," fought for restrictive immigration policies that discriminated against those who were not of "Nordic" or "Aryan" descent.[6] In the 1920s the immigration laws were changed to reflect these prejudices. Low quotas were established for white people from nations or areas outside of those that had supplied the bulk of the American population before 1890. In the minds of many, true Americans were not merely white but also northern European. In fact, some harbored doubts about the full claim to "whiteness" of swarthy immigrants from southern Italy.

After immigration restriction had relieved ethnic and racial anxieties, the status of the new immigrants gradually improved as a result of their political involvement, their economic and professional achievement, and a decline in the respectability of the kind of scientific racism that had ranked some European groups below others. World War II brought revulsion against the genocidal anti-Semitism and eugenic experiments of the Nazis, dealing a *coup de grâce* to the de facto hierarchy that had placed Anglo-Saxons, Nordics, or Aryans at the apex of American society. All Americans of European origin were now unambiguously white and, for most purposes, ethnically equal to old-stock Americans of Anglo-Saxon, Celtic, and Germanic ancestry. Hierarchy was now based exclusively on color. Paradoxically, it might be argued, the removal of the burden of "otherness" from virtually all whites made more striking and salient than ever the otherness of people of color, especially African Americans.

The civil rights movement of the 1960s was directed primarily at the legalized racial hierarchy of the southern states. The Civil Rights Acts of 1964 and 1965 brought an end to government-enforced racial segregation and the denial of voting rights to blacks in that region. But the legacy of four centuries of white supremacy survives in the disadvantaged social and economic position of blacks and other people of color in the United States. The impoverished, socially deprived, and physically unsafe ghettos, barrios, and Indian reservations of this nation are evidence that ethnic hierarchy in a clearly racialized form persists in practice if not in law.

One-Way Assimilation

Policies aimed at the assimilation of ethnic groups have usually assumed that there is a single and stable American culture of European, and especially

English, origin to which minorities are expected to conform as the price of admission to full and equal participation in the society and polity of the United States.[7] Assimilationist thinking is not racist in the classic sense: it does not deem the out-groups in question to be innately or biologically inferior to the in-group. The professed goal is equality—but on terms that presume the superiority, purity, and unchanging character of the dominant culture. Little or nothing in the cultures of the groups being invited to join the America mainstream is presumed worthy of preserving. When carried to its logical conclusion, the assimilationist project demands what its critics have described—especially in reference to the coercive efforts to "civilize" Native Americans—as "cultural genocide."

Estimates of group potential and the resulting decisions as to which groups are eligible for assimilation have varied in response to changing definitions of race. If an ethnic group is definitely racialized, the door is closed because its members are thought to possess ineradicable traits (biologically or culturally determined) that make them unfit for inclusion. At times there have been serious disagreements within the dominant group about the eligibility of particular minorities for initiation into the American club.

Although one-way assimilationism was mainly a twentieth-century ideology, it was anticipated in strains of nineteenth-century thinking about Irish immigrants, Native Americans, and even blacks. Radical white abolitionists and even some black antislavery activists argued that prejudice against African Americans was purely and simply a result of their peculiarly degraded and disadvantaged circumstances and that emancipation from slavery would make skin color irrelevant and open the way to their full equality and social acceptability.[8] These abolitionists had little or no conception that there was a rich and distinctive black culture that could become the source of a positive group identity, and that African modes of thought and behavior had been adapted to the challenge of surviving under slavery.

If the hope of fully assimilating blacks into a color-blind society was held by only a small minority of whites, a majority probably supposed that the Irish immigrants of the 1840s and 1850s could become full-fledged Americans, if they chose to do so, simply by changing their behavior and beliefs. The doctrine of the innate inferiority of Celts to Anglo-Saxons was not even shared by all of the nativists who sought to slow down the process of Irish naturalization.[9] A more serious problem for many of them was the fervent Catholicism of the Irish; Anglo-Protestant missionaries hoped to convert them en masse. The defenders of unrestricted Irish immigration came mostly from the ranks of the Democratic Party, which relied heavily on Irish votes. Among them were strong believers in religious toleration and a high wall of separation between church and state. They saw religious diversity as no obstacle to the full and rapid Americanization of all white-skinned immigrants.

The most sustained and serious nineteenth-century effort to assimilate people who differed both culturally and phenotypically from the majority was aimed at American Indians. Frontier settlers, military men who fought Indians, and many other whites had no doubts that Indians were members of an inherently inferior race that was probably doomed to total extinction as a result of the conquest of the West. Their views were graphically expressed by General Philip Sheridan when he opined that "the only good Indian is a dead Indian." But an influential group of eastern philanthropists, humanitarian reformers, and government officials thought of the Indians as having been "noble savages" whose innate capacities were not inferior to those of whites. Thomas Jefferson, who had a much dimmer view of black potentialities, was one of the first to voice this opinion.[10] For these ethnocentric humanitarians, the "Indian problem" was primarily cultural rather than racial, and its solution lay in civilizing the "savages" rather than exterminating them. Late in the century, the assimilationists adopted policies designed to force Indians to conform to Euro-American cultural norms; these included breaking up communally held reservations into privately owned family farms and sending Indian children to boarding schools where they were forbidden to speak their own languages and made to dress, cut their hair, and in every possible way act and look like white people. The policy was a colossal failure; most Native Americans refused to abandon key aspects of their traditional cultures, and venal whites took advantage of the land reforms to strip Indians of much of their remaining patrimony.[11]

In the early twentieth century, the one-way assimilation model was applied to the southern and eastern European immigrants who had arrived in massive numbers before the discriminatory quota system of the 1920s was implemented. Although some nativists called for their exclusion on the grounds of their innate deficiencies, other champions of Anglo-American cultural homogeneity hoped to assimilate those who had already arrived through education and indoctrination. The massive "Americanization" campaigns of the period just prior to World War I produced the concept of America as a "melting pot" in which cultural differences would be obliterated. The metaphor might have suggested that a new mixture would result—and occasionally it did have this meaning—but a more prevalent interpretation was that non-Anglo-American cultural traits and inclinations would simply disappear, making the final brew identical to the original one.[12]

Before the 1940s, people of color, and especially African Americans, were generally deemed ineligible for assimilation because of their innate inferiority to white ethnics, who were now thought capable of being culturally reborn as Anglo-Americans. Such factors as the war-inspired reaction against scientific racism and the gain in black political power resulting from mass migration from the South (where blacks could not vote) to the urban North (where the franchise was again open to them) led to a significant reconsideration of the social position of African Americans and threw a spotlight on the flagrant denial in the southern states of the basic constitutional rights of African Americans. The struggle for black civil rights that emerged in the 1950s and came to fruition in the early 1960s was premised on a conviction that white supremacist laws and policies violated an egalitarian "American Creed"—as Gunnar Myrdal had argued in his influential wartime study, *An American Dilemma*.[13] The war against Jim Crow was fought under the banner of "integration," which, in the minds of white liberals at least, generally meant one-way assimilation. Blacks, deemed by Myrdal and others as having no culture worth saving, would achieve equal status by becoming just like white Americans in every respect except pigmentation.

When it became clear that the civil rights legislation of the 1960s had failed to improve significantly the social and economic position of blacks in the urban ghettos of the North, large numbers of African Americans rejected the integrationist ideal on the grounds that it had been not only a false promise but an insult to the culture of African Americans for ignoring or devaluing their distinctive experience as a people. The new emphasis on "black power" and "black consciousness" conveyed to those whites who were listening that integration had to mean something other than one-way assimilation to white middle-class norms if it was to be a solution to the problem of racial inequality in America.[14]

It should be obvious by now that the one-way assimilation model has not proved to be a viable or generally acceptable way of adjusting group differences in American society. It is based on an ethnocentric ideal of cultural homogeneity that has been rejected by Indians, blacks, Asians, Mexican Americans, and even many white ethnics. It reifies and privileges one cultural strain in what is in fact a multicultural society. It should be possible to advocate the incorporation of all ethnic or racial groups into a common civic society without requiring the sacrifice of cultural distinctiveness and diversity.

Cultural Pluralism

Unlike assimilationists, cultural pluralists celebrate differences among groups rather than seeking to obliterate them. They argue that cultural diversity is a healthy and normal condition that does not preclude equal rights and the mutual understandings about civic responsibilities needed to sustain a democratic nation-state. This model for American ethnic relations is a twentieth-century invention that would have been virtually inconceivable at an earlier time. The eighteenth and nineteenth centuries lacked the essential concept of the relativity of cultures. The model of cultural development during this period was evolutionary, progressive, and universalistic. People were either civilized or they were not. Humankind was seen as evolving from a state of "savagery" to "barbarism" to "civilization," and all cultures at a particular level were similar in every way that mattered. What differentiated nations and ethnic groups was their ranking on the scale of social evolution. Modern Western civilization stood at the apex of this universal historical process. Even nineteenth-century black nationalists accepted the notion that there were universal standards of civilization to which people of African descent should aspire. They differed from white supremacists in believing that blacks had the natural capability to reach the same heights as Caucasians if they were given a chance.[15]

The concept of cultural pluralism drew on the new cultural anthropology of the early twentieth century, as pioneered by Franz Boas. Boas and his disciples attempted to look at each culture they studied on its own terms and as an integrated whole. They rejected theories of social evolution that ranked cultures in relation to a universalist conception of "civilization." But relativistic cultural anthropologists were not necessarily cultural pluralists in their attitude toward group relations within American society. Since they generally believed that a given society or community functioned best with a single, integrated culture, they could favor greater autonomy for Indians on reservations but also call for the full assimilation of new immigrants or even African Americans. Boas himself was an early supporter of the National Association for the Advancement of Colored People (NAACP) and a pioneering advocate of what would later be called racial integration.

An effort to use the new concept of culture to validate ethnic diversity within the United States arose from the negative reaction of some intellectuals to the campaign to "Americanize" the new immigrants from Eastern and Southern Europe in the period just before and after World War I. The inventors of cultural pluralism were cosmopolitan critics of American provincialism or representatives of immigrant communities, especially Jews, who valued their cultural distinctiveness and did not want to be melted down in an Americanizing crucible. The Greenwich Village intellectual Randolph Bourne described his ideal as a "transnational America" in which various ethnic cultures would interact in a tolerant atmosphere to create an enriching variety of ideas, values, and lifestyles.[16] The Jewish philosopher Horace Kallen, who coined the phrase "cultural pluralism," compared the result to a symphony, with each immigrant group represented as a section of the orchestra.[17] From a different perspective, W. E. B. Du Bois celebrated a distinctive black culture rooted in the African and slave experiences and heralded its unacknowledged contributions to American culture in general.[18] But the dominant version advocated by Kallen and Bourne stopped, for all practical purposes, at the color line. Its focus was on making America safe for a variety of European cultures. As a Zionist, Kallen was especially concerned with the preservation of Jewish distinctiveness and identity.

Since it was mainly the viewpoint of ethnic intellectuals who *resisted* the assimilationism of the melting pot, cultural pluralism was a minority persuasion in the twenties, thirties, and forties. A modified version reemerged in the 1950s in Will Herberg's conception of a "triple melting pot" of Protestants, Catholics, and Jews.[19] The revulsion against Nazi anti-Semitism and the upward mobility of American Jews and Catholics inspired a synthesis of cultural pluralism and assimilationism that made religious persuasion the only significant source of diversity among white Americans. Herberg conceded, however, that black Protestants constituted a separate group that was not likely to be included in the Protestant melting pot. He therefore sharpened the distinction between race or color and ethnicity that was central to postwar thinking about group differences. Nevertheless, Herberg's view that significant differences between, say, Irish and Italian Catholics were disappearing was challenged in the 1960s and later, especially in the "ethnic revival" of the 1970s, which proclaimed that differing national origins among Euro-Americans remained significant and a valuable source of cultural variations.

The "multiculturalism" of the 1980s operated on assumptions that were similar to those of the cultural pluralist tradition, except that the color line was breached and the focus was shifted from the cultures and contributions of diverse European ethnic groups to those of African Americans, Mexican Americans, Asian Americans, and Native Americans. Abandonment of the earlier term "multiracialism" signified a desire to escape from the legacy of biological or genetic determinism and to affirm that the differences among people who happened to differ in skin color or phenotype were the result of their varying cultural and historical experiences. Under attack was the doctrine, shared by assimilationists and most earlier proponents of cultural pluralism, that the cultural norm in the United States was inevitably European in origin and character. Parity was now sought for groups of Asian, African, and American Indian ancestry. This ideal of cultural diversity and democracy was viewed by some of its critics as an invitation to national disunity and ethnic conflict.[20] But its most thoughtful proponents argued that it was simply a consistent application of American democratic values and did not preclude the interaction and cooperation of groups within a common civic society.[21] Nevertheless, the mutual understandings upon which national unity and cohesion could be based needed to be negotiated rather than simply imposed by a Euro-American majority.

Group Separatism

Sometimes confused with the broadened cultural pluralism described here is the advocacy of group separatism. It originates in the desire of a culturally distinctive or racialized group to withdraw as much as possible from American society and interaction with other groups. Its logical outcome, autonomy in a separate, self-governing community, might conceivably be achieved either in an ethnic confederation like Switzerland or in the dissolution of the United States into several ethnic nations. But such a general theory is a logical construction rather than a program that has been explicitly advocated. Group separatism emanates from ethnocentric concerns about the status and destiny of particular groups, and its advocates rarely if ever theorize about what is going to happen to other groups. Precedents for group separatism based on cultural differences can be found in American history in the toleration of virtually autonomous religious communities like the Amish and the Hutterites and in the modicum of self-government and immunity from general laws accorded to Indian tribes and reservations since the 1930s.

The most significant and persistent assertion of group separatism in American history has come from African Americans disillusioned with the prospects for equality within American society. In the nineteenth century, several black leaders and intellectuals called on African Americans to emigrate from the United States in order to establish an independent black republic elsewhere; Africa was the most favored destination. In the 1920s, Marcus Garvey created a mass movement based on the presumption that blacks had no future in the United States and should identify with the independence and future greatness of Africa, ultimately by emigrating there. More recently, the Nation of Islam has proposed that several American states be set aside for an autonomous black nation.[22] At the height of the Black Power movement of the 1960s and early 1970s, a few black nationalists even called for the establishment of a noncontiguous federation of black urban ghettos—a nation of islands like Indonesia or the Philippines, but surrounded by white populations rather than the Pacific Ocean.

The most recent version of black separatism—"Afrocentrism"—has not yet produced a plan for political separation. Its aim is a cultural and spiritual secession from American society rather than the literal establishment of a black nation. Advocates of total separation could be found among other disadvantaged groups. In the late 1960s and 1970s, Mexican-American militants called for the establishment of the independent Chicano nation of Aztlan in the American Southwest,[23] and some Native American radicals sought the reestablishment of truly independent tribal nations.

Group separatism might be viewed as a utopian vision or rhetorical device expressing the depths of alienation felt by the most disadvantaged racial or ethnic groups in American society. The extreme unlikelihood of realizing such visions has made their promulgation more cathartic than politically efficacious. Most members of groups exposed to such separatist appeals have recognized their impracticality, and the clash between the fixed and essentialist view of identity that such projects entail and the fluid and hybrid quality of group cultures in the United States has become increasingly evident to many people of color, as shown most dramatically by the recent movement among those of mixed parentage to affirm a biracial identity. Few African Americans want to celebrate the greater or lesser degree of white ancestry most of them possess, but many have acknowledged not only their ancestral ties to Africa but their debt to Euro-American culture (and its debt to them). Most Mexican Americans value their cultural heritage but do not have the expectation or even the desire to establish an independent Chicano nation in the Southwest. Native Americans have authentic historical and legal claims to a high degree of autonomy but generally recognize that total independence on their current land base is impossible and would worsen rather than improve their circumstances. Asian Americans are proud of their various cultures and seek to preserve some of their traditions but have shown little or no inclination to separate themselves from other Americans in the civic, professional, and economic life of the nation. Afrocentrism raises troubling issues for American educational and cultural life but hardly represents a serious threat to national unity.

Ethnic separatism, in conclusion, is a symptom of racial injustice and a call to action against it, but there is little reason to believe that it portends "the disuniting of America." It is currently a source of great anxiety to many Euro-Americans primarily because covert defenders of ethnic hierarchy or one-way assimilation have tried to confuse the broad-based ideal of democratic multiculturalism with the demands of a relatively few militant ethnocentrists for thoroughgoing self-segregation and isolation from the rest of American society.

Of the four models of American ethnic relations, the one that I believe offers the best hope for a just and cohesive society is a cultural pluralism that is fully inclusive and based on the free choices of individuals to construct or reconstruct their own ethnic identities. We are still far from achieving the degree of racial and ethnic tolerance that realization of such an ideal requires. But with the demographic shift that is transforming the overwhelmingly Euro-American population of thirty or forty years ago into one that is much more culturally and phenotypically heterogeneous, a more democratic form of intergroup relations is a likely prospect, unless there is a desperate reversion to overt ethnic hierarchicalism by the shrinking Euro-American majority. If that were to happen, national unity and cohesion would indeed be hard to maintain. If current trends continue, minorities of non-European ancestry will constitute a new majority sometime in this century. Well before that point is reached, they will have the numbers and the provocation to make the country virtually ungovernable if a resurgent racism brings serious efforts to revive the blatantly hierarchical policies that have prevailed in the past.

CHAPTER 2

The Historical Construction
of Race and Citizenship
in the United States

Nationalist ideologies have often associated membership of a nation-state (existing or imagined) with primordial ethnic identities. Nations have thus been regarded as extended kin groups or communities of descent.[1] In the context of European history, the ethnic basis for citizenship was most fully articulated in Germany during and after the process of unification and in the nations of Eastern Europe that emerged within the Austro-Hungarian empire and became independent after World War I. France and Great Britain have manifested a more complex relationship between ethnicity and citizenship. The former has combined a strong sense of its ethnocultural identity with the universalistic republicanism fostered by the revolution of 1789, and the latter has been a multinational kingdom under a relatively benign English hegemony. American identity and citizenship have not been based in any compelling and consistent way on the ethnocultural character of its population. But, more than the nations of Europe, it has made physical "race," especially as represented by differences in skin color, a determinant of civic and social status.

The founding document of the American republic declares: "All men are created equal; that they are endowed by their Creator with certain unalienable rights; that among these are life, liberty, and the pursuit of happiness." If followed literally, the Declaration of Independence of 1776 would have signalled the birth of a nation in which the only qualification for equal citizenship would have been membership in the human race. (Women were then generally subsumed under the category of "men" or "man.") But the Constitution that created the federal union in 1789 condoned exclusions and inequalities based on race or color as well as gender. Although it used euphemisms to refer to the institution of slavery, the Constitution accommodated itself to the desire of the southern states to consign people of African descent to permanent servitude. For purposes of representation and taxation, each slave was to be counted as three-fifths of a free person. Other provisions had the effect of denying to the federal government the power to legislate against slavery where it existed under state law.[2]

Also significant for the future of black-white relations was the fact that the Constitution provided no definition of national citizenship that might have precluded the states from discriminating on the grounds of race. The only mention of citizenship in the Constitution is in Article IV, section 2: "The citizens of each State shall be entitled to the privileges and immunities of citizens in the several States." This clause gave no precise content to the rights of a citizen and appeared to make national citizenship derivative of state citizenship. The Constitution, however, did give the federal government the power to determine the qualifications for naturalization. Most Americans acquired citizenship by birth in accordance with the British tradition of *jus soli*, which was based originally on the right of the king to command the allegiance of all those who happened to be born in his domain.[3] But it was up to Congress to prescribe the conditions under which immigrants could become citizens. The Naturalization Act of 1790 provided relatively easy terms: two years' residence, "good character," and an oath of allegiance to the Constitution. But the right to citizenship through naturalization was limited to "free white person[s]."[4] There was no prospect of Asian immigration at this time, and Indians within the nation's borders were ineligible for naturalization because the tribes to which they belonged were considered, in the words used later by Chief Justice John Marshall, "domestic dependent nations."[5] It is likely, therefore, that the restriction was aimed mainly at the free people of African descent who circulated within the Atlantic world.

There was no recorded debate on naturalization and the color bar; the Congress was merely following the precedent of several states, which had earlier used the power they possessed over naturalization under the Articles of Confederation to limit the privilege to whites.[6] The lack of controversy was indicative of the powerful consensus that had emerged since the first blacks had arrived in Virginia 171 years earlier that people of African descent belonged to an inferior race unqualified for the social and political rights originally associated with the status of free subjects of the British Crown and later with what was due to citizens of the American republic.[7] That assumption derived initially and primarily from the association of African ancestry with slavery or enslavability, but rationalizing and mystifying the economic incentive to take advantage of African vulnerability were the phobias and anxieties that came to be associated with physical difference and especially dark skin pigmentation.[8]

What citizenship meant in the pre–Civil War period is revealed in Supreme Court Justice Bushrod Washington's 1823 enumeration of the rights that were implied in the privileges and immunities clause. Basic among them were "protection by the government; the enjoyment of life and liberty, with the right to acquire and possess property of every kind, and to pursue and obtain happiness and safety, subject nevertheless to such restraints as the government may justly prescribe for the good of the whole." A long list of more specific rights ensued, including "the benefit of the writ of habeas corpus" and equality under the law, "to which *may* be added the elective franchise, as regulated and established by the laws or constitution of the state in which it is to be exercised."[9] It would prove significant that access to the suffrage was viewed here as a possible concomitant of citizenship, but not as an essential one. In 1823 some states still limited the franchise to property holders and taxpayers, although such restrictions were in the process of being eliminated. White women were citizens for most purposes, but were denied the suffrage until 1920. The extension of manhood suffrage in the 1820s and 1830s was done in a blatantly racist fashion. In some states blacks with property who had previously possessed the right to vote were disfranchised at the same time that all white males were made eligible to vote. The political system that was emerging has been aptly described as a "*Herrenvolk* democracy."[10]

Although the right to vote was not firmly established as a prerogative of citizenship, being denied it when all other males could exercise it clearly relegated black men to an inequality of political status that made them less than full citizens. The Supreme Court's Dred Scott decision of 1857, which declared that free blacks could not be citizens of the United States, reflected the realities of the time, if not, as was claimed in Chief Justice Taney's decision, the intentions of the framers of the Constitution. The federal government discriminated against blacks in the pre–Civil War period by forbidding them from becoming naturalized citizens, carrying the mail, or being issued passports for foreign travel. The states, including the northern states that had abolished slavery, added to the disabilities associated with race in antebellum America. Besides denying free blacks the right to vote, most states prohibited them from testifying in court against whites, serving on juries, attending common schools, and having equal access to common public amenities or facilities. Some even forbade free blacks from other states from entering their jurisdictions.[11]

As the controversy over the extension of slavery to the federal territories heated up in the 1850s and propelled the nation toward civil war, both sides invoked white supremacist ideologies to support their positions. Southern defenders of the expansion of slavery used arguments derived from science and the Bible to maintain that the enslavement of blacks was a "positive good" wherever it existed. Northern advocates of "free soil"—those who would limit slavery to where it already existed under state law—sometimes contended that one of the greatest evils associated with the expansion of the South's "peculiar institution" was that it would entail bringing blacks into regions that could otherwise be homogeneously white. To a considerable extent the southern cause in the sectional controversy of the 1850s was hierarchical biracialism and the northern one was white homogeneity, or total black exclusion. The popularity in moderate antislavery circles of schemes to colonize freed blacks outside the United States reflected a belief in the impossibility of equal citizenship for African Americans. One of those who most cherished the utopian vision of an America without either slavery or blacks was Abraham Lincoln.[12]

The Dred Scott decision, with its formal and categorical denial of citizenship rights to African Americans, was in effect for little more than a decade. It was overturned in the wake of a civil war that occasioned the abolition of slavery and the enlistment of blacks, including freed slaves, in the army that was fighting to preserve the Union against the southern secessionists. Emancipation did not itself entail citizenship, as was evident from the status of antebellum "free Negroes." But military service did. The classical definition of citizenship in a republic, which remained an influential aspect of American republicanism before the enfranchisement of women in the twentieth century, was closely associated with the bearing of arms. He who was asked to fight for the republic also had a right to participate in the deliberations that preceded a resort to arms. According to the historian Linda Kerber, "arms-bearing for the Union was an experience that came before citizenship and helped set the terms for it. Black men risked their lives for the Union . . . and the claim that they had bought their rights with their blood suffused constitutional debate and also the discourse of Reconstruction."[13]

The Fourteenth Amendment to the Constitution, ratified in 1868, provided the first substantive and potentially enforceable conception of national citizenship. Its purpose was to provide legal equality for the emancipated slaves, most of whom had been loyal to the Union, in order to protect them against the oppressive designs of ex-Confederates, who, under the lenient Presidential Reconstruction of 1865–1866, had passed discriminatory state laws that approximated slavery in a new guise. Section 1 of the amendment set forth the basic terms: "All persons born or naturalized in the United States, and subject to the jurisdiction thereof, are citizens of the United States. No State shall make or enforce any law which shall abridge the privileges and immunities of citizens of the United States; nor shall any State deprive any person of life, liberty, and property, without due process of law; nor deny to any person within its jurisdiction the equal protection of the laws." The intention clearly was to establish a birthright citizenship that would include African Americans. The amendment was not, however, meant to apply to Indians, whose membership in tribes who had made treaties with the United States was thought to place them beyond the direct jurisdiction of the nation and therefore not entitled to its constitutional protections. It is also noteworthy that "equal protection of the laws" was provided to all persons, not just citizens. As a result aliens, including aliens deemed ineligible for citizenship because of racially discriminatory naturalization laws, could sometimes gain judicial relief from unfair and unequal treatment by appealing to the amendment.[14]

The Fourteenth Amendment did not by itself eliminate the racial qualification for naturalization, which continued to be restricted to "free white person[s]." Recognizing an inconsistency in its overall Reconstruction policy, in 1870 Congress amended the immigration laws by extending to immigrants of African descent the right to become naturalized citizens. By adding blacks rather than extending the right to all immigrants, Congress deliberately made Asians the only nonwhites who were "aliens ineligible for citizenship." Beginning at the time of the 1849 Gold Rush, Chinese immigration to California had been proceeding apace. Since these newcomers differed physically and culturally from the native white population—in addition to being nonwhite they were non-Christian—they were the targets of a xenophobic reaction that was particularly strong on the West Coast. They were welcomed only by employers, especially railroad builders, who wished to take advantage of their services as workers who could be hired for less than whites. The discrimination and abuse that they encountered in the West did not elicit much sympathy in the East. The stereotypes of the Chinese as filthy, diseased, heathenish, and willing to work for wages no white man would accept circulated nationally and created a set of negative expectations.[15] According to the racialized anthropology or ethnology of the mid- to late nineteenth century, both blacks and Chinese were naturally inferior races lacking the innate capacity for self-government and democratic citizenship that all white males supposedly possessed. But because of their usefulness to the Union cause in the Civil War and to the Republican Party during Reconstruction, blacks were granted a dispensation—a temporary immunity from extreme prejudice and discrimination. The Chinese could make no such claims on influential segments of white opinion.

The period between the end of Reconstruction in 1877 and World War I saw the triumph of a broad-gauged racism that included not merely people of color but also subcategories of Europeans. It was the heyday of what the political scientist Rogers M. Smith has called "ascriptive" Americanism—the belief that what fully qualified someone for American citizenship was a bloodline that could be traced to northwestern Europe.[16] The process of invidious differentiation began with the Chinese Exclusion Act of 1882, the first legislation that prohibited a specific racial or ethnic group from entering the country. By the 1890s southern states were segregating African Americans by force of law, a practice that the Supreme Court in the notorious 1896 *Plessy v. Ferguson* decision found to be compatible with the Fourteenth Amendment. (Its supposition was that separate facilities could somehow be made equal. It was not until the 1954 decision in the case of *Brown v. Board of Education* that the court recognized the falsity of this assumption.) One by one, between 1890 and 1910, southern states effectively nullified the Fifteenth Amendment passed in 1870, which prohibited denial of the right to vote "on account of race, color, or previous condition of servitude." They did so by establishing qualifications for the suffrage that made no mention of race, but were clearly intended to be used (and were in fact used) to deprive most southern blacks of access to the ballot box. The brutal lynching of African Americans for real and imagined crimes or simply for violations of racial etiquette became routine in many parts of the South and occurred occasionally in the North as well. By the turn of the century the power of white prejudice had made a mockery of the Fourteenth Amendment's promise of equal citizenship.[17]

The racialization of immigrants from Southern and Eastern Europe began in the 1890s with the rise of the immigration restriction movement and culminated in the discriminatory quota system that was implemented by the Immigration Act of 1924. It has been alleged by some historians that immigrants from Italy and parts of the Austro-Hungarian or Russian empire were not considered to be "white" when they first arrived.[18] This may be true in some cases. There were questions about whether Sicilians in southern Louisiana should go to white schools, black schools, or separate schools of their own. But in general the racism directed at the "new immigrants" was not color-coded. There were in fact two distinct systems of hierarchical racial classification that were operative around the turn of the century. The one that was based primarily on color—white over black, brown, and yellow—could rationalize the total exclusion or legalized segregation of the stigmatized group. The one that associated the cultural characteristics of certain European nationalities with their genetic makeup—and also at times found a physical correlative in nonchromatic features like head shape— won less popular adherence and had a more limited impact. Many nativists believed that a more or less coercive program of assimilation could turn Italians, Greeks, and Slavs into good Americans, provided that there were not many of them to deal with. Most of them did not advocate prohibition of immigration from Southern and Eastern Europe or the segregation and disfranchisement of those already in the country. They merely contended that allowing such people to enter the country in large numbers was endangering the national culture and the quality of the nation's breeding stock or gene pool. Hence their numbers should be reduced to manageable proportions. On the level of popular invective, Jews and Italians were sometimes distinguished from "white men." But no one seriously doubted that they were members of the same white or Caucasian "great race" as old-stock Americans. It was the importation from England and Germany of the notion that "the little races" of Europe could be ranked—with Nordics, Teutons, or Anglo-Saxons possessing characteristics superior to those of Latins or

Slavs—that informed the racist ideology of the upper-class leaders of the immigration restriction movement.[19]

Anti-Semitism also reared its ugly head in the United States in the early twentieth century. Although less virulent than the variety that had emerged in France, Germany, Austria, and czarist Russia, it became acceptable in elite circles in the East and Midwest and led to at least one notorious lynching in the South.[20] The kind of racist anti-Semitism that came to hideous fruition in Nazi Germany and the Holocaust did not become politicized in the United States in the way that white supremacy did, at least in the southern states. But it did result in a pervasive pattern of discriminatory access to higher education, certain professional and business opportunities, housing, social clubs, and hotels or resorts. It was not pigmentation, even in a symbolic sense, that inspired American anti-Semitism. Hostility derived from two principal factors: the traditional Christian belief that Jews were religious and cultural subversives, and resentment at the competitive success of Jews in some lines of endeavor (which led to the charge that they habitually engaged in sharp practice). Prejudice against Jews may have been more intense and durable than that directed at Italians, Greeks, and Poles, but it did not approach the virulence of anti-black and anti-Asian sentiment.[21]

In the early twentieth century, Japanese immigration to California aroused fears that the United States faced a "yellow peril." As a result, the Japanese government was induced to limit voluntarily the emigration of its nation-als to the United States in return for the promise of better treatment of those who were already in the country. But the "Gentlemen's Agreement" of 1907 did not prevent the State of California from passing a law in 1912 that denied Japanese immigrants the right to buy land in the Golden State. Asian immigrants were not only denied access to naturalization but were also being deprived of the "equal protection of the laws" supposedly guaranteed to "all persons" by the Fourteenth Amendment. The Darwinian conception of a "struggle for existence" among the races aroused fears that evolution-ary success—"survival of the fittest"—would go to the most prolific race rather than to the most intelligent and moral. The teeming masses of Asia were regarded as a serious threat to white hegemony throughout the world. Within the United States, once Asian immigration had been curtailed and it had been determined that the black population was not increasing faster than the white, the most pressing concern was the fact that Southern and Eastern European immigrants had larger families than old-stock Americans. It was in this context that President Theodore Roosevelt warned of "race suicide." One solution was for the native-born to have more children; an-other was to curtail further immigration of people of inferior stock, a goal that was accomplished in 1924.

What lay behind the multitargeted racism and xenophobia that crested in the early twentieth century? The stresses and strains of a rapidly modernizing society would seem to provide a large part of the explanation. Anxieties and insecurities always intensify at a time of massive social and economic transformation. It was around 1900 that the United States ceased to be a predominantly agricultural and rural society and became one that was principally urban and industrial. Consequently, time-honored ways of life, sources of authority and prestige, and even ways of making a living were being threatened. The class and status order was being reconstructed in a way that created new winners and losers.

One of the most persuasive psychosocial explanations of intensified racism is that people who feel threatened by forces that they cannot control or even understand will scapegoat the ethnic or racial Other. The most compelling example is the way that losing World War I heightened German anti-Semitism and gave the Nazis a demonology that they could exploit in their drive for power. The nature of the sense of threat or danger to native-born white Americans from a specific group—blacks, Asians, or "new immigrants"—differed in each case, but the mechanism was the same. The Other was blamed for one's own failures and inadequacies, whether they be cultural, sex- and gender-related, or simply economic. Native-born white workers, at a time of bitter and often violent conflict between labor and capital, had good reason to fear the use by employers of blacks and Asians as strikebreakers or replacement workers. But they succumbed to racism when they disdained extending the boundaries of the working class to include workers with a different skin color and attributed their cooperation with union-busting employers to innate servility rather than to the pressure of economic circumstances.[22]

In the South, the increasing numbers of whites who were losing ground economically as a result of the vicissitudes of the cotton-based economy eventually turned on blacks rather than mobilizing *with* blacks against the landlords, merchants, banks, and corporate enterprises that were exploiting the landless proletarians of both races. In the words of W. E. B. Du Bois, "the white group of workers, while they received a low wage, were compensated in part by a sort of public and psychological wage. They were given public deference and titles of respect because they were white. They were admitted freely with all classes of people to public functions, public parks, and the best schools."[23] The economically dominant middle and upper classes obviously benefited from encouraging divisions among the disadvantaged, but it would be simplistic to view them as nothing more than self-interested and cynical manipulators. They also saw the world in racial and ethnic, as well as class, terms, and they could imagine themselves to be philanthropists rescuing the masses of their racial compatriots from degrading associations. Elite whites in the South could afford to be more paternalistic in their treatment of blacks than the poorer whites who were competing with them economically. But this did not mean that they were less racist. Their self-image as gentry with roots in a slaveholding class required that they be surrounded by blacks who could be forced to play the role of childlike servants and dependents.[24] In the North, members of the old Anglo-American elite deflected the "status anxiety" arising from new wealth onto the immigrants who were allegedly threatening their cultural hegemony as charter members of America's "cultivated classes."[25]

Such social pressures and tensions help to explain why there had to be scapegoats, but they do not fully explain why particular racial or ethnic groups were chosen to play the role. Preexisting stereotypes, such as the image that arose before emancipation of African Americans as natural slaves or the view of the backward and heathenish Chinese sent back by missionaries before the era of immigration, helped to predetermine their selection as targets of prejudice and discrimination. It also gave to the stereotypes the kind of content that could intensify the hostility or contempt that they aroused. The social construction of race should be viewed as a complex process in which the immediate contexts provided by structural relationships interact with the cultural legacies of earlier relationships or contacts to produce a license to hate or denigrate the Other.

The period between World War I and the 1970s saw a sustained and partially successful struggle to expand the meaning of substantive American citizenship to cover groups previously excluded and to include rights and privileges not previously extended to those born or naturalized in the United States. The achievement of women's suffrage in 1920 strengthened the connection between citizenship and suffrage. The granting of U.S. citizenship to all American Indians in 1921 was a mainly symbolic act that had little or no practical effect on the lives of Native Americans who lived on impoverished reservations, but it did at least universalize birthright access to American nationality. After the discriminatory restriction of immigration in the 1920s, the status of those who had previously arrived from Eastern and Southern Europe or were the children and grandchildren of foreign-born parents gradually improved. This process has somewhat misleadingly been called "whitening." What is undeniable is that many "white ethnics," as they later came to be called, stressed their own pigmentation as a basis for gaining acceptance as Americans.[26] The Democratic Party of the 1930s, which under the banner of the New Deal greatly enhanced the role of the federal government in social and economic affairs, appealed to the white ethnics and represented their interests as part of a coalition of minorities that constituted a new majority. It also promulgated a new concept of social citizenship by entitling most working Americans to old age pensions and unemployment benefits.

African-American voters were part of the New Deal political coalition. The large numbers who migrated to the North in the 1910s and 1920s regained the right to vote, thereby creating an incentive for urban politicians to provide some favors or benefits in return for their support. Congressmen whose margins of victory might depend on the "Negro vote" were likely to vote for federal antilynching legislation or against the confirmation of a notoriously racist nominee for a Supreme Court judgeship.[27] The New Deal was more responsive to black interests than any political movement since Radical Republicanism, but it fell far short of providing equal citizenship for African Americans.[28] Because the white South was also part of the New Deal coalition, the Roosevelt administration did not openly challenge the southern pattern of segregation and disfranchisement or even support federal legislation against lynching. Furthermore, the exclusion of servants and farm laborers from the protections of social security denied to much of the black population the benefits of the new social citizenship.

Although there was not a substantial advancement in the cause of civil rights for African Americans during the 1920s and 1930s (apart from some Supreme Court decisions against flagrant denials of equal justice), the intellectual justification for the differential treatment of racialized groups came under attack. A new school of anthropologists attributed human diversity to culture rather than genetics, and studies of human intelligence began to question the notion that there were significant differences in the intellectual endowment of various "races."[29] But it was not until World War II that ideological racism was challenged to such an extent that it became intellectually disreputable—a necessary precondition for an assault on legalized white supremacy. Gunnar Myrdal's classic study of the status of African Americans, *An American Dilemma*, published in 1944, won considerable acclaim for its contention that discrimination against blacks was in contradiction to "the American creed" of equal rights and opportunities for all.[30] This argument made sense only if blacks were included among the "men" or full-scale human beings to which the Declaration of Independence applied. Those racists who viewed blacks as innately unqualified for full citizenship were put on the defensive during and immediately after World War II because of the similarity of antiblack ideology to the anti-Semitism of the Third Reich. The NAACP's call for a double victory, over Nazism abroad and racism at home, resonated with many Americans.

Revulsion against Nazi racism was not in itself sufficient to make racial equality under the law and at the ballot box a high national priority for politicians and policymakers. It took the Cold War and the struggle with communism for "the hearts and minds" of Africans and Asians to create a climate of opinion conducive to the achievement of equal legal and political rights for blacks in the United States. The initial effect of the Cold War was to retard the struggle for civil rights. During the McCarthyite "red scare" of the late 1940s and early 1950s, progressive causes of all kinds fell under the cloud of suspicion that they were Communist-inspired. By the late 1950s and early 1960s, however, paranoid fears of domestic subversion had receded and the international rivalry of the United States and the USSR had become a struggle to gain influence over the decolonized new nations of Africa and Asia. In this context, policymakers began to realize that the practice of Jim Crow was an enormous propaganda liability. Historians and political scientists have recently documented what was long suspected: the success of the civil rights movement in the 1960s depended heavily on "reasons of state" as they were perceived by influential Cold Warriors. Just as the need to preserve the Union against the secessionists had made emancipation seem necessary a century earlier, the need to defend the "free world" against Soviet communism gave impetus to the struggle for African-American legal and political equality that came to fruition in the Civil Rights Acts of 1964 and 1965.[31] Highlighting such pragmatic considerations is not meant to imply that the agency of black protestors and demonstrators was unimportant. It was when nonviolent resisters confronted and exposed the hatred and injustice of the Jim Crow regime—as in Little Rock, Arkansas, in 1957 or Birmingham, Alabama, in 1963—that the headlines around the world put the United States in the embarrassing position of preaching democracy but conspicuously failing to practice it.

In retrospect, 1965 can now be seen as a high point of racial egalitarianism in the United States. In that year the effective and enforceable Voting Rights Act made African Americans full citizens of the polity. In the same year a new immigration law was passed that abolished discriminatory national quotas. Both actions had significant results. Access to suffrage led to a rapidly growing number of black elected officials, to the point where the proportion of blacks in the national House of Representatives began to approach their percentage of the total population. The end of racial and ethnic qualifications for immigration made it possible for large numbers of Asians and Afro-West Indians to come to the United States and become naturalized after five years. This influx and the legal or illegal entry of millions of Mexicans and other Latin Americans created a greater degree of racial and ethnic diversity than the nation had ever known. Some have predicted that by the mid-twenty-first century the United States will have a "nonwhite" or non-Euro-American majority—a demographic situation that already exists in California.

Do these developments mean that the United States has achieved the egalitarian dream derived from a literal reading of the Declaration of Independence and ceased to be a society permeated with racial prejudice and discrimination? What has happened since 1965 makes it clear that formal legal and political equality does not automatically entail equal citizenship. Full citizenship requires more than extending formal rights; it should also mean that the newly included are accorded enough respect to make them feel that they truly belong to the nation. As the French revolutionaries understood, a democratic republic requires fraternity as well as legally acknowledged liberty and equality. If a minority is generally disliked or resented, it will be discriminated against in an extralegal or de facto fashion unless the government acts vigorously to protect its members.

By any objective standard, African Americans continue to be greatly disadvantaged in comparison to their white compatriots. Blacks are now more residentially segregated from whites than they have ever been; they earn on the average only about three-fifths as much as whites, are twice as likely to be unemployed, and have only about one-eighth as much property or net worth. More than half of all the convicts in American prisons are African Americans. They also fall far below general American standards in such indices of well-being as life expectancy, infant mortality, unwed motherhood, and susceptibility to HIV/AIDS.[32]

A major reason for the disparity is, of course, the accumulated disadvantages resulting from a long history of enslavement and racial oppression. The current call for "reparations" is based on a belief that African Americans have been the victims of a human-made historical disaster for which the entire society should assume responsibility. Clearly, enslaved blacks made an enormous contribution to the economic growth of what became the richest nation in the world, a veritable "land of opportunity" for native and foreign-born whites. Simple justice might seem to require that the white beneficiaries of the uncompensated toil that laid the foundations for national growth and prosperity should be taxed to pay the debt. But there is little or no chance that the white majority will be willing to make the sacrifices required. Affirmative action policies in employment and education would be another way to begin to overcome the handicaps resulting from past discrimination, but the courts have held that "racial preferences" cannot be justified on such grounds. The failure to use race-specific policies to overcome historically created inequalities could mean the indefinite perpetuation of these inequalities. Black degradation confirms the prejudices of whites without a sense of history, and encourages alienation and bitterness among blacks, who may rightly feel they lack the respect that substantive citizenship should entail.

But the current situation of blacks and other racialized minorities, such as Mexican Americans, is not merely the residue of past injustice. The partial dismantling of the welfare state is depriving the poor, who are disproportionately black and brown, of access to the social citizenship adumbrated by the New Deal. Furthermore, active discrimination in access to housing, employment, loans, medical care, and education persists. The antidiscrimination laws are either inadequately enforced or fail to cover some of the more subtle ways in which racial bias is expressed. The situation of African Americans has certainly improved somewhat in the last half-century. To a much greater extent than in the past, high achievers can rise to positions of power and prestige. For the growing African-American bourgeoisie the privileges associated with class to some extent overcome the liabilities associated with race. But poorer blacks, confined to the inner-city ghettos from which the middle class has largely fled, suffer from a double handicap of race and class that is extraordinarily difficult to overcome.[33]

The social construction of a "Latino" or "Hispanic" ethnoracial category has differed in significant ways from the racialization of African Americans. Since the time that substantial numbers of Mexicans were incorporated into the United States as citizens under the terms of the Treaty of Guadalupe Hidalgo in 1848, Mexican Americans have, for the most part, been officially classified as white. But the extent to which they have been discriminated against, segregated, and discouraged from voting—particularly in the southwestern United States, where virtually all of them were concentrated until quite recently—belies that designation and has made them socially, if not legally, people of color. The current census categories of "Hispanics" and "non-Hispanic whites" suggest that Latinos without obvious Indian or black ancestry are still white in some sense but may nevertheless be treated as Other. Difficult to determine is the extent to which the prejudice against Latinos in general, and Mexican Americans and Puerto Ricans in particular, is "racial" (based on the phenotypic effects of varying degrees of Indian or African, as well as Spanish, ancestry) or cultural (resulting from the fact that Latino groups have been more prone to maintain their ethnic and linguistic distinctiveness than immigrants from Europe). The "greaser" stereotype applied to Mexicans suggests revulsion at their physical appearance, but the current agitation for "English only" laws highlights the alleged threat to Anglo-American culture from the persistence of Spanish as the lingua franca in Latino communities.

The pan-Hispanic identity affirmed by Latinos themselves is primarily cultural. (What else could it be, given the great diversity of ancestries and phenotypes?) Latino intellectuals have been in the forefront of the campaign for multiculturalism in the United States. Noting that the American concept of individual rights does not normally include the right to remain culturally distinctive, they have advocated a new "cultural citizenship" that includes the right to be different without being denied the respect and recognition that full citizenship should entail.[34] A question remains, however, as to whether the pan-Hispanic identity is the natural outgrowth of cultural commonalities or a defensive reaction against the tendency of Anglo-American society to lump all Latinos together and "racialize" them. The differences among Mexicans, Puerto Ricans, Cubans, Dominicans, Central Americans, and South Americans might seem, from an objective perspective, to outweigh a similarity based mainly on language.

In the case of Asian Americans, the racializing tendencies of American society and the group solidarities that they may evoke are even more evident. Asians or "Mongolians" were one of the primary classifications of the racist anthropology that originated in the eighteenth century and culminated in the early twentieth. Yet the groups currently considered Asian in the United States are culturally quite diverse. They include not only Japanese, Chinese, Koreans, and Vietnamese, but also the South Asians who were often regarded as Caucasians or Aryans by earlier generations of physical anthropologists. The killing a few years ago of a Chinese American mistaken for a Japanese by unemployed auto workers who blamed Japanese competition for their plight shows how racists can disregard ethnic or national distinctions. But pan-Asian defensive solidarity seems to be somewhat less developed or urgently advocated than the movement for pan-Hispanic identity. Anti-Asian prejudice has declined considerably since the turn-of-the-century panic about the "yellow peril"—most precipitously in the years since the internment of Japanese-American citizens during World War II (perhaps the most blatantly racist act of the United States government since the Civil War).

Currently, Asians still suffer from subtle forms of discrimination, such as glass ceilings preventing Asian engineers employed by large corporations from moving from production to management as readily as their white counterparts. But, in comparison to African Americans and even Mexican Americans, Asian Americans appear to be on the way to being assimilated by the Euro-American majority. On the whole, they seem less insistent than Latinos that there be respect for their cultural distinctiveness. (The diversity of languages among them deprives bilingualism of its capacity to serve as a rallying point.) Furthermore, high rates of intermarriage between Asians and whites and the apparent freedom of their offspring to choose their own racial identity create the possibility that the privileged American race of the future will be of mixed European and Asian ancestry.[35] Despite the current absence of a strong trend in this direction, it is also possible to conceive of a growing tolerance of cultural diversity and an increasing acceptance of Latinos as full-fledged members of American society. Were it not for the continuation of a massive influx from south of the border, second- and third-generation Mexican Americans might currently be in a position analogous to that of Americans of Italian descent in the decades after immigration restriction. (During the period from the 1920s to the 1940s most Italian Americans inhabited a social and cultural world of their own but were nevertheless being assimilated economically and politically.)

Harder to imagine is extending to African Americans the degree of respect and recognition that would make them full and equal citizens in substance as well as in legal forms. No other ethnoracial group was enslaved for two and a half centuries in what became the United States or, despite the attainment of *de jure* citizenship in 1868, was subjected to such an elaborate and comprehensive system of legalized discrimination and segregation. There is a long history of the incorporation of groups that initially inspired hostility and discrimination but which were able to exploit their putative whiteness to gain entry at the expense of the perennial Other—the African Americans who remain to the present day the principal "negative reference group" against which white—or nonblack—America persists in defining itself.[36]

Our understanding of the social construction of race and citizenship in the United States can be enhanced if we enrich the kind of comparative perspective that was briefly invoked at the beginning of this chapter. France and Germany are two European countries that have dealt with ethnoracial diversity in ways that are often contrasted. The United States is often paired with France as an exemplar of "civic nationalism," while Germany is designated as the prime exponent of "ethnic nationalism."[37] The American pattern, as we have described it, is actually a peculiar hybrid of these two types. What is distinctive about it is the coexistence of a universalistic affirmation of human rights and a seemingly contradictory set of exclusions based on race or color. Although the egalitarian ideals expressed in the Declaration of Independence, Abraham Lincoln's Gettysburg Address, and Franklin D. Roosevelt's "Four Freedoms" speech seem to apply to all humankind, the America that was experienced by blacks, Indians, Asians, Mexican Americans, and at times even some categories of immigrants from Europe was often one of racialized hierarchy. One way that Americans could avoid blatant contradiction was to define the Other as subhuman or inherently childlike and thus incapable of self-government or democratic citizenship. Liberty and equality could continue to be celebrated but as the prerogative of the *Herrenvolk*, or at least its male members, rather than as a universalistic recognition of the rights of humanity.

France, the other classic example of civic nationalism, has also failed to live up to the principles set out in its charter of universal rights—"*les droits de l'homme.*" Initially, the French Revolution inspired a consistent cosmopolitanism that went to the point of making foreigners resident in France the legal and political equals of native-born inhabitants. But the wars in which the French republic became embroiled after 1793 aroused a xenophobic nationalism that resulted in the persecution of aliens and in effect made the rights of man the prerogative of a select group designated as citizens. The access to citizenship in the French Republic has not been based strictly on *jus soli*, like the English and American, but was originally based on *jus sanguinis*, like the German. What has made France much more hospitable to immigrants than Germany is that birthright citizenship was extended to the third generation in 1851 and to the second in 1889.[38] The fact that those born in the French colonies of North Africa before independence are considered birthright citizens and that automatic citizenship comes to the children of all immigrants when they reach maturity means that contemporary France has made citizenship relatively easy to obtain. But serious proposals to make the second generation meet rigorous standards to qualify for citizenship, as well as the calls for banning immigration from non-European sources emanating from Jean-Marie Le Pen and his *Front National*, demonstrate a persistent French proclivity for xenophobia. But the ethnic side of French nationalism—defense of *la culture française* from alien influences—can be distinguished from American racism. No sharp color line has been drawn in France. In fact, survey data show that the French are less prejudiced against Francophone blacks than against new arrivals from North Africa, who are distinguished from the native French by culture and religion rather than by skin color.[39]

If one is willing to adopt an expansive definition of racism, one could say that the French version is culture-coded, whereas the American is color-coded. Of course the French are not completely immune from color prejudice, and Americans have been known to have xenophobic reactions to cultural difference. But there is a significant relative difference. In general, and especially in recent times, the American "melting pot" has been more tolerant of ethnic and religious diversity than cultural assimilation *à la française*. Exclusion in the American case has normally been based on color or some other concept of innate "racial" difference. The French, on the other hand, have been most antagonized by what they take to be a willful resistance to the absorption of French culture. Haitian immigrants have been received much more hospitably in France than in the United States. But strong adherence to Islam has often been deemed by the French to be an insuperable obstacle to assimilation, a view that is shared by adherents of both the dominant tradition of secular republicanism and the minority right-wing persuasion based on Catholic traditionalism.[40] Despite allegations of Arab-American support of terrorism and anti-Semitism, the rapid growth of Islam in the United States has occasioned relatively little concern or anxiety, except in some quarters after the shock of 9/11.

In apparent contrast to both the United States and France, German identity and citizenship have been rooted in a relatively pure and highly exclusionary form of ethnic nationalism. In France the revolutionary republican state engendered the nation, and in the United States the founding fathers created a political structure that would give meaning to American nationality in the absence of any distinctive ethnic identity. (The free population of the United States in 1789 was predominantly English in origin, but, having revolted against English rule, Americans could scarcely establish a unique identity based on cultural antecedents.) But in Germany cultural and linguistic nationalism preceded the establishment of a unified nation-state. Furthermore, the German cultural nationalism that preceded the unification of 1870 derived much of its content from the romantic revulsion against the Enlightenment doctrine of universal human rights. In the German conception it was the collective soul of a people—the *Volksgeist*—that had the right to self-determination, not the independent rational individuals of democratic political thought.

The German immigration law of 1913 carried the principle of *jus sanguinis* to its logical conclusion. Germans living abroad and their descendants had an automatic and perpetual claim to German citizenship, but people born in Germany who were not of German stock could not become naturalized. In the words of Roger Brubaker, "The 1913 law severed citizenship from residence and defined the citizenry more consistently as a community of descent."[41] During the Nazi era the concept of German citizenship became completely racialized when all those whose families had acquired citizenship in earlier times but who could not claim Aryan descent—mostly Jews and Slavs—were stripped of their German nationality.

Germany's ethnoracial conception of citizenship survived defeat in World War II. The law of 1913 remained in effect, although some very recent modifications have made citizenship through naturalization somewhat easier for non-Germanic immigrants. What has not changed at all is the eligibility for instant citizenship of those of remote German ancestry who may have lived abroad for generations—for example, the Volga Germans of Russia who left their German-speaking homelands in the eighteenth century. The children and grandchildren of Turks who came as guest workers thirty or forty years ago are still regarded as foreigners and face many obstacles if they wish to be naturalized. In 1992, 400,000 Turks who were born in Germany retained their resident alien status.[42]

The role of race in the construction of citizenship in Germany and the United States can be fruitfully compared. The unavoidable Enlightenment context for the creation of American nationality made racists assume that the dominant whites stood for humanity in general and were worthy of all the human rights specified by eighteenth-century philosophers. But blacks, Indians, and Asians were "races," which meant that they lacked the attributes needed for exercising the responsibilities of democratic citizenship. A narrower and more ethnic strain can also be detected at certain points in American history, namely the belief that only those of Anglo-Saxon, Germanic, or Nordic ancestry were qualified to hold the reins of self-government. But the ability of immigrants from the Celtic, Latin, and Slavic regions of Europe to claim whiteness and thereby distinguish themselves from blacks and Asians made these more exclusive assertions of racial priority unavailing in the long run. In the German case, the process began not so much with the racialization of the Other as with the self-racialization of the Germans. They became "the master race," with a right to rule over other Europeans and non-Teutonic Caucasians. This vision was permeated with anti-Enlightenment particularism. Jews became the prime target of German racism because they seemed to represent everything the *Volkisch* Germans rejected—universalism, cosmopolitanism, rationalism, an aptitude for commerce and finance, artistic innovation—in short, modernity.[43]

If Jews were the scapegoats for German antimodernism, blacks and to a lesser extent other people of color served to buttress the American self-concept as the most modern of nations—the vanguard of human progress. The African-American stereotype, in contrast to the German-Jewish, was of a people incapable of being modernized rather than of one that was too modern for its own and everyone else's good. When the United States and particularly the South evinced signs of social and economic backwardness, it was easy to put the blame on the presence of "primitive" African Americans. When the United States became an imperial power seeking to transform the world in its own image, it was similarly easy to blame the resistance and recalcitrance that it encountered on the racial deficiencies of "the colored races."

But there is some hope to be derived from an account of the social construction of race and citizenship in the United States. To contend that race has been socially constructed is also to maintain that it is not natural or inevitable. What has been constructed can also be torn down or "deconstructed." To some extent this has already happened with the overthrow of legalized segregation, racially motivated voting restrictions, and discriminatory immigration quotas. In this chapter I have been very critical of the United States. But I am also proud of the fact that racial injustice have never been unchallenged. Sustained protest and resistance from its victims have aroused a sympathetic response from at least some of the beneficiaries of white supremacy. The national conscience—the desire to live up to the standard of human rights set forth in the Declaration of Independence—has usually needed to be supplemented by "reasons of state" or persuasive claims that the national interest is adversely affected by racism to become efficacious. But at least it shows that white Americans are capable of recognizing priorities higher than the maintenance of racial privilege. That may be something we can build upon.

CHAPTER 3

America's Diversity in Comparative Perspective

The United States has always had a diverse population, but in the past few years the question of how to reconcile persistent racial and ethnic differences with the need for national unity and hopes for the fulfillment of our democratic ideals has been raised more insistently than ever before. During the late nineties President Bill Clinton's commission on race held hearings throughout the country in search of solutions. Central to the great debate on affirmative action is the question of what can and should be done to make America's institutions reflect the diversity of its population. Although theorists from various disciplines have concluded that racial and ethnic identities are "social constructions" and not primordial facts of nature, those identities matter greatly to those possessing them and significantly shape their public attitudes and behavior. Politicized group consciousness is not limited to minorities. As recent studies of the construction of "whiteness" remind us, it is also an attribute of Euro-Americans reacting to the presence or assertiveness of those designated as racially "Other."[1] Group membership may be produced by shared historical experience and social status and not by genes or cultural essences, but ethnoracial identity provides a locus from which most Americans view the world and is a major determinant of whom they vote for, hire or promote, associate with, and welcome as neighbors.

Old-stock Americans of British or northern European extraction have traditionally responded to a perceived increase in ethnic diversity in one of two ways—assimilation or exclusion. Those thought capable of being "Americanized" or "civilized" were to be subjected to a process of cultural adaptation and transformation; those deemed essentially and permanently different and inferior were either denied the right to immigrate or, if they were already here, were denied citizenship rights and relegated to a lower castelike status outside of the enfranchised community as defined by a racialized social contract. Before the civil rights era, which opened the possibility of integrating African Americans into the mainstream and simultaneously lowered the barriers to Asian immigration, the majority's vision of a "real" America that was racially and culturally homogeneous obscured the importance and persistence of group differences.

Since the late 1960s, the classic solutions of exclusion and assimilation have both lost viability, and the notion that America may be permanently diverse and "multicultural" has gained increasing acceptance. Some, especially members of minorities, have celebrated the new pluralism, while others have lamented it and sought to limit its effects. Two main causes of this acknowledgment of diversity are, first, a growing awareness that the campaign to integrate African Americans into a culturally homogenized and color-blind society, which climaxed in the early 1960s, has failed to achieve its objective; and, second, an increase in the numbers and visibility of non-European immigrants, especially Asians and Latinos, who seek to retain significant elements of their cultural heritage.

There were, of course, many observers of American society who recognized its de facto racial and ethnic diversity before the late 1960s. The concept of the "melting pot" was premised on a sense of cultural differences that would eventually be overcome or transcended. In reaction to Anglo-American assimilationism, immigrant and cosmopolitan intellectuals of the early twentieth century promoted a benign and circumscribed cultural pluralism based on European national origins. By midcentury, it had become customary to celebrate the nation's tolerance for the diverse religions and cultural preferences of white ethnic groups.[2] At the same time, relations between whites and people of color, especially African Americans, continued to be framed by a racial-caste hierarchy based (at least in the minds of the upper caste) on biological rather than cultural differences. Latinos were in an ambiguous, intermediary position—not quite white but not clearly non-white. Privately and in their basic attitudes, a substantial fraction of white Americans (possibly a silent majority) still adheres to this pre-1960s conception of racial hierarchy, and a militant fringe speaks and acts aggressively on its behalf, but the doctrines associated with it are no longer acceptable in public discourse. Most of the intellectual critics of multiculturalism, those who view it as a threat to national unity, reject biological racism as emphatically as do those who hail the new emphasis on an egalitarian diversity as an enrichment of American life.[3]

America has of course been diverse in other historically important ways: identities based on class, religion, region, and gender have also encouraged assertive group consciousness, often in complex interrelationships with race and ethnicity. We all have several identities, and the one that achieves priority may vary according to personal or historical circumstances. If racial and ethnic differences have assumed greater autonomous prominence in public discourse today than at any time in the past, it may be because other sources of identity have receded in importance. Sectional differences, in conjunction with the black-white racial division, were of course central to both the mid-nineteenth-century crisis over slavery and the antisegregation struggle of the late 1950s and early 1960s. But regionalism as a prime source of identity, while still alive, weighs less heavily than in the past.

Class consciousness came to the fore in the major labor upheavals of the Gilded Age and again during the Great Depression; but, to the intense regret of social democrats and socialists, and despite the recent growth of economic inequality, it fails to shape our current politics in a decisive way. Catholic immigration and resulting waves of anti-Catholicism made religious differences seem critical to many Americans in the 1850s, 1890s, and 1920s, but today religious pluralism is not a vexing issue for most Americans (except to the extent that the new Religious Right has been seeking governmental endorsement for some of their beliefs). For better or worse, none of these sources of difference receives as much attention today as ethnoracial diversity. To be sure, gender and questions associated with it have recently become the focus of great concern, but the framing context is a heightened emphasis on what sociologists used to call "ascriptive" identities; thus gender, sexual orientation, and disability have been linked with race and ethnicity as apparently immutable conditions that deserve recognition as facets of the new multicultural reality. Those on the left who deplore identity politics and hope for a revival of class-based coalitions of the economically disadvantaged (such as the sociologist and former radical activist Todd Gitlin) are in need of better explanations of how and why race, ethnicity, and gender have seemingly trumped class as a basis for protest against the powers that be.[4]

From a detached and deterministic perspective that provides little hope for a resurgence of class consciousness, the distinguished sociologist Daniel Bell has argued that the increased salience of racial and ethnic identities in the United States and elsewhere is the inevitable result of the great transformation from industrial to postindustrial society. For him, conceptions of class that made sense in an economy based on heavy manufacturing industries with masses of manual workers are no longer appropriate in an era when information and services are central to the economy. Racial and ethnic identities, he argues, fill the vacuum left by the obsolescence of class.[5]

Another prominent sociologist of the older generation has recently provided a more specific explanation for the rise of multiculturalism. Recanting his earlier view that blacks were destined to be assimilated into the American mainstream in the manner of earlier European immigrants, Nathan Glazer now acknowledges that such integration is not occurring and is unlikely to occur. The result is that the ideal of ethnic assimilation has lost its viability, and that "we are all multiculturalists now." It is certainly true that other identity movements were inspired to some extent by the disillusionment of many blacks with the integrationist ideals of the civil rights movement, once it became clear that substantive equality for African Americans would not flow directly from the abolition of segregation laws and government-authorized discrimination. But the rise of Latino and Asian-American group consciousness has independent sources. Nativist and racist responses to an increase of non-European immigration have provoked a defensive solidarity within communities that are actually quite diverse in culture and national origin but find themselves subject to collective stereotyping and color-conscious discrimination by Euro-Americans.[6]

If class consciousness is not a prime mover in politics, structural class differences may nevertheless be a hidden linchpin for the politics of race and ethnicity. The current focus on ethnoracial pluralism—as either a threat to national cohesion or the path to a more just and democratic America—gains some of its intensity from its close correlation with class, as was the case with the interaction of race and region in southern and African-American history before the 1960s. The poor are disproportionately black, Latino, and Native American, and (as William Julius Wilson has argued in the case of African Americans) poverty, unemployment, lack of education, and mean streets are often a more immediate obstacle to equal opportunity than is intentional and systematic racial discrimination.[7] Within black and Latino minority communities, class differences have been growing between the minority benefiting directly from affirmative action and the larger number who are unprepared to take advantage of it. Class, in the broad sense of differential access to income, wealth, and education, has exacerbated racial or ethnic divisions within society as a whole—the stereotype of an out-group tends to be based on its less successful and less law-abiding members—and within minority communities themselves by making it more difficult for relatively affluent and well-educated elites to represent effectively the communities of descent to which they belong.[8]

Just as race and region were hopelessly entangled at an earlier time, race and class are now so intertwined that one cannot hope to deal with one without confronting the other as well. Many historians would argue that this has always been the case, but my contention would be that the nexus has never been so transparent. The declining significance of regionalism as a source of identity and solidarity and the demise of constitutionally sanc-tioned racial discrimination have created a new situation in which race and class are more clearly and intimately associated than ever before.

It might be noticed that I have said very little about culture per se as a source of division and an object of concern. I tend to agree with K. Anthony Appiah that enduring cultural differences are not the core of the problem.[9] For reasons that will become clear when comparisons are made with other "multicultural" societies, the unity of the United States, in my opinion, is not imminently endangered by the presence of irreconcilable ethnic cul-tures. There is in fact a relatively high degree of consensus on basic values among ethnoracial groups. The differences that exist are not of the kind that are likely to lead to constitutional group representation, secession, or ethnic cleansing. This is the good news. The bad news is that color-coded or phenotypic racism persists as a source of social hierarchy and economic inequality. This is not to deny that groups vary in cultural values and behavioral norms. But I will argue that they do not do so to an extent that rules out the possibility of an agreement on the fundamental principles that are essential to the achievement of a cohesive democratic nation.

The United States is not unique in its growing awareness of the challenge of ethnic pluralism to its national traditions. In a search for closely comparable cases, we can rule out the nations cobbled together after World War I out of the remnants of the Austro-Hungarian and Ottoman empires that have recently broken up or seem likely to. In such cases as Yugoslavia and Czechoslovakia, ethnic groups were to a great extent territorially based, and release from the strong centralized control of Communist governments brought secessions, partitions, civil war, and ethnic cleansing. Since American racial and ethnic groups are not territorially based but are dispersed throughout much of the nation, there is no real possibility that multiculturalism will lead to "another Bosnia," as some alarmists have contended.

The former Soviet Union is also too different to justify close comparisons. What has occurred there is really the disintegration of a multinational empire created by the czars and perpetuated by the Communists. It is the last chapter in the demise of the empires that dominated much of the world at the beginning of the nineteenth century—Spanish, Ottoman, Austro-Hungarian, English, French, Dutch, Portuguese, and Russian. The rise of new independent nations within the former Soviet Union brings to a final conclusion the golden age of multinational empires that lasted for several centuries and is therefore more comparable to the decolonization of Africa and Southeast Asia than to the American encounter with ethnoracial diversity.[10]

As the "first new nation" that seceded from one of the great empires, the United States has never really conceived of itself as an imperial power in the traditional sense even when it has acted imperialistically. The acquisition of the Philippines and Puerto Rico as a result of the Spanish-American War was more a historical accident than the result of a conscious and calculated ambition to establish a colonial empire. The independence of the former was projected soon after it was acquired, and the continued possession of Puerto Rico with its commonwealth status is an anomaly that has played little or no role in America's conception of itself as a world power. The choice of independence, continued commonwealth status, or statehood for Puerto Rico is of great concern to the inhabitants of the island and their compatriots on the mainland but seems to matter little, one way or another, to most Americans.

American expansionism has generally taken the form of incorporating new territories and their populations into a federated nation-state rather than a multinational empire, a process that was normally preceded by an influx of white American settlers deemed capable of self-government. If Americans had wanted to establish a multinational empire, they could have seized "All Mexico" when they had the chance in 1847.[11] The acquisition of the noncontiguous territories of Hawaii and Alaska led ultimately to the admission of new states rather than the establishment of permanent colonies. It in no way overlooks or excuses the long history of America's imperialist intervention into the internal affairs of other nations, especially in the Western Hemisphere but also in Asia, to point out that the United States has lacked conventional imperialist ambitions and has generally eschewed colonial possessions and direct or indirect rule over overseas populations, unless it could regard such domination as a step toward incorporation or independence. Americans have been intensely nationalistic and at times aggressively expansionist but not, I would argue, imperialistic in the classic Old World sense. Hence the United States has not had to confront colonial rebellions or ethnic secessions, except in the single case of the Filipino uprising against the imposition of American rule at the turn of the century.

Nevertheless, according to the Canadian political philosopher Will Kymlicka, the United States is, despite itself and contrary to its self-conception, a multinational state.[12] The inhabitants of Puerto Rico, Guam, and American Samoa, as well as Native Americans living on reservations and the Inuit of Alaska, have a special status as national minorities. Currently, a burgeoning movement among native Hawaiians is demanding similar recognition and a land base to go with it. But the cultural distinctiveness, remoteness, and relatively small numbers of these groups have left them out of most discussions of American pluralism. When assimilation of minorities was the dominant aim of liberal reformers, such groups were not usually considered among those slated to be added to the melting pot. In the nineteenth century, to be sure, there was an effort at what amounted to the forced assimilation of Native Americans, but in the early twentieth century this dream faded, both because Indians themselves refused to commit cultural suicide and because the rise of scientific racism among whites concerned with Indian affairs encouraged a belief that Indians, like blacks and Asians, were unassimilable for genetic reasons.[13]

Current advocates of multiculturalism usually include Native Americans among the groups possessing distinctive cultures that deserve to be respected and preserved. But the fact that Indian tribes do have territorial bases, inadequate though they may be, and a special legal and constitutional status based on treaties with the United States government (Chief Justice John Marshall's description of Indian tribes as "domestic dependent nations" is still roughly accurate) makes their situation and prospects quite different from those of immigrants from Asia and Latin America. Immigrants, as Kymlicka points out, have made a voluntary decision to move from one nation to another. National minorities, on the other hand, have been forced to accept alien rule. Consequently, justice for them may require, as it does not for voluntary immigrants, that they have the right to special forms of communal self-government and group representation.[14]

Canada, unlike the United States, has a large, territorially based, national minority—the French speakers of Quebec. Hence its fundamental political arrangements require a special status for one of its provinces if Canada is to remain one nation. The closest American analogue is New Mexico, with a substantial Spanish-speaking population that was supposedly guaranteed full American citizenship by the Treaty of Guadalupe Hidalgo in 1848 but often saw its rights trampled on by Anglo settlers. The state constitution continues to prescribe bilingualism for some limited purposes, but visitors to that state see little evidence of it.[15] A difference of course is that French speakers have remained the overwhelming majority in Quebec, while indigenous Spanish speakers are a minority in New Mexico. Some observers have expressed the fear that continued Mexican immigration may eventually create a Chicano Quebec in the Southwest. But the increase of Spanish speakers through immigration, even when they do come to constitute a majority in California or Texas, would not, in theory at least, confer the right to limited self-determination that, according to Kymlicka, may legitimately be accorded to conquered peoples in a multinational state.

Although the United States does have national minorities, it does not have a national minority that is currently capable of controlling a state, in the way that the French dominate the province of Quebec. Justice for national minorities and indigenous populations is a moral responsibility that the nation ought to take more seriously than it has, but it is not a requirement for the survival of the Union itself, as is the case in Canada. Civic cohesiveness in the United States depends primarily on adjusting successfully to the diversity that has been created by past and present immigration, voluntary in the case of Asians and Mexicans and involuntary in the case of African Americans. A vital and perplexing issue that may be illuminated by other comparisons is whether one model of multiculturalism works both for non-European immigrants who have recently come voluntarily in search of a better life and for those who were brought much earlier in chains for forced labor on plantations and who still carry the mark of their origins in their pigmentation, as well as by such relatively subtle indicators as speech patterns and body language.[16]

The United States shares with several other industrialized countries the questions of how to manage the diversity created by recent immigration from "the world outside the West" and whether an increase in cultural heterogeneity can be reconciled with national self-images inherited from the past. The term "multiculturalism," as well as debates over its meaning, desirability, and legal or political implications, is common to the nations of

Western Europe and to the British Commonwealth countries of Canada, Australia, and New Zealand. In the latter three cases, the problem of diversity is compounded, as in the United States, by questions involving the land and other rights of indigenous populations. It would take a book, if not several, to do justice to the variations in policy and public discourse involving ethnoracial diversity in all these countries. But, on the basis of a broad general knowledge of recent developments in some of them, it is possible to detect a spectrum of responses to multiculturalism, ranging from Canada on one extreme to France and Germany on the other.

The Canadian government has officially endorsed multiculturalism to the extent of directly subsidizing institutions and organizations devoted to "cultural retention" and the maintenance of communal solidarity among immigrant groups, including those from Asia and the Caribbean. This policy is not apparently, as is often supposed, the result of significantly more egalitarian attitudes among Canadians of European origin than can be found among whites in the United States. A recent sociological study of "realities of ethnicity in Canada and the United States" shows on the basis of extensive survey data that there is surprisingly little difference between the basic attitudes of the white citizens of these two North American nations toward immigrants of color. Despite the myths that Canada is a "mosaic" and the United States has been a "melting pot," racial prejudice and xenophobia exist to about the same extent in both countries. Differences in public policy and discourse between Canada and the United States must be explained by other factors and particularly by the ethnoracial context that preceded large-scale nonwhite immigration in recent years. In Canada, the special status of Quebec has compelled a recognition of polyethnicity that sets a precedent for the toleration and even encouragement of the cultural diversity resulting from immigration.[17]

In the United States, the volatile history of black-white relations tends to influence policy and attitudes toward Latino and Asian immigrants. Affirmative action, which was originally conceived as a response to the special disadvantages of African Americans, has been extended to some predominantly immigrant minorities. The current debate over the legitimacy of affirmative action is fueled in part by growing hostility to non-European immigration. It is no accident, therefore, that the characteristic Canadian response to immigrant disadvantage is to promote the cultural autonomy and solidarity of ethnic groups, while that of the United States is either to provide affirmative action for individuals or—if the current assault on affirmative action is successful—to rely simply on "the free market" to provide the kind of opportunities for self-help that earlier European and some contemporary Asian immigrant groups have found sufficient for a relatively high rate of economic success and social mobility—if not for the immigrants themselves, at least for their children and grandchildren.[18]

It is mostly the persistence of palpable black disadvantage that makes a majority of Americans continue to favor some form of "affirmative action," even if they are uneasy about, or opposed to, straightforward "racial preferences" as an aspect of that policy. English-speaking Canadians, on the other hand, do not see why other minorities should not have some semblance of the linguistic and cultural rights traditionally accorded to the Quebecois even as they resist Quebec's demands for greater political autonomy. The problem of Quebec seems to them more soluble in the context of an inclusive multiculturalism than as a reflection of the simple polarity between English and French Canada that inspires the secessionist movement.[19]

Since the 1950s, almost all Western European nations have received large numbers of immigrants from outside of Europe—in the case of the former imperial powers, mainly from their own former colonies. In the period of economic expansion and low unemployment between the mid-1950s and the late 1960s, newcomers were welcomed as a necessary supplement to the domestic labor force, or more specifically as people who would do the kind of menial work that natives were no longer willing to undertake. But the economic slowdown that began in the late sixties and early seventies created tighter labor markets and a movement toward the restriction of immigration that has stemmed the flow but left open the question of how to deal with the substantial numbers who were already there and wished to remain.

The rise of anti-immigrant racism was noticeable first in Britain in the heyday of Enoch Powell in the 1960s. During that decade Britain adopted the dual policy of drastically restricting nonwhite immigration from the Commonwealth and passing antidiscrimination laws, modeled to some extent on those of the United States, to encourage the fair treatment of immigrants of color who were already resident in the United Kingdom.[20] Prejudice based squarely on pigmentation appears to be stronger in Britain than in other Western European countries and has inhibited official recognition of ethnic differences among non-European immigrants. Popular racial terminology often designates both Afro-West Indians and South Asians as "blacks," thereby ignoring the cultural gulf between these two immigrant communities. A shared experience of discrimination has at times created a tenuous antiracist solidarity among people of color, and the egalitarian white Left has generally endorsed this black-white view of British race relations.

Paul Gilroy, the Afro-British cultural critic and sociologist, has traced the race problem in the United Kingdom to an insular nationalism that identifies Britishness with a distinctive physical type and way of life.[21] The British have never been noted for receiving foreigners into their national community with open arms, and they have reserved their greatest revulsion for those who seemed to deviate most from the physical and cultural norms of the island's historic populations. Unlike American proponents of the melting pot or French advocates of total assimilation into the universal republic, they have rarely proclaimed or celebrated their capacity to "Anglicize" ethnic strangers.

Although it addresses the persistent problem of color prejudice, the American civil rights or antidiscrimination model has not proved a fully appropriate response to the increase of diversity in British society. The Atlantic-centered black-white dichotomy fails to respond adequately to the fact that Britain has twice as many inhabitants of Asian as of African descent and that many South Asians claim to be subjected to discrimination and abuse more because of their culture than because of their pigmentation. Recently, a serious debate has developed about whether an American-style civil rights approach really makes sense for Britain. Representatives of the substantial Muslim minority from Pakistan and India have objected to being lumped together with Afro-West Indians as victims of prejudice and discrimination based on skin color and have contended that religion rather than race is central to their identity and the main source of their disadvantage.[22] They have therefore argued that Islam should be accorded the same legal status as Christianity. This issue came to the fore in the Salman Rushdie affair, when Muslims noted that there was a law against blasphemy that applies only to Christianity. It is also a thorny problem for British education because of the requirement that there be some form of religious instruction in state-supported schools. (Normally, of course, it is Christian.)[23] The current trend in Britain is to accord greater public representation for Islamic communities and organizations. The growing Muslim population of the United States suffers from the suspicion that some of its members support Middle East "terrorism," but separation of church and state protects it reasonably well from government-sanctioned religious discrimination.

Currently it is the France of Jean-Marie Le Pen and the *Front National* and Germany with its violent attacks by racist skinheads on Turks and other immigrants that have taken center stage in the Western European drama of ethnic conflict and accommodation. No European nations have responded to the challenge of a more culturally diverse population by adopting the Canadian solution of systematically subsidizing and promoting cultural retention and minority group solidarity or (except to a limited extent in Britain) the American option of state-mandated affirmative action policies to enhance the opportunity of individuals from disadvantaged racial and ethnic minorities.

The Netherlands, where the influx has been mainly from Indonesia and Surinam, has probably come the closest to developing a comprehensive multiculturalism that includes aspects of both American- and Canadian-type policies. A strong tradition of state-subsidized religious pluralism has made the Dutch less resistant than other Europeans to the institutionalization of diversity. The government encourages voluntary affirmative action policies in the corporate sector and in educational and other institutions and has fostered tolerance for the cultural autonomy of such groups as the Moluccan islanders from Indonesia who wish to adhere as much as possible to their traditional way of life. Multiculturalism is an honorific term among the Dutch, but opinions differ on the extent to which the rhetoric of diversity and inclusion has succeeded in overcoming the subtle prejudices and structural impediments that stand in the way of substantive equality for the new immigrant minorities.[24]

For reasons that are radically different in the two cases, Germany and France have provided relatively barren ground for the growth of multiculturalism. German identity and citizenship are rooted in a relatively pure form of ethnic nationalism. Immigrants of remote German ancestry—for example, the Volga Germans of Russia who left their German-speaking homelands in the eighteenth century—are eligible for instant citizenship. On the other hand, the children and grandchildren of Turks who came as guest workers thirty or forty years ago are still regarded as foreigners and face many obstacles if they wish to acquire German citizenship. Four hundred thousand Turks born in Germany retained the status of resident aliens in 1992. Recent legislation makes it somewhat easier for Turks born in Germany to become citizens, but since the government does not recognize dual nationality, few take advantage of the opportunity. German multiculturalism normally takes the form of encouraging Turks to organize themselves as a "national minority" in order to bargain more effectively with the German state. Turkish leaders and antiracist Germans also advocate limited political rights for resident aliens, such as access to the municipal franchise.[25]

The United States long had a racial qualification for citizenship through naturalization. According to the Immigration and Naturalization Law of 1790, only free white immigrants were eligible for citizenship. As part of the postemancipation reforms of the Reconstruction era, the privilege was extended to black newcomers, but it was not until World War II that Asians became eligible for naturalization. The Fourteenth Amendment made citizens of all persons born in the United States (except Indians on reservations, who had to wait until 1924). Since 1868, therefore, the rights of American nationality have been conferred automatically on the children of all immigrants, whatever their race or ethnicity. Recent proposals to deny citizenship to the children of illegal immigrants would break a long tradition and might require a constitutional amendment. Americans may have once had what amounted to a white racial nationalism that contradicted the general principles of civic nationalism that the founding documents of the nation professed, but never, at least officially, a culturally based ethnic nationalism like that of the Germans.[26]

French nationalism, like the American, is professedly of the "civic" as opposed to the "ethnic" variety. Indeed the French virtually invented the idea that a nation could be based on the equal rights and general will of all of its loyal inhabitants. Unlike Germany, France has long been an immigrant-receiving society. What has limited French toleration of other cultures is a powerful ethnocentrism that tends to regard French culture as a universal norm to which all immigrants, whatever their origins, should be able and willing to conform, at least in public. The republican Left, in the spirit of the French Revolution, has favored government policies that are thoroughly secular and even antireligious. The Right, on the other hand, tends to conceive of France as a Catholic country with a traditional culture that is a continuation of what existed under the *ancien régime*. France's state-supported universalist republicanism and its unofficial cultural chauvinism are equally inhospitable to the idea of France as a multicultural nation. Full assimilation is the classic republican solution, and total exclusion is the aim of Le Pen and his supporters. French policy and traditions make no distinction among immigrant groups. The only categories that officially matter are French citizens and foreigners. The rationalistic universalism of the republican Left lacks respect for cultural particularity, especially if it takes a religious form, and the intolerance of the Right extends to anything that is not traditionally French and Christian, preferably Catholic. The French government has nevertheless made some pragmatic adjustments to ethnic diversity. In 1981 the ban on cultural associations based on national origins was lifted, and these ethnic organizations have subsequently received public subsidies for activities that seem likely to facilitate the integration of their members into French society. But such policies have had the unintended effect of intensifying ethnic identities and thus impeding assimilation.[27]

To a greater extent than in Britain, French "racism" is a response to cultural rather than phenotypical differences. The furor over the Muslim girls who wore headscarves to school, which resulted in their being banned in 2004, brought out the hostility of much of the republican Left to any expression of religious commitment in the public sphere and the nativist Right's intolerance of Islam and prejudice against former colonial subjects.[28]

Michael Walzer has recently argued that American liberalism is traditionally more tolerant of cultural diversity than is French republicanism. The French have developed, he contends, a more powerful and coercive concept of assimilation than have the Americans. Although France has received many immigrants, it could never be described as "a nation of immigrants." Newcomers have been expected to become thoroughly French in their public personae, and most of them have. In America, according to Walzer, "children are taught that they are citizens of a plural and tolerant society—where what is tolerated is their own choice of cultural membership and identity."[29] European immigrants have of course been the main beneficiaries of this cultural toleration. At least in recent times, no price has had to be paid for celebrating one's Irishness, Italianness, Jewishness, or Polishness—in fact, vote-seeking politicians from other ethnic groups customarily join in the festivities. Currently, expressions of Asian and Latino cultural specificity also invite the participation of candidates for office, as evidenced by the controversy over whether or not Vice President Al Gore was raising funds when he spoke at a Buddhist temple in 1996.

But before glorifying American tolerance and condemning the lack of it in the French, we need to recall the American color line, which has denigrated people not so much because of culture but because of race as a supposed fact of nature that endowed groups distinguishable on the basis of skin color or nonwhite ancestry with differing degrees of intelligence, character, and capability. Racism in the American sense has had its adherents in France, especially on the far right, but their views have long been less influential in public policy and discourse than are the opinions of those who have defined human diversity primarily in terms of cultural differences. Sociological surveys suggest that the French are significantly less prejudiced against black Africans or West Indians than against Muslim North Africans, who are as light-skinned as many French but who are believed to constitute a cultural threat.[30]

The French may need multiculturalism more than Americans do and are likely to resist it more vigorously, but Americans need what the African National Congress of South Africa calls "non-racialism" more than the French. A confusion between the need to overcome phenotypic racism, which remains a more basic problem for the United States than for France, and the need for cultural toleration, which is not so difficult a challenge for Americans, has at times muddied debates over multiculturalism in both countries.

Walzer's description of American liberalism's capacity for cultural toleration provides some grounds for optimism in the current campaign for a full acknowledgment of the cultural rights of immigrants who are not of European origin. But one cultural issue has come to the fore that has provoked a resurgence of nativist sentiment—the question of language retention and bilingual education. Several state legislatures have recently passed laws recognizing English as an official language. Controversies concerning the linguistic rights of immigrants are not without precedent in American history. The issue of whether immigrants have the right to be instructed in their own language arose in the late nineteenth century in the case of German-medium schools in the Midwest. Laws passed against teaching in German created a political storm in Wisconsin and Illinois in the late 1880s that led to their repeal when many German voters switched parties. During World War I, however, virtually all use of German in public schools, even teaching it as a foreign language, was suppressed. Nebraska went so far as to forbid the teaching of all foreign languages in its schools, but this extreme version of "English Only" was declared unconstitutional by the United States Supreme Court.[31]

Today the language in question is Spanish, and programs in the public schools to begin instruction in Spanish and then gradually move to English have come under intense attack. Bilingual education, the printing of electoral ballots in various languages, and the conduct of public business in Spanish in some localities have led to a movement to amend state and federal constitutions to mandate the use of English in all governmental functions. Comparatively speaking, however, the United States does not yet have a serious problem of linguistic diversity. The world is filled with countries that are deeply divided among language groups that claim equal rights with others—from South Africa with its eleven official languages to Canada and Belgium with two each. If the Spanish-speaking population of the United States continues to grow to the point where Latinos are a majority in some states, it is conceivable that demands for official bilingualism will be made on the state level. The experience of other countries suggests to me that such a policy would not be disastrous so long as many people can be induced to learn and use more than one language, as is currently the case in such polyglot nations as Belgium, South Africa, Canada, Switzerland, and India. It would enrich the culture of the border states of California, Texas, Arizona, and New Mexico, to say nothing of improving intergroup and international relations, if all students in these states were required to learn a modicum of Spanish in public schools, just as English-speaking Canadians and Flemish-speaking Belgians must take some French.

Michael Walzer's liberal prescription of "state neutrality" as a basis for ethnic toleration may not be an adequate response to the current situation of increasing diversity. The political philosophers Jürgen Habermas and Amy Gutmann argue that the achievement of individual rights in an ethnically diverse democratic society requires (in the words of Gutmann) not only "respect for the unique identities of each individual, regardless of gender, race, or ethnicity," but also "respect for those activities, practices, and ways of viewing the world that are particularly valued by, or associated with, members of disadvantaged groups, including women, Asian Americans, African Americans, Native Americans, and a multitude of other groups in the United States." According to Habermas, "A correctly understood theory of rights requires a politics of recognition that protects the integrity of the individual in the life context in which his or her identity is formed."[32]

Such an expansion of the American equal rights tradition to include such cultural rights—protection against being disadvantaged by one's "cultural context"—would presumably require government enforcement, just as policies protecting individuals against discrimination for such ascribed characteristics as gender and race currently do. Affirmative action based on cultural ethnicity exists already to some extent in its coverage of Latinos who are phenotypically white, but the principle has never been clearly acknowledged. The acceptance of a "politics of recognition" and the right to a "cultural context" might well include groups not currently covered by affirmative action, such as Arab Americans.

Critics of multiculturalism will at this point predict the "disuniting of America." What kind of consensus can we hope for if cultural differences are accorded this level of official protection and recognition, even if it is on the liberal basis of an extension of individual rather than group rights? "Complex societies," Habermas argues in response, "can no longer be held together by a substantive consensus on values but only by a consensus on the procedures for the legitimate enactment of laws and the legitimate exercise of power." Martin E. Marty, the eminent historian of American Christianity, has used the precedent of toleration for all religions to prescribe such a value-neutral policy for the United States—in his terms a recognition that the nation is an "association" rather than a "community."[33] Since American nationality is supposedly premised on the commitment to democratic institutions and procedures and not on an officially sanctioned set of cultural values, we should be in a much better position to accept such a conception of what holds us together than are such nations as Habermas's Germany, which has traditionally affirmed an ethnocultural nationalism.

The United States, however, may not be as "complex" as the plural societies to which Habermas's formula would obviously apply. As the political scientist Jennifer Hochschild has contended, United States citizens, with few exceptions, affirm "the American dream" of material success through individual effort. Her study of opinions about race and class in America shows that even the most underprivileged African Americans tend to accept this ideal in principle even if they are unable to live up to it in practice.[34]

Most voluntary immigrants, from whatever source, have come to America primarily with the aim of improving the material circumstances of themselves and their families.[35] This ideal of America as a land of economic opportunity for individuals and families is not shared by traditionalist Native Americans and Hawaiians, nor by some religious communities, such as the Amish and Hutterites; and their historically sanctioned rights to practice a communalism contrary to American individualist norms must be respected. But most Americans, of whatever ethnoracial background, place a high value on individual opportunity to prosper and attain a decent standard of living. From this perspective, the challenge before us is to make life chances for material betterment equally available to everyone regardless of race, ethnicity, or gender. The debate on affirmative action centers on the question of whether special consideration needs to be given to members of historically disadvantaged groups to ensure a "level playing field." (I happen to think that it does, but I will not argue the case here.) America therefore shares with many other nations the challenge of how to accommodate increasing ethnic diversity through immigration from non-European sources, but our basic values and democratic principles may permit us to cope with this mixing of populations more effectively than the principal nations of Western Europe can.

What is truly unique about America's diversity, at least when compared to the other modern industrialized nations in which multiculturalism has become an issue, has been the continuous presence throughout our national history of a substantial and radically disadvantaged minority descended from the involuntary immigrants that the slave trade brought from Africa during the colonial period and for a short time thereafter. As a result, most white Americans, past or present, have had some direct experience of racial advantage or favoritism signifying that their ethnic status was higher than that of African Americans. The American liberal tolerance for ethnic diversity that is praised by Michael Walzer has traditionally stopped at the color line. Nathan Glazer, who views multiculturalism itself as a regrettable if necessary response to the failure to assimilate blacks into the mainstream of American life, begs the question as to whether liberal multiculturalism is an adequate response to the persistent low status of African Americans in the de facto ethnoracial hierarchy.

Will Kymlicka's broad comparative study *Multicultural Citizenship* distinguishes between national minorities (conquered indigenous communities) and immigrant minorities. He has wise things to say about what would constitute a just policy in each case—basically partial autonomy and group representation for the former and an enforceable equality of rights and opportunities for the latter.[36] But African Americans are neither a national nor a voluntary immigrant minority. They were incorporated by force like indigenous peoples, but, like free immigrants, they came from elsewhere and lack a territorial base within the United States. The perennial debate among African Americans between separatists and integrationists—which has included such voices as that of W. E. B. Du Bois, who were really searching for a middle ground—can be seen as an effort to situate the black American experience in relation to Kymlicka's dichotomy. Nationalists have in effect argued that blacks are the equivalent of a national minority that deserves communal autonomy and group representation, while integrationists have in effect accepted the immigrant analogy, if not as a current reality at least as an ideal to be pursued.[37] The castelike character of black status, especially in the South and before 1965, was not truly analogous to that of any group in British, French, Dutch, Canadian, or Australian domestic society in the late nineteenth and twentieth centuries, although one can find some equivalency in the colonies of the European nations. The anthropologist John Ogbu suggested in 1978 that the best analogies for understanding the African-American situation are not ethnic minorities of the usual sort but rather lower castes such as the Burakhumin of Japan and the untouchables of India—groups that have traditionally been relegated to menial roles, socially segregated, and prohibited from intermarrying with the upper caste or castes.[38]

But the caste analogy, although useful as a corrective to simply considering African Americans another minority, is not perfect either. It suggests a permanence and fixity of status that are contradicted by the history of black-white relations in the United States. Blacks in the South of the Jim Crow era may have been very like a caste, but the civil rights movement destroyed the legal basis for such a status. Currently, I would suggest, African Americans are caught between the legacy of caste and the possibility of being included as another ethnic group in a multicultural America. The evolution from "a caste to a minority" that Vernon Williams traces in the sociological thought of the early to mid-twentieth century has not yet been fully achieved in social reality.[39] To me this means that black-specific and not just race-specific policies may be necessary. Affirmative action, which does not usually apply to Asians, may become unnecessary for Latinos, or at least some Latino groups, at some point in the near future and yet remain a justifiable policy for blacks so long as extralegal racism perpetuates aspects of color caste.

It is highly significant, I think, that intermarriage between African Americans and whites, although increasing, is much lower than that between Asian and Euro-Americans or between Latinos and Anglos. Furthermore, polls reveal that a majority of whites continue to oppose black-white marriages on principle.[40] Such data might be taken as evidence of the survival of caste consciousness among a significant proportion of the American population. A multiculturalism that treats all people of color as equally disadvantaged and in need of the same kind of assistance to compete successfully in the American economy and achieve full and effective representation in government and civil society will not, in all probability, suffice to bring full justice and equality to African Americans. To repair the damage done by almost four centuries of enslavement, segregation, white-on-black violence, and pervasive caste discrimination, we will have to go beyond the mere toleration of differences that is often prescribed by liberal multiculturalists and reach for the higher ground of interracial and intercultural democracy.

CHAPTER 4

John Higham's Plural America

This essay is devoted to an appraisal of the work of John Higham, particularly his
book Hanging Together: Unity and Diversity in American Culture, *edited by*
Carl J. Guarneri (New Haven, CT: Yale University Press, 2001).

* * *

Specialization on increasingly narrow subjects is the dominant trend in
American historical scholarship. Rarer and rarer, at least in the academy,
are generalists dealing with broad stretches of the past or souls who work in
more than one of the usual specialties or move readily from one to another.
The new "micro-history" is less concerned with making connections and
establishing general patterns than with recapturing the experiences and
appreciating the achievements of those who were overlooked by previous
generations of historians. Recording the doings of elite white males has
taken a backseat to accounts of marginalized groups—women, African
Americans, Latinos, low-skilled workers, and poor people generally. Much
of value has come from social and cultural history "from the bottom up," but
it has deprived us of a unifying vision of the nation's past across the divides
of gender, race, ethnicity, and class.

During a distinguished career of more than half a century, which ended
with his death in 2003, the historian John Higham resisted the trend toward
greater specialization, while at the same time showing a deep understanding
of the plight of oppressed or marginalized groups that have sought higher
status both within historical memory and in society at large. He focused his
main attention on those immigrants who have been victims of xenophobia,
but he also responded sympathetically to the situation of African Americans. Higham's work, as reflected in the collection of his essays edited by
his former student Carl Guarneri, cut across at least three major subfields
of American history that do not normally interact very much and made
memorable contributions to each of them. These fields are ethnicity and race

in American life and thought since the Civil War; the history of American culture (both popular and elite) in the nineteenth and early twentieth centuries; and the history of historical interpretation. *Hanging Together* makes it possible to assess the full achievement of a very creative historian. It will become clear as we do so that Higham, in his own singularly judicious and good-tempered fashion, was an engaged intellectual in close touch with contemporary cultural trends and controversies, particularly over changing perceptions of the American past.

Born in 1920, Higham came of age in the Great Depression.[1] Although his parents came from a midwestern Protestant background, he grew up in a multiethnic neighborhood in Queens, had Jewish and Catholic friends, and thus became sensitive from an early age to the diverse character of American society. (These interactions were strictly with what were later called "white ethnics"; few if any blacks, he later noted, could be found in Queens in those days.) When he was an undergraduate at Johns Hopkins in the late 1930s and a graduate student at the University of Wisconsin in the 1940s, his political inclinations were toward the left but not the far left. Initially drawn to the democratic socialism of Norman Thomas, he became by the 1950s the kind of "independent liberal" who refused to take sides in Cold War ideological conflicts. His Wisconsin dissertation on the history of American nativism, which became his seminal first book, *Strangers in the Land*,[2] the first comprehensive account of anti-immigrant sentiments and actions between the Civil War and the 1920s, was influenced by the "progressive" school of American historiography originated by Charles A. Beard, which stressed the causal significance of economic conditions and class interests. But Higham was not an economic determinist in Beard's sense. It is clear from his account that ideas and cultural concerns shaped the aims of the nativist movements in ways that were independent of the economic stimulus that may have set them in motion. For example, he recognized that racist ideas and stereotypes were already embedded in the culture when nativist publicists and politicians appealed to them in justification of policies such as discriminatory quotas aimed at Italians, Irish, and Jews. Over the years Higham would move further away from economic or materialist explanations and give increasing weight to cultural factors.

Strangers in the Land was well received when it came out in 1955, and it has remained to this day the standard account of America's anti-immigrant ideologies, movements, and policies. Higham argued that nativism tended to be most virulent in periods of economic crisis but that international developments, such as World War I and the Bolshevik Revolution, had a major independent impact in increasing hostility toward immigrants. He would later call the historians he considered most prominent in the 1950s—Richard Hofstadter, Daniel Boorstin, and Louis Hartz—the "consensus school," which meant that they deemphasized social and ideological conflict in favor of the notion that Americans had always agreed on fundamental liberal capitalist values and were thus spared the class conflicts that led to the rise of socialism and fascism in Europe.[3] But Higham's own work stressed social conflict more than consensus, although not in familiar socialist or Marxist terms. In making ethnic or racial divisions count for at least as much as those associated with class, his work somewhat resembled that of C. Vann Woodward, whose great books *Origins of the New South, 1877–1913* and *The Strange Career of Jim Crow* appeared in 1951 and 1955 respectively.[4]

Woodward was somewhat closer to the explanations based on economic conflict than Higham was, but he also made it clear that racism was deeply rooted in southern culture and not just an improvised weapon in the struggles of classes or interest groups. If Woodward, Higham, and Kenneth Stampp (who in 1956 demolished the image of the happy and harmonious slave plantation of the Old South[5]) are taken to be the representative U.S. historians of the 1950s, one could easily argue that the dominant theme they shared was not so much consensus as an emphasis on the need to shift from a model of conflict based strictly on class to one rooted at least partially in racial or ethnic differences.

But Higham did share one trait with those he called the consensus historians (I'm thinking here particularly of Richard Hofstadter)—a willingness to generalize broadly about American society and politics and to put forward moral and cultural criticism of the tendencies he discerned. A strong disapproval of aggressive nationalism, whether invoked against minorities at home or "enemies" abroad, ran throughout his work. Higham also shared the consensus historians' view that American society cohered, to the considerable extent that it did, because of a core of common values. He sought to understand the relationship between what held the nation together and what threatened to tear it apart.

Higham's second major book was to have been a cultural history of the Gilded Age, which for him was the watershed between the old republic of the antebellum era and the modern colossus of the twentieth century. Brilliant essays on the cultural transformations of the 1850s and 1890s, both included in *Hanging Together*, were the fruit of this work. They reveal Higham's rare talent for uncovering the common elements in elite and popular culture that can be said to reflect the spirit of an age. In his essay on the 1890s, for example, Higham establishes connections among such seemingly diverse phenomena as violent sports, ragtime music, naturalistic fiction, and pragmatic philosophy, all of them developments that broke with convention. But the big book never got written, to some extent at least because of the way the 1960s drew Higham's attention back to issues involving ethnicity and race. He marched with C. Vann Woodward, John Hope Franklin, and other liberal historians at Selma in 1965. Like many academics of his generation, he was disconcerted and to some degree estranged by the radical, countercultural movements of the late

1960s and early 1970s, which seemed to him to glorify division, disruption, and separatism. The Black Power movement and the student protests that he encountered on the University of Michigan campus made him a critic of the New Left, although a relatively calm and judicious one who remained sympathetic to some of the movement's goals if not its methods.

The title essay in *Hanging Together,* which was originally Higham's presidential address to the Organization of American Historians in 1974, was in part a response to the divisiveness of the day. But it approached the topic of "divergent unities in American history" from a detached, nonpolemical, almost Olympian perspective. He found three ways in which Americans had historically found common ground. First was the "'primordial' unity" arising from place, kinship, ancestry, and other "inherited relationships" (for example, membership in an Indian tribe or origin in a particular Italian village, Eastern European shtetl, or Chinese district). Second was the "ideological unity" based on the individualist and libertarian values common to dissenting Protestantism and the Enlightenment political thought that sanctioned the American Revolution. The great nineteenth-century crusade against slavery was built upon a widely shared conviction that slavery was incompatible with these values. Finally came the "technical unity" resulting from the ways that modern forms of specialized knowledge and bureaucratic organization promoted cooperation and coordination. Large corporations, government agencies, interest group lobbies, and professional associations would be among the centers of unifying tendencies.

Higham characterized the Progressive Era between 1898 and 1918 as a time when there was a "fertile amalgamation" of "democratic ideals" and "bureaucratic techniques." This, he found, was particularly the case whenever scientific methods were used to achieve humanitarian goals or when unbiased empirical investigations were required to establish the facts to which reformers needed to address themselves. More recently, however, he found that technical unity seemed to triumph at the expense of both primordial bonds and ideological unity, although the latter forms of solidarity did assert themselves spasmodically. Higham concluded that "each of these adhesive forces—the primordial, the ideological, and the technical—has something to contribute to our complex society, and each of them survives within it. If we can discover how to align the technical with the primordial so that each offsets the other, and give to ideology the task of challenging both, we may raise to a new level one of the great enduring principles of our ideological heritage: the importance of diversity, the value of countervailing power."

In essence Higham was saying that American unities are themselves plural and even contradictory but that they nevertheless must be made to work together in some ways if we are to have a decent and progressive society.

Higham's commitment to studying American history as a totality rather than a set of fragments did not make him a scholarly isolationist. In order to gain a broader perspective on the United States, he championed, and to some extent practiced, comparative history. The major essay on comparative immigrations that he contributed to *The Comparative Approach to American History*, edited by C. Vann Woodward in 1968,[6] is not included in this collection except in the "distilled form" he used in a 1991 address in Australia. Missing, therefore, is Higham's provocative argument that America's twentieth-century mass culture, unlike that of some other immigrant-receiving societies, was invented by immigrants for immigrants. (Among the cultural forms that ethnic entrepreneurs and artists pioneered in their efforts to divert a largely immigrant audience were the first comic strips, vaudeville, and Tin Pan Alley. As he points out, they also contributed significantly to popular journalism, radio broadcasting, and the early film industry.)

Around this time, Higham also expressed the intention to carry out a comparative history of group relations on three multiracial islands—Hawaii, Fiji, and Mauritius. Although many historians were skeptical about the value of such a project (some of the most cynical even wondered if it was designed to provide the opportunity to do research in paradisiacal locations), I regret that he was not able to carry it out. Hawaii might well serve as a model for group relations in a future America in which there is a nonwhite majority. Understanding how it has achieved relative harmoniousness in contrast to the intense ethnic conflict elsewhere in the United States might be very instructive.

The revival during the late sixties and early seventies of Higham's interest in issues involving race and ethnicity came to fruition in a collection of insightful essays—*Send These to Me: Jews and Other Immigrants in Urban America*, published first in 1975 and then in substantially revised form in 1984.[7] Higham found that anti-Semitism in the United States owed relatively little to the cultural and intellectual animus against Jews that had arisen in Europe. The American variant, he wrote persuasively, was primarily a social phenomenon reflecting the insecurities of middle- and upper-class gentiles at a time of great social mobility. In his broad discussion of ideas about group relations in America, Higham advanced the concept of "pluralistic integration," distinguishing between the periphery of an ethnic group, which is open to assimilation or cultural amalgamation, and the core that seeks to preserve as much tradition and autonomy as possible. (For example, religious Jews and Jewish organizations preserve the core, but many individual Jews collaborate with gentiles in secular organizations, become successful in the larger society, and intermarry with non-Jews to such an extent that the core group becomes greatly concerned.) Here as elsewhere, Higham was attempting to mediate between the advocates of a coercive, one-way assimilationism and the champions of ethnic particularism and self-segregation.

Between the mid-seventies and the mid-eighties the question of what was the best model for group relations in the United States lost some of its salience. But in the "culture wars" of the late eighties and early nineties the issue of "the one versus the many" or how much "pluribus" is compatible with "unum" came back with a vengeance. Black nationalism revived in the form of Afrocentrism, and members of other nonwhite groups affirmed their distinctive identities under the banner of "multiculturalism." The last two essays in *Hanging Together*, both written in the early nineties, contain Higham's response to the new pluralism.

His essay "Multiculturalism and Universalism," originally published in *The American Quarterly* in 1993, was one of the most cogent and balanced of the many critical evaluations of the recently intensified celebration of diversity. Higham exposed what he took to be the misconceptions or simplifications associated with the multicultural movement but managed to avoid the polemicism and disdainfulness of other liberal critics. Harking back to his New Deal, democratic socialist roots, he took multiculturalists to task for paying only lip service to class as a source of identity and a basis for mobilizing a political movement while making race, ethnicity, and gender the only differences that really mattered. The lower class, he observed, was often composed of minority ethnic groups, and he argued that class affiliation could unify Americans across ethnoracial divisions. He also contended that social justice, with due recognition of cultural differences, could acquire legitimacy and effectiveness from the universalistic commitment to democracy and human rights that was held to be the national creed. Rather than imposing an intolerant uniformity, American universalism could be the basis for establishing a balance between unity and diversity.

In "The Future of American History," first published in 1994 and the most recent of the essays in *Hanging Together*, Higham responded to the current efforts of some younger historians to denationalize history: "Celebrating diversity and deconstruction, the insistent pluralism of our post-Marxist era rejects any claim to centeredness in the forms of experience. In short, postmodernism calls for destabilizing and decentering an integrated national history."

Higham had no objection to internationalizing history by pursuing subjects that necessarily cross national borders, such as the history of migrations, intellectual and social movements, and scientific or technological innovations. But he wanted to make it clear that the choice of some historians to investigate subjects that could not be confined within a single nation-state, for example, the United States, does not delegitimize the work of other historians who continue to write history based on the national experience. Some advocates of "internationalizing American history" have repudiated the kind of comparative history that takes nation-states as its "units of analysis." Higham found this view shortsighted. Despite globalization, nations still matter and have certainly mattered greatly in the past as sources of identity and as the centers of power over people's lives. Nations successfully claim the allegiance of most citizens and can make them go to war, pay taxes, and obey laws. Arguably, nationalism is the most influential ideology of the modern world and "deconstructing" it, as Higham suggested, will not make it go away as a historical force, any more than deconstructing race eliminates racism's horrendous impact on its victims.

Higham's effort to save American history from the postmodernists risked the charge that he was an advocate of a chauvinistic "American exceptionalism." He called for the investigation of "Americanness," not simply as nationalist "myth, symbol, and ideology" but also as an unarticulated sentiment of "belonging, of being at home"; but this intention scarcely made him an American exceptionalist. Although the term has been recently applied to anyone who believes that the American past has unique or distinctive features, its proper meaning is the once prevalent notion that the United States departs from a general pattern that applies to all of the advanced, industrial societies of Western Europe. To maintain, as Higham did, that all nations are exceptional in the sense that they have cultural and institutional features that do not exist elsewhere or do not exist elsewhere in precisely the same combination is to use common sense rather than succumb to national chauvinism.

Playing down the significance of national peculiarities, Higham convincingly argued, risks homogenizing historical experience to an intolerable extent. Does it really make sense to deny that there is, or at least has been, a characteristic or typical American, English, French, or German mode of life, thought, and perception? There may be an increase in postnational institutional power—through multinational corporations and international organizations, for example. But people in many parts of the world remain little affected by them. The fact that Western nations are becoming more diverse internally is a more serious problem for those who believe in unifying national traits or characters, but historians have a responsibility to identify and analyze the historically constructed core cultures against which the new pluralist movements are reacting.

The two major essays of the 1990s, written when John Higham was well into his eighth decade, reflect the persistence of his desire to reestablish connections or sources of unity both within a historiography that he saw as overspecialized and within an American society that he viewed as too racially and ethnically segmented. His search was for a middle ground. He advocated both historical writing that absorbed the new cultural and social history into some kind of higher synthesis and a society that accepted diversity and assimilation as complementary and compatible processes rather than as antitheses. These efforts were entirely commendable, in my opinion. There have been far too many false dichotomies and oversimplifications in the discussion of group relations in the United States. The notion that people either assimilate and lose an original identity or remain outside the

American mainstream is false to the historical experiences of many ethnic groups—as any close observer of, say, Italian-American or Polish-American history is aware. Equally misleading and pernicious is the claim of parochial nationalists and separatists that those who interact with the larger culture are betraying their "roots." Establishing a common ground through general adherence to liberal-democratic ideals and practices does not preclude ethnic diversity any more than it conflicts with the variegation of religious belief and affiliation. Indeed, as is obviously true of religious toleration, it mandates a respect for differences.

But ethnic pluralism may still constrict individual freedom if race and ethnicity are seen as primordial and inescapable—fixed forever by the sheer fact of ancestry or skin color. The "essentialist" view of ethnicity, as set forth, for example, in the philosopher Horace Kallen's contention that you can change everything except the identity of your grandfather, ignores the fact that the importance people attribute to personal ancestry may vary greatly and should, at least from the standpoint of liberal-democratic theory, be a matter of personal choice. What makes the problem of black and white in America so intractable is the extent to which identities erroneously considered fixed and permanent carry with them built-in assets or liabilities.

Also generally persuasive is Higham's assertion that nations and national identities remain legitimate, indeed essential, objects of historical inquiry. Those who claim otherwise are in danger of ignoring the extent to which the values and ideas that derive from cultural nationality influence almost everything that we do and say. As Americans, we have a certain cultural "given" that we cannot avoid confronting, unless we choose to be expatriates or hermits. We do not, for example, question the value of democracy and personal liberty (although what we mean by such terms may vary greatly). But Higham's search for comparative insights affirms the need for the kind of cosmopolitanism that will give us some distance from Americanness. And that distance is needed if Americans' ideological traditions are to be adjusted to the changing circumstances of the twenty-first century.

My only criticism of Higham's recent essays is that they may have been a bit alarmist in their assessment of the dangers arising from recent assertions of "multiculturalism" by representatives of various racial or ethnic minorities. He was far less apocalyptic than his fellow liberal and near-contemporary Arthur M. Schlesinger Jr. was in *The Disuniting of America*,[8] and his strictures on identity movements for not paying enough attention to the salience of class seem to me entirely persuasive. But he fell a bit short of what seems to me a fully fair and balanced assessment of the latest assertions of cultural pluralism. For example, his criticism of ethnic studies programs in universities concentrated on the ones that have been overly political and ignored those that have achieved intellectual depth. Of course a calmer perspective is now possible than was the case in the late eighties and early nineties because of the recent subsiding of the "culture wars." We no longer hear so much about the "disintegration" or "balkanization" of America.

But differing reactions may also come from differing regions. In the Northeast multiculturalism has often been associated with African-American cultural nationalism and especially with Afrocentrism. Louis Farrakhan, Leonard Jeffries, and Molefi Asante are sometimes taken as its exemplars. If this is what is meant by multiculturalism, it is indeed a disintegrative movement. In California, however, where African Americans are greatly outnumbered by Latinos, and Asians are relatively more numerous than elsewhere, multiculturalism has come to signify something rather different. The emphasis here, at least in intellectual and academic circles, is increasingly on group interaction and cooperation rather than separation. A high rate of intermarriage and the emergence of many young people who proudly affirm a mixed or multicultural identity suggest how porous group boundaries are becoming. When Stanford introduced an undergraduate major in Comparative Studies in Race and Ethnicity a few years ago, many teachers anticipated that most of the students would choose the ethnically specific tracks—African-American, Chicano, Asian-American, and Native American. (The major originated in part as a response to the demands of Chicanos and Asian Americans to have ethnic studies programs of their own equivalent to the one already existing for African Americans.) In fact, a substantial majority elected a comparative studies track that required working on more than one group and on general patterns of race and ethnicity, not only in the United States but in other countries as well. A large proportion of the students identified themselves as being of mixed race rather than as members of a single minority group.

My own experience is that the sizable minority of students who can claim only a white identity interact with those who consider themselves "people of color" with much less tension than might have been the case a decade ago. All of this mixing and blurring of identities is taking place under the auspices of multiculturalism or "diversity." Something like John Higham's ideal of "pluralistic integration" is perhaps being fulfilled on California campuses. The common ground is acceptance of what amounts to a human right to affirm a traditional identity or construct a new one out of the collision of groups and cultures in our increasingly diverse society. The historical basis for such possibilities can be found in Higham's work over the years.

PART TWO

Slavery and Racism: Historiographic Interventions

CHAPTER 5

The Skeleton in the Closet

Three books are evaluated in this chapter—Slave Narratives, *edited by William L. Andrews and Henry Louis Gates Jr. (Library of America, 2000),* Born in Bondage: Growing Up Enslaved in the Antebellum South *by Marie Jenkins Schwartz (Cambridge, MA: Harvard University Press, 2000), and* Soul by Soul: Life Inside the Antebellum Slave Market *by Walter Johnson (Cambridge, MA: Harvard University Press, 1999).*

* * *

I.

One hundred and thirty-five years after its abolition, slavery is still the skeleton in the American closet. Among the African-American descendants of its victims there is a difference of opinion about whether the memory of it should be suppressed as unpleasant and dispiriting or commemorated in the ways that Jews remember the Holocaust. There is no national museum of slavery and any attempt to establish one would be controversial. In 1995, black employees of the Library of Congress successfully objected to an exhibition of photographs and texts describing the slave experience, because they found it demoralizing. But other African Americans have called for a public acknowledgment of slavery as a national crime against blacks, comparable to the Holocaust as a crime against Jews, and some have asked that reparations be paid to them on the grounds that they still suffer from its legacy. Most whites, especially those whose ancestors arrived in the United States after the emancipation of the slaves and settled outside the South, do not see why they should accept any responsibility for what history has done to African Americans. Recently, however, the National Park Service has begun a systematic review of exhibits at Civil War battlefields to make visitors aware of how central slavery and race were to the conflict.

Professional historians have not shared the public's ambivalence about remembering slavery. Since the publication of Kenneth Stampp's *The Peculiar Institution* in 1956 and Stanley Elkins's *Slavery* in 1959, the liveliest and most creative work in American historical studies has been devoted to slavery and the closely related field of black-white relations before the twentieth century. In the 1970s, there was a veritable explosion of large and important books about slavery in the Old South.[1] But no consensus emerged about the essential character of antebellum slavery. What was common to all this work was a reaction against Stanley Elkins's view that slavery devastated its victims psychologically, to such an extent that it left them powerless to resist their masters' authority or even to think and behave independently.[2] If slaves were now endowed with "agency" and a measure of dignity, the historians of the seventies differed on the sources and extent of the cultural "breathing space" that slaves were now accorded. For Herbert Gutman, it was the presence among slaves of closely knit nuclear and extended families; for John Blassingame, it was the distinctive communal culture that emanated from the slave quarters; for Eugene Genovese, it was the ability to maneuver within an ethos of plantation paternalism that imposed obligations on both masters and slaves.[3]

Clearly there was a difference of opinion between Blassingame and Gutman, on the one hand, and Genovese on the other, about how much autonomy the slaves possessed. Genovese conceded a "cultural hegemony" to the slaveholders that the others refused to acknowledge. But even Genovese celebrated "the world that the slaves made" within the interstices of the paternalistic world that the slaveholders had made. At the very least, slaves had their own conceptions of the duties owed to them by their masters, which were often in conflict with what the masters were in fact willing to concede. Although all the interpretations found that conflict was integral to the master-slave relationship, the emphasis on the cultural creativity and survival skills of the slaves tended to draw attention away from the most brutal and violent aspects of the regime—such as the frequent and often sadistic use of the lash and the forced dissolution by sale of many thousands of the two-parent families discovered by Gutman.[4]

There was also a tendency to deemphasize physical, as opposed to cultural, resistance by slaves. Relatively little was said about rebellion or the planning of rebellion, running away, or sabotaging the operation of the plantation. From the literature of the 1970s and 1980s, one might be tempted to draw the conclusion that slaves accommodated themselves fairly well to their circumstances and, if not actually contented, found ways to avoid being miserable. Out of fashion was the view of Kenneth Stampp and other neo-abolitionist historians of the post–World War II period that the heart of the story was white brutality and black discontent, with the latter expressing itself in as much physical resistance as was possible given the realities of white power. Interpretations of slavery since the 1970s have tended to follow Genovese's paternalism model when characterizing the masters or analyzing the master-slave relationship and the Blassingame-Gutman emphasis on communal cultural autonomy when probing the consciousness of the slaves. Tension between the cultural hegemony and cultural autonomy models has been the basis of most disagreements.

Beginning around 1990, however, a little-noticed countertrend to both culturalist approaches emerged. The work of Michael Tadman on the slave trade, Norrece T. Jones on slave control, and Wilma King on slave children brought back to the center of attention the most brutal and horrifying aspects of life under the slaveholders' regime.[5] Tadman presented extensive documentation to show that the buying and selling of slaves was so central to the system that it reduces any concept of slaveholder paternalism to the realm of propaganda and self-delusion. "Slaveholder priorities and attitudes suggest, instead, a system based more crudely on arbitrary power, distrust, and fear," he wrote.[6]

What kind of paternalist, one might ask, would routinely sell those for whom he had assumed patriarchal responsibility? Building on Gutman's discovery of strong family ties, Jones maintained that the threat of family breakup was the principal means that slaveholders used to keep slaves sufficiently obedient and under control to carry out the work of the plantation. There was no paternalistic bargain, according to Jones, only the callous exercise of the powers of ownership, applied often enough to make the threat of it credible and intimidating. Like Jones, Wilma King likens the master-slave relationship to a state of war, in which both parties to the conflict use all the resources they possess and any means, fair or foul, to defeat the enemy. She compared slave children to the victims of war, denied a true childhood by heavy labor requirements, abusive treatment, and the strong possibility that they would be permanently separated from one or both parents at a relatively early age. She presented evidence to show that slave children were small for their ages, suffered from ill health, and had high death rates. The neo-abolitionist view of slavery as a chamber of horrors seemed to be reemerging, and the horror was all the greater because of the acknowledgment forced by the scholarship of the seventies that slaves had strong family ties. What was now being emphasized was the lack of respect that many, possibly most, slaveholders had for those ties.

A recent book that eschews theorizing about the essential nature of slavery but can be read as providing support for the revisionists who would bring the darker side of slavery into sharper relief is *Runaway Slaves: Rebels on the Plantation* by John Hope Franklin and Loren Schweninger.[7] This relentlessly empirical study avoids taking issue with other historians except to the extent that it puts quotation marks around "paternalistic." It has little or nothing to say about slave culture and community. Its principal sources are

not the many published narratives of escaped slaves, such as the ones now
made available by the Library of America, but rather newspaper accounts,
legal records, and the advertisements that describe runaways and offer a
reward for their return.

The latter sources are especially useful because they contain candid descriptions of lacerated backs, branded faces, and other physical evidence of
cruel treatment. Few runaways actually made it to freedom in the North.
Most remained in relatively close proximity to their masters' plantations and
were eventually recaptured. It was generally young men who absconded, but
they did so in huge numbers. Few plantations of any size failed to experience
significant absenteeism. Franklin and Schweninger are unable to determine
"the exact number of runaways," but conclude very conservatively that there
had to have been more than 50,000 a year. Slaves ran off for a variety of
motives—to avoid being sold or because they wanted to be sold away from
a harsh master, to avoid family dissolution or to find kin from whom they
had already been separated, to avoid severe whipping or as a response to
it. The picture that emerges from the many vivid accounts of individual
acts of desertion is of an inhumane system that bears no resemblance to
the mythical South of benevolent masters and contented slaves. It is even
hard to reconcile with the more sophisticated view that most slaveholders
conformed to a paternalistic ethic that earned a conditional acquiescence
from many of their slaves.

The masters found in this book are cruel and insensitive and the slaves
openly rebellious. Although it rarely brought freedom, the mode of resistance
described in *Runaway Slaves* could have positive results for the deserters.
In some cases, they successfully made their return contingent on better
conditions, or at least avoidance of punishment. In other words, running
away could be a kind of labor action, the closest approximation to a strike
that was possible under the circumstances.

II.

But of course most slaves did not run away and some plantations did not have
serious problems of desertion. Franklin and Schweninger might therefore
be exposing only one side of a complex reality. The deep discontent of the
deserters is obvious, but was their attitude typical or exceptional? To answer
this question, it would be helpful to have direct testimony from slaves who
stayed as well as those who fled. There are two principal sources of slave
testimony—the published narratives from the nineteenth century, some of
which have been collected by William L. Andrews and Henry Louis Gates
for the Library of America, and the interviews with elderly ex-slaves conducted in the 1930s by WPA writers. Selections from the interviews are now

available in a book-audio set, published in conjunction with the Library of Congress and the Smithsonian Institution. Reading these books and listening to the tapes conveys, if nothing else, a sense of how diversely slaves could be treated and how variously they could respond to their circumstances. The narratives written by fugitives stress, as might be expected, the abuse and oppression from which their authors have fled. But the WPA interviews include some that convey nostalgia for kindly or honorable masters and suggest that paternalism could, in some instances, be an ethical code as well as a rationalization for servitude.

One could conclude therefore that some masters were genuine paternalists who made their slaves grateful that their owners were among the decent ones (unlike, for example, the owner of a neighboring plantation who had a reputation for cruelty), while others were ruthless exploiters who treated their human property simply as tools of their own greed and ambition. Both bodies of sources have built-in biases that detract from their authority, as Franklin and Schweninger suggest in explaining why they made little use of them: "Suffice it to say that many of the persons who inhabit the pages of recent studies are either far removed in time and space from the South they describe, or, due to conventions, or the purpose of a diary, are less than candid in their observations."

An earlier generation of historians considered the kind of narratives collected by Andrews and Gates unreliable because they had allegedly been ghostwritten and embellished by white abolitionists for purposes of antislavery propaganda. Recent research, however, has established the authenticity of most of them. Original claims for their authorship and the existence of many of the people and events they describe have been verified. But how representative of the slave population in general were the life experiences and attitudes of these literary fugitives? They had to be literate to write their stories, and 95 percent of the slaves were unable to read and write. Four of the six accounts of escapes from the South to the North presented in *Slave Narratives*—those of Frederick Douglass, William Wells Brown, Henry Bibb, and William and Ellen Craft—feature fugitives who had white fathers. Two of them—Henry Bibb and Ellen Craft—were so light-skinned that they were able to pass for white.

Mulattos may have been a substantial minority of the slave population of the Old South, but literate, light-skinned mulattos were rare. It is nevertheless telling evidence of the callousness of southern slaveholders that most of the children they sired with slave women were unacknowledged and kept in servitude, rather than being emancipated by their fathers, as was more likely to be the case in other slave societies. To attain freedom, the fugitives of mixed race had to use their degree of whiteness or access to education (which allowed them to forge documents) as devices for deceiving their pursuers. Upon arrival in the North, their value to the abolitionists came partly from the pathos that could be generated among color-conscious Northerners by the thought that someone who looked white or almost white could be a slave, especially if she were a beautiful young woman at the mercy of a lustful master. But the sexual exploitation of slave women of any pigmentation was a harsh reality, as the narrative of Harriet Jacobs, who went to extraordinary lengths to avoid the embraces of her owner, clearly illustrates.[8]

The testimony collected by WPA interviewers in the 1930s suffers from very different and perhaps more severe limitations. Most of it, including much of what is included in *Remembering Slavery*, the recent selection edited by Ira Berlin, Marc Favreau, and Steven F. Miller, comes from those born in slavery but emancipated as children.[9] Very few of them experienced slavery as adults and those who did were into their nineties by the time they were interviewed. Seventy- or eighty-year-old memories are notoriously fallible and can be distorted as a result of what may have happened more recently. Some of those who had lived through the era of lynching and Jim Crow segregation might view their experience as children who had not yet experienced the worst of slavery with a certain amount of nostalgia.

In most cases, moreover, the interviewers were southern whites, and blacks at the height of the segregation era in the South would have been reluctant to express their true feelings about how their inquisitors' forebears had treated them. One would therefore expect the oral testimony to make servitude seem more benign than it actually was. But despite these inherent biases, there is in fact much evidence in *Remembering Slavery* to support the view that slavery was legalized brutality. Whipping, it is clear, was virtually omnipresent. Helplessly watching a parent being severely flogged was etched in the memory of many of the interviewees, and a surprisingly large number had been whipped themselves by masters or overseers, despite their tender ages. Sam Kilgore was exceptional in having a master who never whipped his slaves, but "Marster had a method of keepin' de cullud fo'ks in line. If one of dem do somethin' not right to dem he say: 'Don't go to wo'k tomorrow Ise 'spec de nigger driver am a-comin' pass an' Ise gwine to sell youse.'"

Whether discipline was obtained by constant use of the lash, by the threat of sale for any misbehavior, or both, the system revealed here is one that relied on fear and coercion rather than on any sense of a patriarch's responsibility to his dependents. There is also evidence in *Remembering Slavery* of what today would be considered the most flagrant kind of child abuse. Her mistress beat Henrietta King, an eight- or nine-year-old accused of stealing a piece of candy, while her head was secured under the leg of a rocking chair. "I guess dey must of whupped me near an hour wid dat rocker leg a-pressin' down on my haid," she recalled. As a result of the pressure, her face and mouth were permanently and severely disfigured.

In the light of such evidence, it is not readily apparent why Ira Berlin's introduction affirms that a paternalistic ethic prevailed among slaveholders.

Was it really true in most cases that "the incorporation of slaves into what planters called their 'family, black and white,' enhanced the slaveholders' sense of responsibility for their slaves and encouraged the owners to improve the material conditions of plantation life"? Material conditions did improve during the nineteenth century, but an alternative explanation is available: slaves were valuable property that was appreciating in value. In the light of their financial interest in healthy, marketable slaves, the real question might be why conditions on the plantations were often so harsh. A slave scarred by whipping depreciated in value, but whippings persisted; slave children were an appreciating asset; but, if Wilma King is correct, they were generally unhealthy and undernourished. (An image from more than one account in *Remembering Slavery* is that of slave children being fed at a trough like pigs.)

Paternalism in one sense of the word may be a by-product of vast difference in power. Those who present no conceivable threat to one's security, status, or wealth may be treated with condescending and playful affection. It is clear from some of the recollections in *Remembering Slavery* that attractive slave children could become human pets of their masters and mistresses. Mature slaves who "played Sambo" could also arouse feelings of indulgence and receive special treatment. But the possession of great power over other human beings can also provoke irrational cruelty. The other side of the coin of paternalism in this psychological sense is sadism.

Berlin is on stronger ground when he notes that "the paternalist ideology provided slaveholders with a powerful justification for their systematic appropriation of the slaves' labor." But the racism that made it possible to consider blacks as subhuman was another possible justification. The two could be synthesized in the notion that blacks were perpetual children and had to be treated as such no matter what their actual ages. But if this was the dominant view, it did not prevent a substantial amount of child abuse.

III.

Slave children are the subjects of Marie Jenkins Schwartz's *Born in Bondage*. It covers much of the same ground as Wilma King's *Stolen Childhood*, but in its effort to understand the master-slave relationship it leans toward the paternalism model more than toward the "state-of-war" analogy invoked by King and Norrece Jones. Consequently it presents a somewhat less horrific impression of what it meant to grow up on a slave plantation. It acknowledges the possibility of sale for adolescent slaves, noting that approximately 10 percent of them were sold from the upper to lower South between 1820 and 1860. But in claiming that "the risk of separation from families through sale was relatively low for very young children," it disregards the frequent sale of men without their wives and young children or of women with infants without their husbands that is acknowledged elsewhere in the book. Schwartz's conclusion that "slaves throughout the South worried about being sold" seems like an understatement in the light of what Norrece Jones has revealed about how masters manipulated intense fears of family separation to maintain discipline.

The conception of paternalism found in *Born in Bondage* is set forth in terms very close to those employed by Eugene Genovese. "The paternalistic bargain that slaveholders and slaves struck," Schwartz writes, "required each to give something to the other. Slaves displayed loyalty to their owners, at least outwardly, and slaveholders rewarded this with better treatment." She concedes that "the paternalistic attitude of owners was not the same thing as real benevolence" and that the slaves, aware of its self-serving nature, obeyed masters and mistresses "without internalizing the owner's understanding of class and race." But playing the prescribed deferential roles made life easier and must have become second nature for some. Children were quick to see the benefit of pleasing their owners, and the sheer presence of large numbers of children on most plantations was one factor encouraging a paternalistic ethos.

Putting aside the unresolved question of whether sincere and durable "paternalistic bargains" were normal or exceptional in slave governance, Schwartz makes the original and useful point that there was an inherent conflict between such paternalism (to whatever extent it may have existed) and the efforts of slaves to maintain a family life of their own. To the degree that masters took direct responsibility for slave children they undermined the authority of the parents and the unity of the slave family. But how likely in fact were slave owners to play such a role in the raising of slave children? Little evidence of this kind of attentiveness appears in the written and oral narratives. Accounts of slave children running about naked or in rags, being fed at troughs, or put to work at a very early age run counter to the impression of slaveholders acting *in loco parentis*. Although it offers some significant new insights, *Born in Bondage* should not displace Wilma King's *Stolen Childhood* and be taken as the definitive last word on growing up under slavery. Rather the two books should be read together as revealing different aspects of a complex reality.

Perhaps the time has come to get beyond the debate between the two schools of thought about the nature of antebellum slavery—the seemingly unresolvable disagreement over whether it can best be understood as resting on a "paternalistic bargain" between masters and slaves or simply on the application of force and fear in the service of economic gain. The reality reflected in the slave narratives and other primary sources is of great variation in plantation regimes. What proportion might be classified as paternalist and what proportion was based simply on "arbitrary power, distrust, and fear" cannot be quantified; it is a question that can be answered only on the basis of general impressions that will differ, depending on which sources are deemed representative and which anomalous. The side that a historian supports might be determined more by ideology or theoretical approach than by a careful weighing of the evidence.

It also seems possible that many slaveholders could fancy themselves as paternalists and act in ways that were totally at odds with their self-image. Walter Johnson's book on the slave market, *Soul by Soul*, in effect transcends the dichotomy by showing that a culture of paternalism and a commitment to commercialism were not incompatible. He also undermines another persistent and contentious either/or of southern historiography, one that also involves the status of paternalism as ideology and social ethos. This is the question of whether "race" (inequality based on pigmentation) or "class" (stratification based on premodern conceptions of honor and gentility) was central to the culture and social order of the Old South.[10]

Johnson takes us inside the New Orleans slave market, the largest and busiest in the South, and discovers that the buyers and sellers of slaves could easily mix the language and values associated with paternalism and commercialism. Unlike later historians, they saw no conflict between their needs for status and sound business practice. "I consider Negroes too high at this time," one slave owner told another, "but there are some very much allied to mine both by blood and intermarriage that I may be induced from feeling to buy, and I have one vacant improved plantation, and could work more hands with advantage." Clearly the purchasers of slaves liked to think that they were doing a favor to those they acquired. They could buy themselves "a paternalist fantasy in the slave market" when they made a purchase that seemed to accord with the wishes of the person being bought, despite the fact that it could also be justified on strictly economic grounds. But, Johnson comments, the proslavery construction of slave-market "paternalism" was highly unstable: it threatened to collapse at any moment beneath the weight of its own absurdity. One could go to the market and buy slaves to rescue them from the market, but it was patently obvious ... that the market in people was what had in the first place caused the problems that slave-buying paternalists claimed to resolve.

Paternalism, Johnson concludes, was "a way of imagining, describing, and justifying slavery rather than a direct reflection of underlying social relations." It was therefore "portable" and could "turn up in the most unlikely places—in slaveholders' letters describing their own benign intentions as they went to the slave market." Paternalism was an illusion but one that was essential to the self-respect of many slaveholders, just as hardheaded commercial behavior was essential to their economic prosperity and social pretensions. As portrayed by Johnson, the slaves were not taken in by paternalistic rhetoric. But they could influence their own destiny in the slave market by the way they presented themselves: "The history of the antebellum South is the history of two million slave sales. But alongside the chronicle of oppressions must be set down a history of negotiations and subversions." Slaves brought to market could subvert their sale to undesirable purchasers by feigning illness or acting unruly and uncooperative, or, putting on a different mask, encourage their purchase by masters who had a reputation for good treatment or who already possessed some of their kinfolk. This form of black "agency" might be considered less decisive or heroic than the running away described by Franklin and Schweninger, but "these differences between possible sales had the salience of survival itself."

On the question of whether slavery and the Old South should be characterized by race or by class domination, Johnson suggests that both were present and that it is impossible to distinguish between them in their day-to-day manifestations. He advances the original and potentially controversial argument that to be truly "white" in the Old South one had to own slaves. Buying a first slave therefore brought racial status as well as a new class position. I would qualify the argument by limiting its application to "black belt" or plantation areas where a substantial majority of whites actually owned slaves. In the southern backcountry and uplands, where nonslaveholding yeomen farmers predominated, the social "whiteness" of anyone who was not black or Indian was beyond question, and it was even possible to regard slaveholding itself as compromising whiteness by creating too much intimacy between the races.

Johnson also contends that differences in pigmentation were a major element in the expectations that purchasers had about the use they could make of the slaves they bought. Dark-skinned slaves were considered healthier and better suited to field labor. Male slaves who were light-skinned but not too light were thought to be good candidates for training in skilled trades. Very light-skinned males were difficult to sell, however, because of the fear that they could escape by passing for white (as Henry Bibb's narrative well exemplifies). Very light-complexioned females, on the other hand, brought high prices as "fancy women" or concubines. This was a color and class hierarchy more often associated with Latin America and the Caribbean than with America's characteristic two-category, white-over-black pattern of race relations. But Johnson argues that the physical aspect of the classification of slaves into different occupational groups was highly subjective and that observers described the pigmentation of slaves differently depending on what use they intended to make of them.

To some extent this was undoubtedly true. But it defies common sense to claim without qualification that "the racialized meaning of [a slave's body], the color assigned to it and the weight given to its various physical features in describing it, depended upon the examiner rather than the examined." It is a useful postmodern insight that race and color are, to a considerable extent, "social constructions." But surely the difference between very light and very dark skin was a physical fact that had an independent effect on the evaluations being made. Except for this one instance, however, Johnson's discussion of the social and cultural construction of reality by whites and blacks in the slave market does not do violence to the inescapable external realities that limited the options and influenced the behavior of the buyers, the sellers, and the sold. By beginning the process of undermining and transcending the sharp dichotomies between paternalism and commercialism, and between race and class—on which historians of the Old South have been fixated for so long—Johnson has advanced the study of African-American slavery to a higher level.

CHAPTER 6

They'll Take Their Stand:
Davis and Genovese

This chapter compares recent works by three prominent historians of slavery—
Inhuman Bondage: The Rise and Fall of Slavery in the New World *by David
Brion Davis (New York: Oxford University Press, 2006) and* The Mind of the
Master Class: History and Faith in the Southern Slaveholders' Worldview
*by Elizabeth Fox-Genovese and Eugene D. Genovese (Cambridge: Cambridge
University Press, 2005).*

*   *   *

For nearly half a century two historians have dominated the field of slavery
studies, broadly conceived. David Brion Davis has been the preeminent
historian of ideas about slavery in the Western world since the early modern
period and has completed two volumes of a projected trilogy: *The Problem of
Slavery in Western Culture* and *The Problem of Slavery in the Age of Revolution,
1770–1823.*[1] He has now taken time out from work on the third volume in
this sequence to produce a general history of slavery and antislavery in the
Americas, especially in the parts of it colonized by the English.

Eugene Genovese has been the foremost authority on the political economy
of antebellum southern slavery and on the emergent ideologies or worldviews
of both masters and slaves. His greatest achievement in dealing with these
subjects is his book *Roll, Jordan, Roll: The World the Slaves Made.*[2] Now he has
written, with his wife, Elizabeth Fox-Genovese (who has also made important
contributions to slavery studies[3]), the first of a projected series of volumes on
"the mind of the master class." These books are meant to increase our respect
for the intellectual abilities and acuity of the Old South's slaveholding elite. This
first volume concentrates on their ideas about history and religion and makes
only passing references to what is generally considered to be the slaveholders'
major intellectual preoccupation—the development of a proslavery argument

to counter the attack from northern abolitionists. This subject, we are told in the preface, will be covered more fully in a subsequent volume.

In a way, these two books show the authors' reversal of direction. Much of the previous work of Elizabeth Fox-Genovese and Eugene Genovese has drawn on Marxist theory to illuminate class relationships and the cultural concerns and ideologies arising from them. In the current volume they produce the kind of intellectual history that some might consider old-fashioned because it concentrates almost exclusively on the ideas themselves rather than on the external circumstances that may have shaped their content and given them salience. On the other hand, Davis, a leading practitioner of intellectual and cultural history, has now gone far beyond the history of ideas and attempted to study New World slavery in all its ramifications, social, economic, and political, as well as intellectual and cultural. Whereas the Genoveses have narrowed the scope of their inquiry to the discourse and habits of mind of a relatively small number of planter intellectuals, Davis has widened his perspective to encompass the history of slavery and the opposition it engendered in Great Britain and its New World colonies, as well as in the United States.

Precisely because of its breadth, *Inhuman Bondage* defies summary; much of it draws heavily on the more specialized work of other scholars. From start to finish Davis stresses the racial aspect of New World slavery, both as its distinguishing feature and the source of its particularly brutal and dehumanizing character when compared to most other forms of bondage in human history. He points out that slaves in the ancient world were of all colors and ethnicities and not easily distinguishable from the free population, which was often similarly diverse (as was the case, for example, in ancient Rome). This lack of a racial justification for servitude facilitated the manumission and subsequent assimilation of many of those who had been enslaved, whether in Greece, Rome, or medieval Europe. Unlike former slaves in the New World, they did not carry the visible marks of their former degradation. Of course slavery always entails cruelty and brutalization. In his introductory discussion of the remote origins of slavery in human history, Davis sees it as an extension of the domestication of animals, an attempt to turn human beings into beasts of burden. As bad as slavery has always been, however, Davis finds it at its worst in the racial form that it took in the New World, where a difference in color and the meanings associated with it were a substantial barrier to humane treatment.

Davis convincingly demonstrates that slavery was central to the history of the New World. His chapter on the origins of the extensive enslavement of Africans and their transport across the Atlantic "is meant to underscore the central truth that black slavery was basic and integral to the entire phenomenon we call 'America.' This often hidden or disguised truth ultimately involves the profound contradiction of a free society that was made possible by black slave labor."

When he narrows his focus to slavery in nineteenth-century America, Davis points out that the United States had "the largest number of slaves in the Western Hemisphere" and concludes that "far from being a marginal misfortune, African-American slavery pulsated at the heart of the national economy and thus at the core of American political culture." When the future of slavery became an issue in national politics and Southerners set about defending their "peculiar institution" against abolitionist denunciation, a commitment to white supremacy was the basis of the southern consensus that emerged. "Virulent racism," Davis contends, "lay at the heart of the South's extremely shaky unity." This unity was precarious because a substantial majority of white Southerners did not own slaves. It was the "crucial function of racism and racial identity" to unify nonslaveholders behind an institution from which they derived no material benefit: "Racial doctrine—the supposed innate inferiority of blacks—became the primary instrument for justifying the persistence of slavery, for rallying the support of nonslaveholding whites, for underscoring the dangers of freeing a people allegedly 'unprepared' for freedom, and for defining the limits of dissent."

For Davis, the only antidote to poisonous racism is a moral and ideological commitment to human equality. Dismissing the more cynical explanations of economic determinists as superficial, he finds that such a commitment lay behind Britain's antislavery movement of the early nineteenth century and its decision in 1833 to emancipate all the slaves in its colonies. In the ideology of "free labor," which was widespread in England, he finds a deeper meaning than a simple belief in the economic superiority of wage labor over slave labor. It reflected "the desire to dignify and honor labor," the labor of those who earned wages as well as those who paid them, and "can be viewed as a way of genuinely recognizing elements of equality in people of subordinate status."

Davis argues that "a fortunate convergence of economic, political, and ideological circumstances" made it possible for Britain to "achieve genuine reform—a reform that greatly improved and uplifted the lives of millions of blacks" and "curbed some of the worst effects of early global capitalism." He concludes his paean of praise for Britain's abolition of slavery by endorsing the historian W. E. H. Lecky's opinion that it stands "as among the three or four perfectly virtuous acts recorded in the history of nations."

Historians are entitled to change their minds, and it may be worth noting that this evaluation of British abolitionism differs somewhat in tone and substance from Davis's discussion of the same topic in *The Problem of Slavery in the Age of Revolution*, published more than thirty years ago. There Davis found that the British antislavery ideology helped the dominant classes to deflect attention from the exploitation of the working classes at home by shifting concern to the plight of slaves in distant colonies. In this way they were able to maintain and strengthen their class-based "cultural hegemony" and undercut the radicalism inspired by the French Revolution. In his new book he puts much emphasis on the influence of Quaker and Anglican abolitionists and the remarkable size of the mass movements in which over a million people would sign petitions to end slavery.

In addition to analyzing abolitionism in Britain itself, *Inhuman Bondage* recounts the dramatic history of the slave rebellions that broke out in the British West Indies on the eve of emancipation. Davis finds that the slaves had some awareness, mainly from their contact with missionaries, of the progress of the abolition movement in Britain. Consequently they refrained from massacring whites when they had the chance for fear of alienating public opinion in the mother country. This restraint is in sharp contrast to the contemporaneous Nat Turner rebellion in Virginia in 1831, when no such considerations impeded the killing of whites.

Perhaps Davis's most original argument is that British emancipation and its consequences help to account for the American South's hysterical reaction to the small and unpopular abolitionist movement that emerged in the antebellum North during the 1830s and 1840s. According to the South's conspiracy theorists, Great Britain was plotting to undermine the American economy by encouraging abolitionism and even slave rebellions in the United States. Also contributing to the fear of a widespread slave rebellion incited by abolitionists was the memory of the revolution in Haiti around the turn of the century. Moreover, the economic decline of the former British slave colonies in the 1840s and 1850s provided a frightening indication of what would happen in the South even if, as was the case in the West Indies, slavery were to be abolished gradually and the owners compensated. "The South's increasing fixation on British abolitionism and the declining economy of Haiti and the British Caribbean," Davis concludes, "helps to explain the Southerners' paranoid, disproportionate response to critics in the North."

Although it is certainly plausible, the contention that an intense Anglophobia was a central element in the slaveholding South's "crisis of fear" needs more documentation than Davis provides in this book. Beyond recognizing an endemic anxiety about the possibility of slave rebellion arising from the memories of Haiti and the Nat Turner revolt, previous historians of southern extremism before the Civil War have given relatively little weight to concerns about Britain's role in fomenting slave uprisings. It is well known that one inspiration for the annexation of Texas in 1845 was a false report that the British were offering to guarantee Texas's independence from Mexico in return for its repudiation of slavery. But Davis sees a much broader and more pervasive concern. Perhaps his forthcoming *Problem of Slavery in the Age of Emancipation* will provide the additional evidence needed to support his hypothesis.

One might have expected Britain's emancipation policy to have been a topic of the slaveholder writings, letters, and conversations described and analyzed in *The Mind of the Master Class* by Elizabeth Fox-Genovese and Eugene Genovese, but I found no mention of it in more than eight hundred pages of text. Perhaps it will be treated in a subsequent volume dealing with political attitudes and the controversy over slavery. This volume is devoted primarily to what "the master class" thought about history (especially ancient and European history) and religion.

The claim of the authors that the book examines the thought or "world-view" of the master class as a whole might be questioned. In fact, they mainly discuss the mentality of a handful of highly articulate planter intellectuals. The same names—Thomas R. Dew, Robert L. Dabney, J. D. B. DeBow, George Fitzhugh, George Frederick Holmes, Louisa McCord, Edmund Ruffin, and James Henly Thornwell—come up repeatedly. The Genoveses make no effort to demonstrate how, or to what extent, this intellectual elite actually spoke for the planter class as a whole, including its less articulate and erudite members. Some use of travelers' accounts reporting conversations with ordinary slaveholders might have enlarged the range of evidence. Another source might have been the correspondence of more typical members of the planter class, some of which is to be found in southern archives.

Despite this limitation of scope, however, the Genoveses' book is extraordinarily erudite. What is most impressive is the authors' ability to tell us what precisely was meant by the innumerable literary and cultural references found in the writings of the slaveholding intellectuals. They seem to have read all the books that their subjects read and talked about, and they are thus able to get inside their minds to a remarkable degree. Dante, Thomas à Kempis, John Bunyan, Sir Walter Scott, and Thomas Carlyle are only a few of the writers cited by the Genoveses who came in for discussion among the cultured southern planters and clergymen they deal with. "Perhaps nothing so impressed Southerners," they write, "as Scott's loving attention to families and local communities."

The Genoveses, as cultural conservatives, have in the past made no bones about their finding contemporary American society and culture repugnant; but, for the most part, they avoid polemics about modern culture in this book. Except to the extent that they subtly empathize with some of the ultraconservative views of those they are writing about, they have provided a reasonably objective account of the diversity of opinion among the planter elite on such subjects as historical revolutions, the cult of chivalry, classical European literature, and especially religion. They write, for example, that "well-educated Southerners ... loved and regarded [Dante] as their own," seeing him as a "premature Protestant," particularly in view of his "opposition to papal intervention in secular affairs."

At only one point did I find the Genoveses making an overt and exaggerated claim for the superiority of the slaveholders' ethics and wisdom over those that have prevailed in the United States since the abolition of slavery. After a seemingly unbiased account of the debate among Southerners about American expansionism and imperialism, in which diverse and even antithetical opinions were expressed (about, for example, the justification of war with Mexico), they somehow come to the conclusion that views among southern thinkers not only added up to anti-imperialism but can be contrasted with the ideology of America's later interventions in world affairs. Here the argument sounds speculative and tendentious:

> By minimizing the suffering of their own black slaves, they defended slavery at home all the more passionately while they struggled in the United States against an imperialist worldview that would subsequently impose unprecedented misery and mass slaughter on the world. The defeat of the slaveholders and their worldview opened the floodgates to the global catastrophe their leading spokesmen had long seen a-borning.

Another finding that seems calculated to improve the image of the slaveholders is more persuasively documented. Their toleration of religious diversity among whites, the authors show, exceeded that of the North (which was beset during this period by virulent anti-Catholic nativism). Although religious beliefs were strongly held and arguments on theological issues could be intense, the rights of Catholics, Jews, and even the ultraliberal Protestant denominations, such as Unitarians and Universalists, to practice their religion and promulgate their faith were respected in the Old South, *provided that they endorsed slavery.* The underlying agreement that held the white South together, politically and socially as well as religiously, was the belief in the rightness of slavery and white supremacy.

Such a commitment is, of course, highly objectionable to modern liberals and makes it difficult for them to see anything of value in the slaveholders' worldview. Although the Genoveses do not condone or defend slavery and racial discrimination, they view the commitment to hierarchy that these institutions entailed as providing the foundation for some commendable qualities. In the prologue to the book they write: "The late I.F. Stone was once asked how he, a prominent spokesman for the radical Left, ... could admire a slaveholder like Thomas Jefferson. If we recall correctly, he replied, 'Because history is tragedy, not melodrama.'"

The underlying argument of their book is that the Old South, in its flawed and "tragic" way, stood for some values that have been sadly neglected in our modern, individualistic society:

> To modern sensibilities it is a preposterous idea that a slave system could engender admirable virtues.... In our own time it seems perverse, not to say impossible, to separate the horror of slavery from the positive features of an ordered and interdependent social system. To Southerners and not just slave-

holders, slavery was a bulwark against the corrosive features of free labor and the loosening of the social bonds that nurtured humane social relations.

For Eugene Genovese the Old South has always been anticapitalist and antiliberal. But until the 1990s he linked this interpretation to Marxian radicalism. In such works as *The World the Slaveholders Made*, one can find an undertone of approbation of the slaveholders—whatever else they might have been, at least they were not liberal or capitalist.[4] But it was clear that for Genovese, socialism and not some kind of traditional society was the right solution for the excesses of individualism that modern society engendered. In *The Fruits of Merchant Capital*, published in 1983, Fox-Genovese and Genovese, in their first collaboration, described the antebellum South as a "hybrid" society in which precapitalist and capitalist values coexisted in a state of apparently unresolvable tension.[5] In *The Mind of the Master Class*, however, they argue that the inherently individualistic character of Protestantism prevented the slaveholders from developing a consistent and coherent worldview. "Protestantism's inherent tendencies toward radical individualism and democratization posed a direct threat to the South's slaveholding social order," they write. This truth was clear to Catholics, who "while denying the inherent sinfulness of slavery, recognized the Protestant origins of an individualism that should logically have rejected slavery." They go on to quote with apparent sympathy a South Carolina priest's pronouncement that "it is only under Catholic governments, where the church can regulate the relative duties between the servant and the master, that slavery can exist as a Christian institution."

By suggesting that for most slaveholders a problem of identity arose from the fact that they had the wrong kind of religion, the Genoveses echo Allen Tate's "Remarks on the Southern Religion" in *I'll Take My Stand*, the 1930 manifesto of the Southern Agrarians. (It is somewhat surprising that the Genoveses do not mention or cite this essay, for its argument is remarkably similar to theirs.) According to Tate, the Old South "was a feudal society without a feudal religion." Its error was that "it tried to encompass its destiny within the terms of Protestantism, in origin, a non-agrarian and trading religion."[6] In the essay Tate does not specifically invoke Catholicism as an alternative, and somewhat ruefully admits his own lack of religious belief. But it is no surprise that he later converted to Catholicism. According to both Tate and the Genoveses, Protestantism inevitably encourages industrialism, capitalism, and laissez-faire liberalism, all of which, in the words of the latter, threatened the South's "simultaneous preference for the corporatism of the family as the fundamental institution of society." (That an ethically or even religiously based democratic socialism might be a third option is a possibility they do not discuss.)

Despite its sympathetic treatment of the corporatism and the close-knit family life that southern bondage helped to engender, *The Mind of the Master*

Class does not condone slavery itself. The authors emphatically acknowledge the inherent cruelty and brutality of the master-slave relationship. Because of the virtually unchecked power that slavery gives to one man over another and the fact that "men are frail creatures bound to abuse power," slavery, they write, "stands convicted as the least defensible of human relations." If one were a believer in Christianity with its Golden Rule, it might seem that the abolitionists were right when they condemned slavery as a sin. Not so, say the Genoveses, provided that one takes the Bible literally, as most Americans in both the North and the South did in the period before the Civil War. They argue convincingly that Southerners had the best of the argument about whether slavery is sanctioned or condemned in Holy Scripture. Not only was slavery a pervasive institution throughout biblical times, but nowhere does either the Old or New Testament explicitly criticize it. Where the southern interpreters of scripture went wrong, the Genoveses concede, was when they attempted to provide a biblical mandate for racial slavery, and not just slavery in general. The notion that blacks in particular were enslaved because God had cursed their alleged ancestor Canaan as punishment for an obscure offense by his father Ham against his grandfather Noah had no basis in scripture. Nowhere in the Book of Genesis is there any indication that Canaan and his descendants were black.

Fox-Genovese and Genovese acknowledge that the Old South, to the extent that its worldview was manifested in the thought of the intellectually active slaveholders they discuss, was a profoundly conflicted and ultimately a fatally flawed society. "Individualism," they conclude, "even in its peculiarly conservative southern form, tends to place the state in hostile relation to society's discrete units, individual and corporate. Herein lies a principal germ of the disintegration of community itself." But the Genoveses do not simply describe this internal conflict; they seem to share it. Although they deplore slavery and racism, they clearly value the "corporate" and traditionalist aspects of antebellum southern life and invite us to regard them as an alternative to the modern society that they deplore. But can one in fact detach the virtues from the vices in this case? Slavery and racism provided the essential underpinning for such hierarchy and community as existed in southern society as a whole. Without racial slavery as the basis of its distinctiveness, the Old South would not have differed all that much from the North.

Although the Genoveses write clearly about the racism that was endemic in the Old South, it does not seem to me that they give it the centrality it deserves. They attribute the loyalty of nonslaveholders to the master class "primarily" to the "rural independence" and relative immunity from government interference that characterized their lives, a form of autonomy that they shared with the owners of slaves. Most other historians have given greater weight to what they describe as a secondary factor—"the comfort of many of the less affluent whites derived from racial stratification." I share Davis's view that the "shaky unity" of the Old South was based primarily on a "virulent racism." One might add that this fierce commitment to white supremacy in a biracial society survived the abolition of slavery itself and pointed ahead to Jim Crow. If, as Davis contends, racism was the heart of the matter, it becomes difficult to find much to admire in "the world the slaveholders made."

Placed in juxtaposition, the two books under review reveal a profound clash of values and ideals. In his celebration of British emancipation and American abolitionism—his affirmation of human progress toward a more just and humane society—Davis puts forward a persuasive version of the modern liberalism that the Genoveses reject. Although both Davis and the Genoveses have strong ideological commitments, and readers are bound to feel drawn to one side or the other on the basis of their own beliefs, both books have great historical weight and strong moral implications, especially when read together.

CHAPTER 7

America's Original Sin

Works presenting three diverse approaches to slavery are discussed here—Challenging the Boundaries of Slavery *by David Brion Davis (Cambridge, MA: Harvard University Press, 2003),* Generations of Captivity: A History of African-American Slaves *by Ira Berlin (Cambridge, MA: Belknap Press/Harvard University Press, 2003), and* The Slaveholding Republic: An Account of the United States Government's Relations to Slavery *by Don E. Fehrenbacher, completed and edited by Ward M. McAfee (New York: Oxford University Press, 2001).*

*   *   *

The institution of slavery has had a profound and lasting effect on American history. Virtually all historians now agree that sectional differences on the slavery issue caused the Civil War. Until the eve of that conflict the slaveholding interest was so economically and politically powerful as to appear virtually impregnable. No one could reasonably have predicted in 1860 that the emancipation of more than four million African-American slaves would come within five years. Nothing short of the needs and emotions aroused by the vast bloodletting required to preserve the Union could, in so short a time, have abolished an institution that had sunk such deep roots in America. Before the war, lawyers, politicians, clergymen, even physical anthropologists had defended it against a northern abolitionist movement that had never gained much popular support. In *Challenging the Boundaries of Slavery,* his brief but incisive reflections on slavery in American and world history, David Brion Davis sums up the economic basis for the slaveholders' power in antebellum America:

> There were strong economic reasons for the broad national reach of American slavery. Southern slave-grown cotton was by far the nation's leading export. It powered textile-manufacturing revolutions in both New England and

England, and it paid for American imports of everything from steel to invest-
ment capital. Moreover, since the price of slaves continued to soar through the
antebellum decades, American slaves represented more capital than any other
asset in the nation, with the exception of land. In 1860 the value of Southern
slaves was about three times the value of the capital stock in manufacturing
and railroads nationwide.

Ira Berlin, in his *Generations of Captivity: A History of African-American
Slaves*, shows that the northern states, despite having gradually emancipated
their own slaves between the Revolution and the 1830s, were deeply implicated in the protection and preservation of slavery in the South. Northern
free blacks agitated vigorously for the freedom of their brethren in bondage,
but the discrimination and violence to which they were exposed in the North
left them for the most part disfranchised, impoverished, and (especially after
the Fugitive Slave Act of 1850) unsure whether they could maintain their
own freedom against slave catchers and kidnappers. Berlin goes so far as to
characterize the free African Americans of the antebellum North as living
in what amounted to "maroon colonies" (analogous to the independent
communities that escaped slaves were able to establish in remote regions of
Jamaica, Guyana, and Brazil). Like maroons, they were isolated from whites
and only precariously free. There were sympathetic white abolitionists, but
they were an unpopular minority, without political power and unable to
develop a plausible strategy to end slavery (at least not until the attempted
secession of southern states in 1861 made it possible to advocate emancipation as a means to preserve the Union).

The Slaveholding Republic—a work left unfinished by Don E. Fehrenbacher when he died in 1997 and ably completed and edited by his onetime
student Ward M. McAfee—reveals for the first time the full extent of the
slaveholders' dominance over the federal government in the period between
the constitutional convention and the election of Lincoln in 1860. It is well
known that a majority of U.S. presidents and Supreme Court justices before
1860 were southern slaveholders and that both of the national political
parties of the period between the 1830s and the 1850s—the Democrats
and the Whigs—deferred to a proslavery faction. But Fehrenbacher also
reveals in detail the myriad ways in which the federal government acted as
the direct agent of slavery and slaveholders. It did so in its governance of the
District of Columbia, its conduct of foreign policy (which included seeking
compensation for slaves carried off in wars or escaping into other national
jurisdictions), and its role in the recapture and return of fugitives who had
made it to "the free states."

These three books, therefore, offer differing perspectives on what might
be considered the original sin of America—the enslavement and brutal exploitation of millions of people of African descent over a period of almost
250 years. From whatever angle it is examined, however, slavery left deep

scars that have not yet healed. Its legacy persists to this day in the failure to extend full equality to African Americans. Slavery and its consequences, these books tell us, were not incidental or secondary aspects of American history but constitute its central theme. Rather than being an exception to the grander themes of liberty and democracy, slavery and the racism it engendered have exposed the shallowness and narrowness of the national commitment to these ideals.

The first basic question that might be asked about the history of African-American slavery is how it originated and what its antecedents were. In challenging the conventional boundaries of the subject, Davis goes back to the enslavement of black Africans resulting from Arab expansion into North and East Africa, which began in the seventh and eighth centuries. The numbers of black slaves imported into the Islamic lands of the Middle East and North Africa during a period of some twelve hundred years may have been as great, if not greater, than the number carried across the Atlantic to the Americas between the fifteenth century and the nineteenth. Neither the Koran nor Islamic law gave any sanction to racism, and Muslims always held white as well as black slaves. But in practice there was a tendency, which may have influenced southern Europeans who came in contact with Islamic slavery in the fourteenth and fifteenth centuries, to discriminate among the slaves on the basis of color; the most arduous and demeaning tasks were reserved for the darker-skinned.

During the late medieval period, southern Europeans, especially Italians, were heavily involved in the slave trade that transported Caucasians from the Dalmatian coast and regions north of the Black Sea to Egypt and Syria, where they were sometimes used to produce sugar. (The word "slave" in English, as well as its homophones in other European languages, has the same root as "Slav.") As Europeans developed a taste for sugar and tried to grow their own on Mediterranean islands, they initially employed such white captives. But two almost simultaneous events—the fall of Constantinople to the Turks in 1453 and the beginnings of a slave trade involving Portugal and sub-Saharan West Africa—changed the source of slavery and gave new impetus to the development of plantation agriculture. The Turkish conquests cut off ready access to Europe's previous sources of both sugar and slaves, encouraging the Portuguese to develop plantation colonies on the eastern Atlantic islands of Madeira, Cape Verde, and São Tomé in the late fifteenth and early sixteenth centuries. By the time Columbus arrived in America, Madeira was a thriving prototype for the use of enslaved Africans to grow sugar and other commercial crops in the New World.

During the next three centuries there occurred the largest shift of population that the world had ever seen, and most of it was from Africa to the Americas by means of the Atlantic slave trade. "By 1820," Davis writes, "at least ten million African slaves had arrived in the New World, as opposed to a grand total of two million Europeans." But the shocking fact is that by 1820 the two million Europeans had become twelve million, whereas the ten million Africans had left only six million descendants. No other set of figures so graphically illustrates the inhumanity of slavery and the slave trade.

What was new about New World slavery was not only the sheer numbers involved, but also "its specifically racial character." Davis points out that "degrading stereotypes of the slave" had long existed but were now for the first time associated exclusively with people of African ancestry. The linkage of Africans with slavery and servility was, he concludes, "at the heart of white racism." There is a perennial debate among historians about the causal connection between New World slavery and white racism. Did racism emerge primarily as a rationale for slavery or did the Africans' physical characteristics and the stereotypes associated with them make them seem uniquely eligible for enslavement? From Davis's account and from what I know of the sources he uses, I would conclude that blacks originally became prime candidates for lifetime servitude not so much because of their race or color as because they were readily available at a time when access to slaves of any other color was severely limited and certainly incapable of meeting the demand for plantation laborers in the New World. But once the association was made between servitude and pigmentation, it would take more than the abolition of slavery itself to remove the stigma associated with blackness.

Although Davis provides a worldwide perspective and covers more than a millennium of servitude, Ira Berlin concentrates on what would become the United States between the early seventeenth century and the era of emancipation and reconstruction. His *Generations of Captivity* is a sequel to an earlier book, *Many Thousands Gone: The First Two Centuries of Slavery in North America*, published in 1998.[1] The first three chapters of the new work summarize the earlier study, and the fourth carries the story forward from the 1820s to the 1860s. Because so much of the book is not really new, readers may underestimate the importance of what has been added. The subtitle—"A History of African-American Slaves"—suggests that the book is not so much a study of slavery in all of its aspects as an effort to convey the everyday life and typical experiences of the slaves themselves. As a practitioner of social history "from the bottom up," Berlin pays relatively little attention to how the masters viewed themselves or to the political and ideological controversies to which the existence of slavery eventually gave rise.

The kind of world that the slaves could make for themselves, he continues to argue here, as he did in his earlier work, depended to a considerable extent on whether they lived in "a society with slaves" or in "a slave society." In the former the labor force was only marginally composed of black people who were owned by whites. Before the end of the seventeenth century the Chesapeake colonies of Virginia and Maryland were such societies, because white indentured servants rather than black slaves did most of the work on the plantations. In a "slave society" slavery was the dominant labor system, and there was a sharp and deep divide between the caste or status group that included the masters and that to which the slaves belonged.

The first or "charter" generations of North American slaves, Berlin contends, were mostly "Atlantic Creoles" who did not come directly from traditional African societies but rather from the cosmopolitan enclaves on the Atlantic rim that served as depots for the seventeenth-century slave trade to Brazil and the sugar islands of the West Indies. They tended to have Spanish or Portuguese surnames, some knowledge of a European language, and a previous exposure to Christianity. In a society not yet committed to a heavy reliance on slavery, these pioneer African Americans were often able to become free, develop skills, and even acquire land and servants of their own. It was not until the late seventeenth and early eighteenth centuries that Virginia and Maryland evolved into true slave societies. As white indentured servants became harder to recruit and as African slaves became available in large numbers and at affordable prices, a class of large slaveholding planters emerged and seized social and political control of the two colonies.[2]

The gradual emergence of a regime dominated by plantations in the Chesapeake colonies and its relatively sudden rise at about the same time in South Carolina provided a setting for what Berlin calls the "plantation generations" of North American slaves. By the early eighteenth century most slaves came directly from traditional African societies and were subjected to a harsher, more closed environment than their "charter generation" predecessors. (Eighteenth-century Louisiana under the French and Spanish went for a time in the other direction, evolving from a slave society to a society with slaves.) The political and social upheavals at the end of the eighteenth century gave rise to the "revolutionary generations," some of whose members gained freedom through private manumissions, as in the upper South, or were gradually emancipated through public action, as in the northern states. To the generations discussed in his early work, Berlin has now added "migration generations" to illuminate what happened to African Americans as a result of the expansion of the plantation system from the eastern seaboard into the Cotton Kingdom of Alabama, Mississippi, Louisiana, and Texas.

Without the support of the American legal and political system, the expansion of slavery through the migration of masters and slaves could not have taken place. In the second chapter of *Challenging the Boundaries of Slavery*, Davis describes the year 1819 as a decisive point for the rest of the antebellum era. The controversy over whether or not Missouri should be admitted to the Union as a slave state coincided with two other seemingly independent developments: the Supreme Court's endorsement of an expanded role for the federal government in fostering economic development and the beginnings in New England of a reinterpretation of the Bible that offered a potential challenge to the scriptural literalism that made slavery acceptable to many Christians. Davis believes that these ideological innovations foreshadowed the clash between slavery and modern liberal capitalism that would be resolved only in the Civil War. But the Missouri Compromise of 1820 allowed for the continued expansion of slavery in a westerly direction and maintained the parity in the number of free and slave states that the South regarded as essential for the preservation of its "rights." In 1819 the slaveholding American republic that Don Fehrenbacher has written about was still strengthening its hold on the government and the law.

In disagreement with the views of one wing of the abolitionist movement, as well as with some recent historians, Fehrenbacher does not view the Constitution itself as a proslavery document. The three-fifths clause, he contends, was a genuine compromise and not a concession to slaveholders. The fraction itself originated as a device for using population as a surrogate for wealth in allocating taxes under the Articles of Confederation. In the deliberations leading to the Constitution it served as an alternative to counting all slaves for the purpose of representation, which would have advantaged slaveholders more than a three-fifths clause. Except for slaves, representation was based on total population, not on the voting population. If women and children were included, why not slaves? Not counting them at all would be to the North's advantage in the Electoral College and the House of Representatives, but would have clearly implied that blacks were not human beings, even inferior ones.[3]

Fehrenbacher does not go so far as to view the Constitution as "antislavery" (as another school of abolitionists would attempt to do), but he does consider it a genuine compromise. It allowed opponents to hope for the gradual elimination of slavery through individual state action, as was beginning to occur in the North, while granting those who benefited from slavery relief from the prospect of direct federal intervention. None of the three clauses in the Constitution that mention slavery—the three-fifths clause, the prohibition of a ban on the international slave trade for twenty years, and the provision for the return of fugitives from one state to another—"recognized slavery as having any legitimacy in federal law. On the contrary, the framers were doubly careful to treat it explicitly as a state institution."

Hence—and this is Fehrenbacher's central argument—the United States was not founded as a slaveholding republic but only became one because of the ability of the slaveholders to impose their will through policies and legislation based on dubious or clearly erroneous interpretations of the Constitution. Fehrenbacher then describes in detail exactly how the slaveholders used their political leverage to further their interests in different activities of the federal government—the administration of the District of Columbia, the conduct of foreign policy, efforts to suppress the African slave trade, federal involvement in the return of fugitive slaves, and decisions on whether slavery would be allowed in federal territories.

Fehrenbacher thus gives new credibility to the view of Abraham Lincoln and the Republicans of the late 1850s that an aggressive slave power was thwarting the desire of the Founding Fathers to put slavery on a "course of ultimate extinction" and was in fact acting to extend and nationalize the South's "peculiar institution." The Republican victory in 1860 was therefore "a sharp break with the past" that had "revolutionary implications for Southerners." It is altogether fitting that Fehrenbacher, long a distinguished and sympathetic interpreter of Lincoln's response to the sectional crisis, should have produced as his last book the most convincing vindication to date of Lincoln's view of the Constitution and its relation to slavery.[4]

But the man who did so much to save the republic from the slaveholders also took at times a very pessimistic view of the future of black-white relations in the United States. On several occasions—as late as 1862—he advocated a total separation of the races through government-subsidized colonization of African Americans somewhere outside the United States. (The American Colonization Society had been advocating this "solution" to the problem of slavery and race since 1817.) Until late in the war, and certainly until after the Emancipation Proclamation of January 1, 1863, Lincoln seemed settled in his belief that the prejudice of whites against blacks was so deep-seated that it would forever prevent the two races from living together in equality.[5]

Did Lincoln's long-standing racial pessimism make him a white supremacist or simply a political realist responding pragmatically to the intense racism of the time? In the third and final chapter of his book Davis discusses the antislavery movement and faults the abolitionists for their lack of realism in an era when the color line was hardening: "However much we deplore the racism of many colonizationists, we cannot deny that their vision of the future was more realistic than that of the later abolitionists." The North's ultimate turn against slavery was not, he suggests, a result of the abolitionists' appeal to conscience and human solidarity. "By continually overreacting to a somewhat neutral, complacent, and racist North, southern militants created an *antislavery* North in the sense that many Northerners felt personally and justifiably threatened by an undemocratic Slave Power." This of course was precisely the sentiment to which Lincoln appealed, setting in motion a process that would result in the abolition of slavery in a nation that remained strongly committed to white supremacy.

One might conclude from the impressions that Fehrenbacher and Davis convey of white racial attitudes and actions that African-American slaves would have been so brutally treated that they would have had little chance to make a life for themselves that provided a measure of dignity and self-respect. But Berlin's account of how the slaves themselves survived the decades just before the Civil War makes them appear self-reliant and creative to an almost superhuman extent when we consider what they were up against.

He makes no claims about the paternalistic benevolence of the masters—quite the contrary—but he nevertheless finds that the slaves for the most part managed to avoid the despair and degradation that their circumstances might have warranted.

The key distinguishing feature of slave experience during this period, according to Berlin, was the forced migration of more than a million African Americans from the older slave states to the newer ones, an uprooting that made being a slave temporarily even more demoralizing than it had been in more stable plantation communities. The huge shift of black people from the seaboard slave states to the Cotton Kingdom of the southwest qualifies in his view as a "second middle passage," recalling the trauma of the earlier Atlantic crossing. The internal slave trade that accounted for most of this movement made the economies of the upper or non-cotton-growing South more dependent on the raising of slaves for the interstate market than on the production of agricultural commodities.

Throughout his book, Berlin emphasizes family and kinship as the basic mechanism for slave survival. His work thus follows in the tradition of the late Herbert Gutman, whose book on the slave family I reviewed more than twenty-five years ago.[6] Although he endorses recent studies showing that family breakup was a common feature of the interstate trade, Berlin contends that black families of a cohesive and emotionally fulfilling kind survived the disruption of previously established relationships. Against the odds and after much suffering, the migrating slaves managed to reestablish a sense of community based on family and kinship. Although fully acknowledging the brutality of the slave trade and the plantation regime, he contends that circumstances could not deprive the slaves of "agency"—the ability to take action in their own interest—and community.

One might expect that an interpretation stressing the slaves' ability to act independently of their masters would make much of the occasions when they directly resisted white authority. But there is very little in *Generations of Captivity* about open rebelliousness or defiance. Much recent scholarship on the lives that the slaves made for themselves finds that "slave resistance" was almost exclusively a matter of slaves struggling to maintain their own culture and has little to say about rebellion, sabotage, purposeful malingering, or running away. If earlier liberal or leftist historians made too much of open rebelliousness or "day-to-day resistance," it may be that the newer emphasis on culture and community, of which Berlin is a leading proponent, does not pay enough attention to more desperate and violent responses to being held in bondage. The basic dilemma of slavery studies "from the bottom up" has always been that too much emphasis on oppression makes African Americans simply victims and thereby denies them a usable past, while too much stress on their ability to act on their own behalf and on their cultural creativity tends to obscure the extreme brutality of the system, making it seem almost benign. The pendulum has swung so far in the direction of creative action by slaves that a corrective may be impending, as some recent studies suggest.[7]

Berlin's concluding point is that two distinctive black cultural traditions were carried over from the era of slavery into that of Reconstruction. One, deriving primarily from northern free blacks, stressed individualism and self-help; the other, coming directly from the slave plantation experience, was a kind of communalism that valued family solidarity over the individual acquisition of wealth and status. Berlin does not explicitly take sides in his evaluation of these two traditions, but I detect here and in some other recent works of African-American history an image of the slave community that seems designed to serve as the basis for a cultural critique of the dominant American ethos of liberal capitalism.[8] Whatever its ethical or philosophical merits, such an approach risks obscuring the realities of slavery by romanticizing an experience that entailed enormous suffering and was in many ways disabling. The right balance between slavery as a source of African-American culture and community and slavery as debilitating oppression has yet to be struck.

CHAPTER 8

The Long Trek to Freedom

This chapter focuses on the emergence of pro- and antislavery sentiment as portrayed in several major studies—Though the Heavens May Fall: The Landmark Trial That Led to the End of Human Slavery *by Steven M. Wise (Cambridge, MA: Da Capo Press, 2005)*, Slave Country: American Expansion and the Origins of the Deep South *by Adam Rothman (Cambridge, MA: Harvard University Press, 2005)*, The First Emancipator: The Forgotten Story of Robert Carter, the Founding Father Who Freed His Slaves, *by Andrew Levy (New York: Random House, 2005), and* Bound for Canaan: The Underground Railroad and the War for the Soul of America *by Fergus M. Bordewich (New York: Amistad, 2005).*

*　*　*

I.

Before the middle of the eighteenth century, slavery was generally accepted in Europe and its colonies as a divinely ordained punishment for original sin or simply as a natural part of the eternal order of things. Yet by then Europeans had stopped enslaving one another for centuries; slavery was a condition mainly imposed on blacks brought from Africa to the New World in order to produce tropical staples for European consumption. England and France in particular had an enormous stake in the slave trade and the plantation system, which were primary sources of prosperity and commercial development for both countries. But very few black slaves were to be found in either England or France, and it was an open question whether slavery could still be enforced in either country.[1] Restricting slavery to particular races and regions opened it to criticism because it deviated from norms in European countries; but, paradoxically, it also meant that those who had little direct contact with slavery could easily put it out of their minds.

The ideas of the Enlightenment were bound to raise fundamental questions whether slavery and the slave trade were compatible with the new ideals of liberty, equality, and rationality. In his 1748 *Spirit of the Laws* Montesquieu considered various justifications for slavery, including the alleged subhumanity of blacks, and showed how unreasonable they were. But the Enlightenment was a two-edged weapon when applied to the kind of servitude that existed in the eighteenth century. Although Enlightenment thinkers developed a conception of universal human rights, they also studied and classified the physical variations among human beings and thus laid the foundations for a concept of biological race that could be used to establish new hierarchies. It became possible to justify slavery on grounds of alleged scientific fact rather than divine fiat, owing to the new sciences of comparative anatomy and physical anthropology. Several prominent Enlightenment thinkers who at times had qualms about slavery, such as Voltaire, Hume, and Jefferson, were convinced that blacks were much inferior to whites in their rational capacities—a belief that allowed apologists for the institution, such as the Jamaican planter Edward Long, to develop a modern and "scientific" defense of black servitude. Enlightenment theories, depending on how they were interpreted and applied, could condemn slavery as a denial of the rights of humanity or defend it as consistent with science and rationality.

As the books by Steven M. Wise, Andrew Levy, and Fergus M. Bordewich make clear, the strongest and most effective opposition to slavery did not come from Enlightenment rationalists but from religious zealots who were inspired by the evangelical or pietistic revivals and the "awakenings" that began in the eighteenth century and continued into the nineteenth. These men of faith discovered that slavery was not just ideologically questionable but contrary to the will of God—a sin that could no longer be tolerated by believing Christians.

Evangelical concern for the souls of enslaved Africans became evident before any visible hostility to the institution itself. The most active and successful missionaries to the slaves of the New World were the Moravians, members of a pietistic sect of Czech and German origin, who were successful in improving the condition of some slaves precisely because they made it clear that they were not opposed to black slavery in principle. They were able to persuade slave owners that they would not harm their interests and in doing so were able to gain influence in places like the Danish West Indies and North Carolina, partly because they conceded that the Bible sanctioned the servitude of Africans even after they had been baptized. But they argued that the divinely ordained status of blacks as "hewers of wood and carriers of water" did not preclude a degree of spiritual equality with whites that required kindly treatment from masters and sometimes even led to the full integration of religious worship.[2]

The pioneers of religious opposition to slavery were the Quakers. From their base in Pennsylvania, mid- to late eighteenth-century Quakers set in motion the American antislavery movement, first within their own community, and then more broadly in the Anglo-American world. Since they were pacifists, the Quakers had no weapons other than peaceful persuasion, but this was enough to make slaveholding incompatible with membership in the Society of Friends. The foremost Quaker exponent of abolishing slavery was Anthony Benezet, whose influence extended from Pennsylvania across the Atlantic. Benezet was a major inspiration for the first important British abolitionist, Granville Sharpe, the main character of Steven M. Wise's book *Though the Heavens May Fall*, which is a thorough and convincing account of the case that led to the official banning of slavery in England in 1772.

Sharpe was not a Quaker himself; in fact he was a highly orthodox member of the Church of England who had strong prejudices against Catholics and Protestant dissenters alike. Wise goes so far as to call him "a religious bigot." But his tireless and ultimately successful effort to end slavery in England was dictated by a conviction that slavery was contrary to scripture. Whereas other biblical literalists found a sanction in holy writ for black servitude, Sharpe found the contrary. His main weapon against it was the English common law. Although not a lawyer himself, he was the prime mover in a series of court actions that led ultimately in 1772 to the decision by Lord Mansfield, chief justice of the King's Bench, that slavery could not exist in the "free air of England."

No one knows how many black slaves there were in England at the time. Estimates of the total run from as low as 3,000 to as high as 40,000; approximately 15,000 seems a reasonable guess. Most of these slaves had been imported from the West Indies or North America by their masters, who expected to be obeyed and served as they had been in the colonies. But unlike Virginia or Jamaica, England did not have slave markets or public authorities clearly empowered to apprehend fugitives and return them to their owners. Consequently, many slaves simply deserted their masters and went to live independently in "free black" enclaves, the largest of which, by far, was in London. Sharpe came into the picture most often when masters sought to capture their vagrant human property and ship slaves back to the colonies for their own use or for sale to someone else. He and his associates used writs of *habeas corpus* to prevent such actions by slave owners and then went on to prosecute some masters for physically assaulting their slaves while seizing them and trying to hustle them on board ships bound for Jamaica or Virginia.

In the first case of this kind that came before Lord Mansfield, the lawyers engaged by Sharpe succeeded in getting a judgment that freed their client but only on the grounds that his status as a slave had not been established. In the subsequent case of 1772, however, there was no doubt that James Somerset, who had been plucked off a ship bound for the West Indies, was legally a slave under colonial law. Here Mansfield faced squarely the issue of whether slavery and English residence were compatible. Dismissing precedents based on *villeinage*, a medieval form of lifetime servitude that had never been outlawed but which no longer existed in practice, Mansfield found no basis for human property under British common law. "The power of a master over his slave has been different in different counties," he concluded. "The state of slavery is of such a nature that it is incapable of being introduced on any reasons, moral or political, but only positive law.... It is so odious that nothing can be suffered to support it but positive law."

In other words, if the British wanted slavery, Parliament would have to legislate it. Such a denial of the legitimacy of English slavery pointed to the subsequent campaign against the slave trade and ultimately against slavery itself in the British colonies.[3]

In 1772, with the American Revolution only a few years away, slavery was legal in all of the American colonies. The struggle for American independence on the grounds specified in the Declaration of Independence cast doubt on the future of slavery. How could a nation that proclaimed that "all men are created equal" enslave some of them? There was a strong presumption during and immediately after the Revolution that slavery was an unjust and harmful institution and that its days were numbered.

It was not only the injustice of slavery that counted against it, but the fact that slavery was seen as having introduced an inherently alien and potentially dangerous black population into what many hoped would become a white man's country (once the Indians were disposed of, that is). Particularly after the uprising in Haiti in the 1790s, the fear of a widespread slave rebellion served as a major impetus to thinking about how to eradicate slavery. Thomas Jefferson objected to it because of its harmful effect on both races and favored emancipation in principle, but he could not imagine slaves being emancipated without the deportation or "colonization" of the freed black population. Lord Mansfield's decision did not turn England itself into a multihued or multiracial nation, as emancipation without colonization would do to the United States.

A lack of such population pressures in the northern states and a limited economic stake in slave labor there led to the gradual emancipation of slaves in those states beginning in the 1780s and 1790s. But south of what became the Mason-Dixon Line antislavery sentiment flickered and then died around the turn of the century. Adam Rothman's *Slave Country: American Expansion and the Origins of the Deep South* is the fullest account we have of how slaveholding in the southern states became not only acceptable but also a source of pride and celebration.

The critical factor, as Rothman's subtitle indicates, was the acquisition of vast new territories suitable for plantation agriculture, especially for the growing of short-staple cotton, a commodity much in demand for the industrial revolution in Great Britain and the northeastern United States.

A flourishing Cotton Kingdom arose in the nineteenth century as the U.S. government obtained the territories that became the states of Alabama, Mississippi, and Louisiana from France and Spain and crushed the Indian resistance in the new Southwest.

Fears that an excess of black people in the seaboard states would lead to a slave rebellion were among the factors that led Congress to abolish the slave trade by 1807. But the question remained where the additional slaves needed in the new territories would come from. The need was met by natural increase in the numbers of slaves and by internal migration. Unlike their counterparts elsewhere in the New World, North American slaves more than reproduced themselves, and the surplus of slaves beyond the labor needs of the states where they were born could be sent westward to man the new cotton plantations, whose prosperity depended on good soil, two hundred frost-free days, and the cotton gin—all of which were available after 1800.

Jefferson and others initially recommended "diffusion" of the seaboard slave population to the new territories in order to prepare the way for gradual emancipation; such movement, it was thought, would ease white racial fears of being overwhelmed or threatened by a growing black population. But eventually the argument for diffusion became a rationale for perpetuating slavery on grounds that spreading out the slave population led to more humane treatment than would have been possible if they were confined to the original slave states. The belief that American slavery was justified as a system of paternalism thus originated as the dominant social ideology of the Deep South.

II.

Robert Carter III, the subject of an impressive new biography by Andrew Levy, was an authentically paternalistic master of the late eighteenth century who kept all his slaves in Virginia and eventually freed them instead of "diffusing" them to the West. Inheriting hundreds of slaves from forebears who were among the greatest planters of Virginia, Carter refused to sell any of them; he gave them considerable independence of action on the many plantations that he owned and avoided the harsh physical punishments that were routinely imposed by other masters. In 1791, he made the extraordinary decision to free all 452 of his slaves while he was still alive.

Through a complicated "Deed of Gift" he began the process by freeing fifteen a year. A Virginia law of 1784 authorizing such private and voluntary manumissions provided an opportunity (which would be foreclosed early in the next century) for Carter and other would-be emancipators of their own slaves. But Carter was unique in the number that he freed and in the fact that he was the only one of Virginia's large slaveholding planters who divested himself completely of human property while he was still alive.

(George Mason provided for the manumission of his slaves after his death, and George Washington did so after his wife's death; Thomas Jefferson, notoriously, freed in his will only his slave mistress Sally Hemmings and their children.)

Carter's inspiration for his action was primarily religious. He was not a particularly well-educated man for a member of his class; as a child he had been allowed to run free and read whatever he wanted without the supervision and intellectual discipline that a tutor would normally have provided. The Enlightenment thought that influenced Jefferson and Madison had relatively little effect on him, although at times he considered himself a deist. His religious peregrinations began in 1777 when he contracted smallpox and had a high fever that lasted several days. In the midst of it, Levy tells us, he had a vision, or what he later described as a "most gracious Illumination." The details of what he saw and felt remain sketchy, but they left him with the impression that he had experienced God directly and had been called to His service. Soon he left the Anglican Church and did the unthinkable for a member of the Virginia planter elite: he became a Baptist, thus joining a church of the plain folk and increasingly of the slaves.

For a time Carter became the major patron of the Baptists in Virginia; in addition to providing financial support for its congregations he traveled about attending as many Baptist meetings as he could. But when the Baptists sought respectability by toning down and eventually repudiating the opposition to slavery that they had announced in 1777, Carter drifted away from them and became an independent religious "seeker." The closest he came to a new religious allegiance was when he fell under the spell of the Swedish mystic and visionary Emanuel Swedenborg, who envisioned a "New Jerusalem" free of slavery and other human iniquities. While under Swedenborgian influence, Carter made a Deed of Gift offering eventual freedom to all his slaves.

Levy has done exhaustive research but we find in his book no full explanation in Carter's own words of what he thought he was doing. He did not write books or tracts or give sermons setting out his religious views and their implications for the slavery question. In fact he was remarkably inarticulate for a man who had such strong opinions and took such dramatic actions. For the most part Levy has to imagine his spiritual life from the evidence of his behavior and a few brief references in his correspondence, which seems to have been mostly concerned with matters of business. I failed to find a single eloquent or even quotable statement of Carter's fundamental beliefs. Precisely why he became "the first emancipator" remains mysterious and ambiguous.

Carter was an idiosyncratic Virginia aristocrat, whose behavior was most unusual. I have to question Levy's view that he was a Founding Father whose emancipatory act can be taken as judgment on the other founders and whose behavior suggests what they could and should have done to rid the country of slavery. Carter had a very marginal part in the American Revolution. He was generally lukewarm about the Patriot cause and remained on the sidelines. Never elected to a major public office, he did nothing in particular to help establish the government that came into existence in 1789. The failure of the great Virginia Founding Fathers—Jefferson, Washington, Madison, and Mason—to prevent the rise of a proslavery South is difficult to attribute to any quality that Carter had that they lacked. They might have done better, but if we acknowledge the political, economic, and ideological obstacles to abolition that Rothman shows were developing, we see that they could also have done worse. At least they provided some ideas that, if consistently acted upon, could inspire later opponents of slavery.

Nevertheless, Levy helps us to understand why the revival of antislavery sentiment in the nineteenth century was based less on the secular egalitarianism of Jefferson than on something like the religious perfectionism of Robert Carter. The centrality of faith and piety to the nineteenth-century abolitionist movement is made clear in Fergus Bordewich's absorbing history of the Underground Railroad, a difficult story to tell because the Railroad was never a centrally organized or well-coordinated undertaking. How it related to the larger abolitionist movement has never been made entirely clear. But beginning in around 1800 and extending up to the time of the Civil War, a variety of groups and individuals helped fugitives escape from the South to Canada or protective enclaves in the upper North. That they made up a movement that could be likened (somewhat misleadingly) to a railroad system was an idea that did not develop until the 1840s, when the railroad itself became a prominent part of the American scene. But Bordewich has made a valiant and generally successful effort to piece together the scattered evidence into a coherent story.

Once again the pioneers were Quakers. Although strictly nonviolent, Quaker activists were willing to disobey unjust laws, such as the Fugitive Slave Acts passed by the U.S. Congress. Because of the Quaker presence and its proximity to slaveholding Maryland, Pennsylvania became a principal way station on the path to Canada. But Quaker communities in Ohio and Indiana were also havens for slaves making their way to Canada via the Great Lakes. Other evangelical Protestants, such as Methodists, Presbyterians, and Congregationalists, became increasingly involved with Railroad activities in response to the development of a more radical and activist antislavery movement in the North in the 1830s. As Bordewich makes clear, their primary motivation was almost always religious. Although many white abolitionists had doubts about the full equality of blacks, they "were exhilarated by the conviction that they were doing what faith demanded of them. They were, after all, assuring their own salvation in a deeply pious era when Judgment Day was as real as the annual spring planting and autumn harvest."

In its earliest years, between 1800 and the 1840s, the Underground Railroad was primarily conducted by humanitarian whites who provided temporary havens for black fugitives and then guided them to the next station on the line to Canada and freedom. For a long time, historians interpreted the entire history of the Underground Railroad as a story of benevolent whites helping essentially passive blacks. Beginning in the 1960s and 1970s, revisionist historians who stressed the initiatives of African Americans themselves described the Railroad as if it were almost exclusively a black endeavor. Bordewich strikes a good balance between the earlier overemphasis on white benevolence and the more recent tendency to ignore it almost completely. White initiative was crucial in the early stages, but as a militant black antislavery movement developed in the North, partly because of agitation by former fugitives such as Frederick Douglass, African Americans increasingly became leaders of the movement. Particularly impressive were the blacks who worked as conductors on the Railroad, such as the legendary Harriet Tubman, whose forays into the South to recruit fugitives and guide them to freedom were only possible because she could pass as a slave herself in order to get close to her potential passengers. But whites remained seriously involved in a genuinely interracial movement, which in some ways anticipated the civil rights movement of the late 1950s and early 1960s.

The movement remained nonviolent until the 1850s. The Fugitive Slave Act of 1850 was the crucial factor leading to an acceptance of violent action to prevent the capture of those who had escaped from slavery. The new law gave the federal government much greater enforcement powers and threatened the freedom of fugitives who had thought they were safe in northern antislavery enclaves. It also increased the chances that blacks who had been born free or legally emancipated would be kidnapped, fraudulently enslaved, and sent south. As federal marshals sought fugitives in black communities, they were sometimes met with lethal resistance. A number of rescues or attempted rescues took place in the early 1850s, some resulting in loss of life on both sides.

Bordewich describes some of these incidents, but it is odd that he does not mention the efforts to rescue Anthony Burns in Boston in 1854, an extremely dramatic and violent affair in which a white abolitionist killed a guard. A large number of federal troops were dispatched to capture Burns; they marched him to a boat in Boston Harbor through an enormous, jeering crowd. No further attempts were made to arrest fugitives in Boston.

Bordewich's omission of the Burns affair is symptomatic of a general problem of the book—its relative neglect of New England as a source of antislavery thought and action. He may be overcorrecting a previous tendency in antislavery historiography to overemphasize New England's contribution to the movement. The actual traffic on the Underground Railroad may have been somewhat lighter than in upstate New York or northern Ohio, but it was substantial. As Bordewich acknowledges at one point, Vermont was a prime haven for fugitives. It may have been the safest state of residence for a fugitive who did not wish to go to Canada.

The turn to violent action against slavery culminated in the actions of John Brown. Since Brown was active in the Underground Railroad for several years and to some extent conceived his raid on Harpers Ferry in 1859 as a large-scale effort to inspire mass desertions from southern plantations, his exploits are a legitimate part of the story Bordewich tells. In December 1858 and January 1859, as a kind of dress rehearsal for Harpers Ferry, Brown forcibly liberated eleven slaves from Missouri plantations, killing one owner before leading them on a long trek to freedom in Canada. Brown has recently become an object of great historical interest.[4]

There has long been controversy over whether or not he was excessively committed to violence. In Kansas in 1856 he presided over the murder of five proslavery settlers who neither owned slaves themselves nor were guilty of any known acts of violence against the antislavery settlers with whom they were competing for control of the territory. Recent discussions of Brown have raised the question whether he was a prototype of the modern "terrorist" driven to extreme actions by religious zealotry and by a belief that there was direct divine sanction for his deeds. In his recent biography of Brown, David S. Reynolds tries to distinguish Brown's kind of terrorism from that of modern suicide bombers and plane hijackers. Reynolds argues that Brown's methods can be justified by the need to challenge the enormous and exceptional evil of slavery, by the lack of other means of dealing with it, and by the better society that was envisioned as a result of taking violent action against it.[5]

In his more general discussion, Bordewich compares the religiously inspired abolitionists involved in the more militant actions of the Underground Railroad with contemporary anti-abortion activists, who attack clinics and commit other illegal acts in response to a "higher law." He concedes that "uneasy questions" remain "about what happens when revealed religion collides with a secular society that shares neither its politics nor its reading of the Scriptures." But he concludes that the faith of the "deeply pious activists of the underground ... was also balanced by a generous idealism, and by an uncompromising devotion to the rights of others" that he suggests would be difficult to find among the more militant members of the contemporary anti-abortion movement. The implied argument here is that slavery was an obvious and flagrant denial of personal liberty, while the woman's "right to choose" might be considered an assertion of that liberty. Bordewich does not resolve the question of the legitimacy of violence and civil disobedience, but by raising it he brings to his account the moral seriousness it deserves.

CHAPTER 9

Redcoat Liberation

The issue of African-American slavery and the American Revolution forms the focus of this essay, principally as discussed in the following books—Epic Journeys of Freedom: Runaway Slaves of the American Revolution and Their Global Quest for Liberty *by Cassandra Pybus (Boston: Beacon Press, 2006)*, Rough Crossings: Britain, the Slaves and the American Revolution *by Simon Schama (New York: Ecco, 2006), and* The Forgotten Fifth: African Americans in the Age of Revolution *by Gary B. Nash (Cambridge, MA: Harvard University Press, 2006).*

* * *

Popular views of the American Revolution usually overlook one aspect of it that sharply contradicts the idealized image of a struggle for liberty against oppression. For the one-fifth of the population that was African-American, freedom meant escape from slavery but not independence from Britain; those seeking emancipation were more likely to find it in places under British control than in territory held by white American revolutionaries. During the war thousands of slaves—estimates run as high as 80,000 to 100,000, or nearly a fifth of the total slave population—deserted their masters at least temporarily. Some simply vanished into the woods, swamps, and mountains of the South. But vast numbers crossed over behind British lines where those willing to join the struggle against the rebels were being offered their freedom as a reward for service to the Crown. Some of those who went to join the enemies of American independence were also inspired by somewhat misleading rumors that the British had abolished slavery. In a landmark legal decision of 1772, Lord Mansfield had decided that slaves brought to England could not be taken back to the colonies by their masters or sold for export. This ruling undermined slavery in Britain and soon led to its disappearance, but it did not affect black bondage elsewhere in the empire.[1]

For the British, welcoming and emancipating runaway American slaves was clearly a pragmatic policy and not an expression of principled hostility to slavery. Loyalists under British protection were permitted to keep or recapture their slaves, and hundreds of thousands of Africans would continue to toil in Britain's Caribbean colonies for another half-century. Moreover, those who fled to the British side were not always well treated or cared for. Large numbers died from disease (especially smallpox, against which, unlike many of the British soldiers, they had not been vaccinated); others were simply left behind to face possible recapture and return to slavery when the British were forced to evacuate their troops by sea. But despite the perils and uncertainties that confronted them, approximately ten thousand slaves sought refuge with the British in Virginia alone after the royal governor, Lord Dunmore, proclaimed freedom for those willing to fight in November 1775. Thousands more came from the Carolinas and Georgia. At the end of the war, between 15,000 and 20,000 escaped slaves remained under British protection in the port cities that had not yet been evacuated, namely New York, Charleston, and Savannah.

In the peace agreement that ended the war a clause was added at the last minute giving the Americans the right to reclaim property that had fallen into British hands. When George Washington, who himself had lost slaves, appealed to Guy Carleton, the British commander in New York, to return the fugitives under his control to their owners, he was rudely rebuffed. Carleton argued that the runaway slaves who had been promised freedom by the British could no longer be considered property and that it would be dishonorable to permit their reenslavement. As a result of this policy roughly nine thousand freed slaves accompanied the last British forces to leave what was now the independent United States of America.

What happened to them subsequently is a complex and ultimately tragic story, one in which the former slaves made heroic efforts to gain freedom and dignity. Some of them were taken to England, where most found themselves begging and starving in the streets of London. Not only were there very few jobs open to them but they did not even qualify for the relief offered destitute Englishmen under the Poor Laws, since they had not been born in an English parish. Seeing their plight, Granville Sharp, the founder of the British antislavery movement, who had recently helped to launch a campaign to abolish the slave trade, drew up a plan for colonizing them in Sierra Leone on the "Grain Coast" of West Africa. In 1787, 411 potential colonists, mostly black men but including a surprising number of white wives, set sail in three ships accompanied by a naval escort. Three hundred seventy-seven of the settlers survived the voyage, but of these, 122 died in very short order, victims of disease and harsh climatic conditions. Those who survived experienced difficulties dealing with indigenous chiefs, who had their own claims to the land the former slaves occupied and hoped to own.

Meanwhile a larger group of escaped slaves had been resettled in Nova Scotia and New Brunswick as part of the Loyalist population that had found refuge there after the Revolution. But the blacks discovered that most of the land promised them remained in white hands, and the best many of them could do was become tenants of the white landowners under terms that resembled indentured servitude or debt peonage. In 1791 the Nova Scotian blacks sent one of their leaders, Thomas Peters, to London to seek help from British humanitarians. Peters managed to induce the patrons of the Sierra Leone colony to invite the discontented blacks in the Maritime Provinces of Canada to emigrate there. This plan promised better economic opportunities for the emigrants and a healthy infusion of population for the struggling colony.

Peters returned to Nova Scotia in the company of Lieutenant John Clarkson, on leave from the Royal Navy and brother of the prominent abolitionist William Clarkson. Between them, Peters and Clarkson recruited about 1,200 emigrants—roughly half of the entire black population of the Maritime Provinces—and in 1792 they set sail for Sierra Leone in thirteen ships. Despite severe storms on the Atlantic, all the ships arrived and so did most of the passengers. As governor of the enlarged colony in its first year, Clarkson was generally fair and efficient, but his tendency to be paternalistic made some of the ex-slave inhabitants crave more freedom and self-government than he seemed willing to grant.

Before long, he had an angry confrontation with Thomas Peters, who may have felt, with some justification, that he was the Moses-like leader who had initiated and inspired this exodus and resettlement and should therefore have been accorded greater recognition and responsibility. After Clarkson returned to England in 1793, his successors proved much more authoritarian and contemptuous of the settlers' desire for self-government than he had been. The result was dissatisfaction, unrest, and eventually open rebellion by some of the settlers against the rule of the Sierra Leone Company. By the late 1790s the colony had lost most of its original humanitarian character and had become, for the most part, a commercial venture directed from London rather than the example of black self-government that Granville Sharp originally had hoped for.

The three books under review all deal with these events, with differences in emphasis and in the amount of detail devoted to particular episodes. The backgrounds of the authors and their more general concerns as historians influence how they approach the common subject of blacks and the American Revolution. Cassandra Pybus is an Australian based at the University of Tasmania, who specializes in the history of African Americans and the African Diaspora. Her *Epic Journeys of Freedom* concentrates on the personal histories of the runaway slaves and provides an unexpected Australian twist to the story. Simon Schama is an Englishman now teaching at Columbia whose historical interests have been remarkably varied, ranging from the history of Dutch art to the French Revolution. He has not previously written about African Americans. His *Rough Crossings* is preoccupied with the interaction between some of the leading figures of Britain's humanitarian movement and the runaways as a group. Gary Nash, a professor emeritus at UCLA, is a leading historian of the United States, specializing in the revolutionary period. His primary concern in *The Forgotten Fifth* is with the experience of African Americans in the Revolution itself and immediately afterward; he is less interested than the others in what subsequently happened to those who left with the British in 1782.

Epic Journeys of Freedom is a well-written and engaging narrative history that also happens to be the fruit of prodigious research. To trace the lives of individual runaway slaves (thirty of whom receive particular attention both in the text and in a biographical appendix), Pybus explored archives and manuscript collections in four countries on three continents—the United Kingdom, the United States, Canada, and Australia. From them she was able to piece together enough biographical information to recover the essential (and often inspiring) life stories of people who would otherwise not be part of the historical record.

We learn, for example, that David George was born a slave in Virginia, and ran away as a boy only to be enslaved by Indians. He was given by them to an Indian agent, fled to the British in 1779, was evacuated from Charleston to Nova Scotia in 1782, and joined the exodus to Sierra Leone in 1791. Within the community of migrating ex-slaves he was a religious leader. While still a slave he helped found the first black Baptist church in the United States. Later he established and ministered to Baptist churches in Nova Scotia and Sierra Leone. Religious activity in general is a central theme of Pybus's account. More than anything else, it was Methodist and Baptist Christianity of an intensely emotional and evangelical kind that provided a sense of community and solidarity to people who were struggling for self-determination under very trying circumstances.

Of special interest among her cast of characters is one who became a fervent Methodist and also bore a distinguished surname. Harry Washington was born in Africa, became the slave of George Washington in 1763, escaped to the British in 1776, and served during the war as a corporal in one of the black units established by the British military authorities. After the war, he was evacuated first to Nova Scotia and then to Sierra Leone. In 1800, he was a leader in an abortive struggle for "settler independence from the Sierra Leone Company." (Had he succeeded he might have become the George Washington of the republic of Sierra Leone.) As punishment for his seditious activity he was exiled from the colony proper and became the leader of an exile community.

Pybus establishes her Australian connection by uncovering the fact that eleven of the convicts transported in 1787 to the new penal colony at

Botany Bay in New South Wales were former slaves who had previously been evacuated from the United States. Since they were only about 2 percent of the initial convict population of the colony, they had little chance to develop a collective identity. But Pybus follows the careers of some of them, especially the rebellious convict known only as Caesar. On several occasions, Caesar deserted the colony and tried to survive on his own in the wilderness or among the aborigines. Eventually he was shot and killed by a bounty hunter. Other black convicts fared better. John Randall served out his sentence, acquired a white wife and a land grant, and ended up as a successful farmer who also served as a constable.

Still, the eventual success of Randall and some other convicts should not be allowed to obscure the misery and deprivation of all the convicts, black and white, in the early years of the settlement. British humanitarians in the 1780s could have sympathy with slaves or even with blacks in general, but they ignored the atrocious treatment of those unfortunate enough to be convicted of a crime—often for what today would be considered a minor offense, such as petty larceny. The long voyage to Australia was more deadly than what Africans typically experienced in the Middle Passage. Pybus notes that "unlike slave cargo, the convicts had no value, so no attention was given to keeping them fit and alive." In the colony itself food was often in short supply, especially during the early years, and mass starvation was narrowly averted.

Pybus does not pay much attention to the question of how Americans could fight for freedom and also own slaves. But one of the most prominent spokesmen for the revolutionary cause, Thomas Jefferson, attracts her attention in a way that will not enhance his reputation. Statements Jefferson made after the war about the slaves from his own plantations who ran off to the British were misleading and self-serving. When, for example, he reneged on some debts owed to British creditors in 1786–1787, he excused his incapacity to pay by claiming that the redcoats had taken away thirty of his slaves, "even though he had lost eighteen at most."

In *Rough Crossings* Simon Schama covers much of the same ground as Pybus (except for the Australian episode) but more from the vantage point of British humanitarians, especially Granville Sharp and John Clarkson, than from that of the runaway slaves themselves. He describes the collective experiences of the slaves clearly and sympathetically, but particular individuals among them do not come alive to the same extent as they do in *Epic Journeys of Freedom*.

Schama's book is divided into two parts—the first called "Greeny" (the nickname of Granville Sharp) and the second "John" (for John Clarkson). By centering on these leaders, who figure scarcely at all in Pybus's account, Schama is writing as much about members of a white elite as he is about ordinary African Americans. He mentions most of the runaway slaves who are included in Pybus's biographical appendix, but only Thomas Peters figures prominently in his account, mainly because of his collaboration with Clarkson in organizing the migration from Nova Scotia to Sierra Leone. As always, Schama writes with verve and mastery, with many fascinating details, although sometimes the details become digressions that impede the flow of the narrative.

When Schama's book was first published last year in the United Kingdom, some reviewers thought it would make Americans very angry because of the way it debunks their national mythology of a virtuous and glorious revolution. At the beginning of the book, Schama reports that an ex-slave in Nova Scotia renamed himself "British Freedom," thus expressing "a belief that it was the British monarchy rather than the new American republic that was more likely to deliver Africans from slavery." Many African Americans during the Revolution and for some time afterward regarded the British as the enemy of their enemy and therefore as their friend. "Whether the British deserved this reputation as the most racially broadminded among nations and empires is, to say the least, debatable," Schama writes. But his only example of Britain's indifference to enslaved blacks in North America is the extent of its sympathy for the Confederacy during the American Civil War. This later history, of course, should not negate a conclusion that at the time of the Revolution, almost a century earlier, the British were indeed more "racially broadminded" than white Americans. And this seems to be the judgment that Schama is implicitly making.

Concerning the relation of slavery to the motives of the American revolutionaries, Schama asserts at one point that "Patriot mobilization in the South" was driven by fears that the kind of slave rebellions that were occurring elsewhere in the Americas (as in Surinam and Jamaica) "might spread north." This anxiety, rather than "any solidarity with captive people elsewhere in the hemisphere," was the dominant motivation. Once the Revolution had commenced, "the most feverish nightmare involved the British actually fomenting black rebellion as a way of intimidating the Patriots."

Schama reinforces this argument by claiming the slaveholders were often skeptical of the Patriot cause until they learned that "British troops would liberate their blacks, then give them weapons, and their blessing to use them on their masters." This belief led them to enlist in a Revolution that they could define (in anticipation of the Confederate cause in the Civil War) as a defense of slavery. Yet something more than this must have been involved, since the substantial minority of slaveholders who remained Loyalists were assured by the British that they could keep or recapture their slaves, and to a considerable extent they were able to do so. Many of the slaves owned by Loyalists ended up after the war on the sugar plantations of Jamaica or Barbados. By some calculations slave owners incurred a greater risk of losing their human property by joining the Revolution than by staying out of it.

One could make a comparison of British and American slavery and attitudes toward the institution on the eve of the Revolution that would put the Americans in a somewhat better light. It is far from clear that there were more abolitionists in Britain in 1775 than in the American colonies. At that time there were only Granville Sharp and a few Quakers.[2] The future United States also had antislavery Quakers (most notably Anthony Benezet, who was an inspiration for Sharp and other pioneers of the British movement) and James Otis, the Boston revolutionary. Although slavery is always cruel and degrading, it is at least arguable that the kind of slavery practiced by the British in the Caribbean was normally harsher than what existed in the North American colonies. No American virtue can be claimed from such a comparison, for the differences were clearly the result of different crops, climate, and other factors.

But it is also true that the American slave population had attained a natural rate of increase by the time of the Revolution, which helps to explain why some colonies, including Virginia, called for the suspension of slave importations and felt aggrieved when the British government refused to acquiesce. The natural increase suggests that conditions on the American plantations were healthier than those that existed in the West Indies, where slaves had to be imported in large numbers to replace those who had been worked to death before they could reproduce.

If slavery was not under attack by Americans during the Revolution itself, this was perhaps because raising the issue would have impeded cooperation in the struggle for independence between the colonies heavily dependent on slavery and those that were not.[3] But after the war there was a period of about twenty years when there was substantial criticism of slavery, and efforts were made, even in parts of the South, to put it, as Abraham Lincoln said, "in the course of ultimate extinction." Although the northern states had begun gradually to abolish slavery, even in Virginia the hold of the institution seemed to be weakening.

Schama makes much of the British having freed ten thousand Virginia slaves during the Revolution, a fact that deserves emphasis. But he does not also say that, as the result of new legislation facilitating manumission, twice that many slaves were voluntarily freed by their masters between 1782 and 1800. As everyone knows, George Washington freed his slaves in his last will and testament. Robert Carter, who is mentioned by Schama as a planter who made desperate efforts to keep his slaves from absconding to the British, freed all 509 of them by a deed of gift in 1791.[4] Another notable emancipator was Richard Randolph, who not only provided in his will of 1796 for the emancipation of all ninety of his slaves, but also provided them with four hundred acres of land on which to live.

To gain insight into how close the United States came to abolishing slavery in the period immediately after the Revolution and why the effort did not succeed, we can turn to Gary B. Nash's *The Forgotten Fifth: African Americans in the Age of Revolution*. The book is based on three lectures given at Harvard in 2004. The first describes the large-scale movement of blacks to the British side during the war, and does so more concisely than Pybus and Schama, but with comparable force and effectiveness. Nash describes the black flight as "the greatest slave rebellion in North American history—one almost too shocking for the American public to contemplate even now."

Whereas Schama makes the British the instigators of this rebellion, Nash suggests that slaves themselves took the initiative; some of them had already gotten in touch with the British and offered to fight the rebels in return for their freedom when Lord Dunmore's proclamation of November 1775 made it an official policy. More than the other writers, Nash pays attention to blacks who did not leave with the British. He describes the emergence immediately after the war of new black leaders and organizations committed to making the ideals of the Revolution—"the right to life, liberty, and the pursuit of happiness"—apply to them as well as whites. In the long run, the ideology of the Revolution would prove to be a crucial asset for African Americans in their struggle for equality.

Nash's second lecture raises the fascinating question, "Could slavery have been abolished?" Historians have generally assumed that the postwar flurry of antislavery sentiment and action was superficial and doomed to failure. Nash boldly suggests otherwise, arguing that the movement came very close to success and failed only because of a lack of astute and effective leadership on the part of those who were in a position to make a difference, namely the Founding Fathers. Most of them regarded slavery as an undesirable and troublesome institution and often seemed on the verge of doing something about it, but they were never quite able to take decisive action. Nash's argument is original and suggestive, but to my mind not entirely persuasive. It can also be argued that the main obstacle to abolishing slavery in the 1780s and 1790s was not inept leadership but rather deeply rooted racial prejudice, the unwillingness of whites to contemplate an egalitarian biracial society. Nash attempts to deemphasize racism as a factor by pointing out that the dominant thought of the period held that the source of racial differences was "cultural environmentalism," a doctrine that, unlike the biological racism of the nineteenth century, made blacks the potential equals of whites in capacities and attainments.

Nash is correct about the difference between late eighteenth- and mid-nineteenth-century racial thinking, but does race prejudice really require an overtly racist ideology? No doubt theories of black inferiority enhanced the power of prejudice, but I would contend that a folk racism not only existed but exerted considerable influence even without an elaborate intellectual rationale. Nash himself refers to "the ocean of white prejudice" that would-be emancipators had to take into account. He also cites with approval the contention of Winthrop Jordan, the leading authority on American racial attitudes in the colonial and early national periods, that there was a "nearly universal" belief among whites that freeing the slaves would "inevitably lead to racial intermixture," which would mean "that civilized man had turned beast in the forest."

It is significant that Jefferson's postrevolutionary proposals for gradual emancipation in Virginia were accompanied by a proviso that those emancipated had to be deported or "colonized" to someplace beyond the nation's borders. His assumption and that of many others who sincerely hoped to see the eventual demise of slavery was that whites and freed blacks could never coexist harmoniously in the same society (especially in cases where the latter were present in substantial numbers).

Nash's last lecture, "Race and Citizenship in the Early Republic," carries us into the nineteenth century and describes, among other things, the founding of the American Colonization Society in 1816, the organization that hoped to transport African Americans to Africa and established the colony of Liberia for that purpose in 1819. For some of its early adherents the objective of this enterprise was not simply to get rid of troublesome free blacks but also to open the door to gradual emancipation. Sending away those freed would allegedly alleviate the racial fears aroused in the white population by the prospect of abolishing slavery.

Was the establishment of the Colonization Society a manifestation of the intensifying racism of the nineteenth century, as Nash suggests, or a carryover from postrevolutionary concerns about blacks, slavery, and the future of the republic? The best answer might be that it was both. It may be that Nash somewhat exaggerates the difference between attitudes toward slavery and race between 1780 and 1800 and those that prevailed during the next two decades. There certainly was some deterioration of the situation of free blacks in the North and a declining disposition to do anything about slavery in the southern states. But in my view the decisive break with the postrevolutionary mentality did not occur until the 1830s and 1840s, when southerners began to defend slavery as a "positive good" rather than a "necessary evil," and a fully developed version of scientific racism became widely accepted and influential in both the North and the South.

CHAPTER 10

Black Hearts and Monsters of the Mind: Race and Identity in Antebellum America

*This chapter on racial ideology and its dissenters chiefly discusses three new approaches—*A Hideous Monster of the Mind: American Race Theory in the Early Republic *by Bruce Dain (Cambridge, MA: Harvard University Press, 2002),* Black Identity and Black Protest in the Antebellum North *by Patrick Rael (Chapel Hill: University of North Carolina Press, 2002), and* The Black Hearts of Men: Radical Abolitionism and the Transformation of Race *by John Stauffer (Cambridge, MA: Harvard University Press, 2002).*

* * *

Before these books appeared in 2002, the intellectual and cultural history of race in postrevolutionary and antebellum America was, generally speaking, a segregated enterprise. The attitudes of those designated as white toward people defined as racially "other," especially blacks, were explored over a period of more than four decades by several historians, including William Stanton, Winthrop Jordan, Reginald Horsman, Alexander Saxton, David Roediger, and myself. The black intellectual and cultural experience has been well covered in the work of Benjamin Quarles, Sterling Stuckey, Lawrence Levine, William H. and Jane H. Pease, James E. and Lois Horton, and Mia Bay. In their different ways the three books under review, two of them especially, seek to obliterate the color line in the history of racial thought and attitudes by presenting blacks and whites, or at least some blacks and some whites, as engaged in a common, interactive discourse. They also suggest that intellectual history—studies of the kind of articulate, creative thought normally confined to elites—may be regaining some of the currency that it had before being overshadowed during the last two or three decades by the study of folk cultures and popular mentalities.

Bruce Dain's *A Hideous Monster of the Mind* is a very competent example of intellectual history as the description and analysis of complex ideas. It summarizes and analyzes the various scientific, cultural, and historical theories about race and race difference that were developed and promulgated in Europe and America in the late eighteenth and early to mid-nineteenth centuries. Dain is a close, incisive reader of texts, and he provides fresh insights into the thinking of Buffon, Blumenbach, Herder, and other founders of European ethnology, anthropology, and cultural studies. Then, crossing the Atlantic, he revisits with new eyes and new insights the principal white Americans who articulated views of race—Jefferson, Samuel Stanhope Smith, Samuel G. Morton, and Josiah Nott, among others. But Dain's most remarkable achievement is bringing into this debate those African-American intellectuals who challenged racist arguments and made a strong case for black equality. Especially impressive among these champions of black claims to freedom and respect were Hosea Easton and James McCune Smith. Until very recently these creative black thinkers have been virtually unknown, certainly as compared to such conspicuous figures as Frederick Douglass and David Walker. Dain also discusses the thought of Walker and Douglass, but he seemingly finds their purely intellectual contributions (as opposed to their roles as publicists or activists) less profound or remarkable than those of Easton and Smith.

If Dain has written superb intellectual history of a fairly conventional kind, focusing on the ideas more than the social and psychological context from which they arose, John Stauffer's *The Black Hearts of Men* is concerned with what race meant in the life experiences of four "Radical Abolitionists"—two black and two white. By writing a comparative or composite biography of Gerrit Smith, James McCune Smith, John Brown, and Fredrick Douglass, Stauffer seeks to shed light on race as a protean, constructed identity. Race as theory or formal ideology seems to play a relatively small role in this process, which, as the title of the book suggests, was more a matter of the heart than the head. John Brown and Frederick Douglass are well known as major actors in the antislavery agitation that helped bring on the Civil War. Douglass was the most prominent of black abolitionists, and Brown of course created a sectional crisis by raiding Harpers Ferry in an unsuccessful effort to trigger a slave insurrection. Gerrit Smith was an extremely wealthy upstate New Yorker who threw himself and his resources into various causes, especially antislavery, but he has not previously received the attention he deserves because he was generally at odds with what historians have viewed as the mainstream of the movement. His support for John Brown's raid on Harpers Ferry and the feverish effort he subsequently made to escape the consequences of his involvement has tarnished his reputation among some historians. James McCune Smith, who has already been mentioned and about whom we will have more to say later, was a New York–born but British-educated black physician and writer who had an extended and sometimes close relationship with Gerrit Smith.

The third book under review, Patrick Rael's *Black Identity and Black Protest in the Antebellum North*, is less overtly interracial than the others, concentrating as it does on the leadership and ideology of the northern free black community. But the book's central thesis is that the northern black protest movement in the era of slavery was squarely in the mainstream of American ideological and cultural developments and even contributed to them. Rael is thus at odds with those contemporary historians who, as he sees it, want to read the cultural nationalism and ethnic pluralism of a later time back into the antebellum period. Then, according to Rael, the physical color line did not correspond to a clear differentiation of culture and values. If I read him correctly, it was only the difference of opinion on race itself—the belief of most whites in congenital black inferiority and the belief of blacks in their fundamental equality—that created a serious divergence of ideologies and beliefs. If whites could simply have overcome their color-coded racism, as (according to Stauffer) individuals like John Brown and Gerrit Smith were able to do, they would have found blacks little different from themselves in culture and values.

Besides affirming actual or potential interracialism, the three books exhibit a number of other features that are likely to influence the historiography of race in America. Rael in particular suggests that it was the experience of free African Americans in the North rather than that of slaves in the South that set the pattern for black identity formation in the post–Civil War period. He notes that the southern black community was fractured by status and color differences to a much greater extent than that of the North—most obviously the gulf between slave and free, but also, in the deep South at least, between black and mulatto. It was, he contends, in the northern states that a single and unified black identity was first constructed. In the 1970s and 1980s, most scholarship on antebellum Africans focused on "the slave community" or "slave culture" and the legacy it provided for subsequent black consciousness. Although they make no explicit claims for the priority of the North in the making of blackness, Dain and Stauffer both put northern African Americans at the center of the black discourse on race. (One reason, of course, was that the only blacks who could engage in public discussion were those in the North.)

Another common feature of all the books is the considerable attention they give to a previously unheralded, almost unknown, figure—James McCune Smith, who now emerges as perhaps the most learned and versatile black intellectual before the rise of W. E. B. Du Bois at the turn of the century.[1] As we have seen, he is one of Stauffer's four protagonists, and he also has a prominent place in both of the other books. McCune Smith was born in New York City in 1813, the son of a slave woman who was in the process of being emancipated. We know little about his father, who was apparently a white merchant. Educated in the excellent African Free Schools that produced several of the most prominent black leaders of the time, he worked for a short time as a blacksmith and then resolved to become a physician. After being refused admittance on racial grounds to American medical schools, he traveled to the University of Glasgow, where he received his M.D. in 1837. Returning to New York as the only academically qualified black physician in the United States, he established a successful interracial practice and ran a profitable pharmacy. But he also found time to coedit an African-American newspaper and write a substantial number of essays for black publications.

In his writings, McCune Smith refuted the claims of scientific racists and criticized white abolitionists for their condescending attitudes toward blacks and their refusal to contemplate violence in the struggle against slavery. He was also a pioneer in the development of statistical social science and provided the definitive refutation of the proslavery propaganda that was based on the 1840 census. (It purported to show an extraordinarily high rate of insanity among free black people in the North as compared to the well-adjusted and "contented" slaves of the South.) His most memorable writing was perhaps the series of ten essays that he published in Frederick Douglass's paper from 1852 to 1854 entitled "The Heads of the Colored People Done with a Whitewash Brush." Satirizing the craniologically based racial typology of the "American School of Ethnology," it described and contemplated the heads of a diverse series of black people as a basis for demonstrating their individuality and humanity.

Nevertheless, McCune Smith remains a somewhat elusive figure, difficult to characterize or fully understand. His writings have apparently not been collected and republished, hence they remain for the most part in the original black periodicals; only one published lecture appears in Rael's very extensive bibliography. Unlike Frederick Douglass, he produced no autobiographical writings; and virtually no personal papers, other than the letters he wrote to Gerrit Smith, have come to light. Stauffer confesses that he can provide little information on the more intimate side of McCune Smith's life because of "the lack of records" (p. 224). He is clearly important enough to deserve a full biography, but writing one will be a formidable task.

The most controversial aspect of the books taken together is the extent to which they depart from what has been the dominant paradigm in the history of race and the black experience in the United States. All of them unabashedly focus on elites or exceptional individuals and thereby eschew "history from the bottom up." None of them would easily qualify as the kind of "social history" that deals with entire communities, or even as "cultural history," if that term means, as it often has in the past two decades or so, the exploration of popular mentalities or "folk thought." Of course intellectual history never really went away, and, as I have previously suggested, these books may be signs of its revival.

Since Dain's announced subject is "race theory," he can scarcely be criticized for limiting himself to fairly elaborate and complex bodies of thought. His book can be regarded as a contribution to the history of science, a thriving enterprise that does not appear to have much of a "bottom-up" dimension. His analysis of individual theories and theorists is often quite original and even surprising. He puts Jefferson's racial speculations in the context of an eighteenth-century "natural history" that was already becoming outmoded. He thus calls into question the prevailing assumption that the Sage of Monticello anticipated the scientific racism of the nineteenth century. Early nineteenth-century versions of "polygenesis"—the theory that the races were separately created species—appear from Dain's account to be less coherent and influential than previously thought. The nineteenth century's most significant contribution to thought about race, which applied to opponents of slavery as well as its defenders, was its divorce of nature and morality. Abolitionists like William Lloyd Garrison and Hosea Easton came down on the side of morality, whatever the natural facts might be. Proslavery racial theorists like Samuel G. Morton and Josiah Nott argued for suppressing feelings of empathy or sympathy for individual blacks when it was a matter of assigning the group to which they belonged to its proper position in society. For Morton and Nott, a "fixed hierarchy of races" (Dain, p. 204) was dictated by the objective study of nature and therefore should be recognized in law and enforced by government.

Focusing on elites when writing the history of theories that purport to be scientific is more obviously justifiable than doing the same thing in dealing with a group's struggle against oppression. Patrick Rael's *Black Identity and Protest in the Antebellum North* challenges what he calls "the community studies/culturalist paradigm." His sources are the public utterances of black leaders rather than the expressive popular customs, behavior, and folklore that historians of African-American culture and consciousness have often relied upon. "I concede without hesitation the elite biases of most of my sources," Rael writes. But he proposes that "we reconsider the realm of public speech as a force in its own right rather than as a mere subordinate to the larger realm of cultural nationalism and culturally based identity politics" (p. 289). One of Rael's prime targets is Sterling Stuckey, who has argued eloquently that pre–Civil War black thought manifested a cultural nationalism with African origins.[2] Rael does not deny that a "slave culture" with African roots existed, only that it could find "little support in the public sphere," where "black resistance grew more from leaders' pragmatic responses to their situation than from their assertion of a distinct cultural 'genius' of

African-descended people" (pp. 48–49). The black protest thought of the antebellum era appealed primarily to the bourgeois values of respectability, character, individual responsibility, and self-help. In other words, it was fully compatible with the main currents of social thought and ideology in northern society as a whole. "Respectability," in fact, was a "master value" (p. 201) for those who spoke for the northern black community, just as it was for increasing numbers of white Americans at the time. By strongly embracing this emerging middle-class worldview, blacks actually helped it to triumph and thus, according to Rael, manifested an unexpected kind of historical agency.

Does this mean that blacks lacked a sense of distinctive identity and nationhood, that their only ambition was to be assimilated into white America? Not at all, Rael answers, and it is here that his argument becomes most original and intriguing. The early to mid-nineteenth-century conception of nationalism, he argues, did not require a strong cultural basis. A sense of peoplehood from whatever source, even simply the experience of being mistreated as a group, could engender nationalist aspirations. A sense of cultural uniqueness could contribute to the construction of such a national identity but was not essential to it. To become self-determining and civilized one had to belong to a nation. If blacks could not be part of the American nation, they would presumably have to have one of their own. On the question of whether such "nationalism" literally required the creation of an independent black state, and if so, where it should be, Rael gives the impression of uncertainty, ambiguity, or the suspension of judgment. Dain in *Monsters of the Mind* records a debate on this issue among African-American intellectuals in the 1820s, which led them to the general conclusion that Haiti could not serve this purpose. When Liberia became independent in 1847, another alternative was provided, but it was one unacceptable to most black leaders because of its association with white-sponsored colonization of freed blacks. The later pan-Africanist ideal of a continent liberated from colonialism was not yet readily conceivable.

Rael, however, is not really concerned with the political and geographical implications of antebellum black nationalism. The group-centered ideology of the protest leaders he cites was, more than anything else, a defensive response to racism. Yet he also takes note of the rise of ethnically and racially based conceptions of nationalism in the mid-nineteenth century and the extent to which black discourse was affected by this creeping essentialism. By the end of the antebellum period, the debate between nationalists (such as Martin Delany) who had come to favor black emigration from the United States to West Africa and those who dreamed of blacks being incorporated into America was really, he concludes, a clash of two emerging examples of "romantic ethnic nationalism" (p. 238), one black and the other simply American.

Rael makes a notable effort to avoid reading modern concepts of race and nation back into the antebellum period. To do so, he believes, would be ahistorical and anachronistic. He suggests that there was no clear distinction at the time between the two terms: they were used interchangeably (as in references to an English or French "race" or to a German "nation" before one really existed). The main difference—and this was why black leaders generally preferred thinking of themselves as a nation—was that "different races were characterized by inequality, but nations seemed to share a fundamental equality" (p. 254). Rael's general approach is compatible with the postmodernist presumption that categories like nation, race, and ethnicity are "socially and culturally constructed," but I believe that one can profitably use transhistorical, "ideal-type" constructions of such categories for purposes of comparative analysis. I agree with Rael that nationalism does not have to be based on what we could call "race" or "ethnicity." In abstract principle, if not unfortunately in practice, the "civic nationalisms" that emerged from the American and French revolutions did not require particular cultural or genetic antecedents. According to the Declaration of Independence and of the Rights of Man, one simply had to be a human being to belong to the nation. It is not until the nineteenth century that nationalism could be thought of as rooted in race or ethnicity. What Rael calls "romantic ethnic nationalism" developed first in Germany and then spread to much of the rest of Europe. It came to Britain and the United States principally in the form of "Anglo-Saxonism."

But to an extent that Rael fails to appreciate, ethnicity (even in the historically very specific form of nineteenth-century romantic nationalism) was a problematic basis for identity in a nation committed simultaneously to equal rights and the maintenance of slavery in a substantial proportion of its territory. Hence "racism"—the belief that innate characteristics relevant to social performance and citizenship are attributable to ancestry, as observable in such physical characteristics as skin color—became a more important source of American nationalism than ethnicity, which expresses itself primarily in what we would call culture—language, religion, moral values, art, traditional customs, etc.[3] On the basis of this kind of approach, one could more readily understand Rael's statement that black thinkers "evinced troubling concessions to the racialism of their day" (p. 284). The terrain on which they had to operate made this almost inevitable. But "racialism," as K. Anthony Appiah has pointed out, is not necessarily "racism,"[4] because it may affirm innate or essential identities without creating a hierarchy by placing one race above another. In my view, a more extensive use of such categories might have sharpened Rael's analysis and placed his findings in a broader context.

On empirical grounds the book can be criticized for exaggerating the hegemony that the middle-class black elite was able to exercise over the black working class. Certainly Leslie Harris's recent book on African Americans in New York before 1863 suggests that there was much more interclass tension and working-class resistance to elite domination than is apparent in Rael's account. The 1837 speech of one Peter Paul Simons, cited by Rael as an isolated and anomalous example of public protest against the elite's cult of respectability and its nonviolent moderation, is seen by Harris as an indication that "many blacks, even some black reformers, were disillusioned with moral and intellectual improvement as the central method to achieve black freedom and equality."[5] Furthermore, the two major black protest leaders that John Stauffer features in *The Black Hearts of Men* moved decisively away from the ideology of liberation through the "moral and intellectual improvement" that Rael finds at the core of black protest.

John Stauffer's book is in many ways a very impressive achievement. Comparative biography is a difficult genre, and it has rarely been done so sure-handedly. His method is to take some common events, experiences, or concerns and then see how each of his four subjects reacted to them and then to each other's reactions. These include the Panic of 1837, the millennialist expectations of the early 1840s, the rise of women's rights as an issue, and the increasingly intense and sometimes violent sectionalism of the late 1850s. (Of course, a degree of unevenness is inevitable here because the four men reacted with varying degrees of intensity to the common stimuli or differed in the extent to which their responses were recorded or have survived.)

The main focus of the book is on the construction of identity in a racially divided society. Its point of departure is the recent literature on the construction of "whiteness." An earlier generation of historians focused on the invention of blackness and took whiteness for granted. But in the work of historians like David Roediger and Matthew Frye Jacobson, it has become apparent that affirming whiteness was essential to European immigrant incorporation into American society and to the containment of class conflict in an industrializing society.[6] Stauffer derives from such literature a sense that the central problem to be overcome if American society is to move beyond race is not merely improving the situation of blacks; it also entails the abolition of whiteness as a source of identity and privilege. To the extent that people think of themselves as white in some significant sense, they are complicit in a racial order that advantages them at the expense of blacks. Stauffer contends that his two "white" protagonists—Gerrit Smith and John Brown—had to overcome their constructed racial identities and make themselves existentially "black" in order to escape the condescending racial attitudes of most other abolitionists and gain the full trust of African Americans.

Paradoxically, however, the two blacks in his quartet end up prescribing race mixture and "amalgamation" as the salvation of America. Frederick Douglass and James McCune Smith, as is also apparent in Dain's discussion of their thought, were not racialists or even black nationalists. What they represent for Stauffer is an anticipation of the modern (or postmodern) attitude that race has no objective reality or fixed meaning and is constantly in the process of being socially and culturally reconstructed. (He describes all four of his subjects as demonstrating "the protean nature of identity politics" [p. 152].) Were Douglass and McCune Smith therefore incipient champions of the "mixed race" identities that many of my students at Stanford are now espousing? Perhaps, but mixed race is still race, and Douglass and McCune Smith, who were conscious of their own mixed ancestry, seemed to entertain the hope that race could be overcome entirely and that America could become genuinely color-blind.

The central character in *The Black Hearts of Men* is Gerrit Smith, who served to a considerable extent as the link between the others. Also, unlike the others, he left behind voluminous personal records. One suspects that at some point Stauffer might have been tempted to write a biography of Smith, and something close to a full biography, at least up to 1860, is embedded in this volume. Smith was a complex and somewhat unstable figure, who, it seems, could hold conflicting beliefs simultaneously—as when he supported both colonization and abolitionism in the early 1830s after most abolitionists had repudiated the scheme of gradually ending slavery by exporting those emancipated to Africa. His endorsement of William Miller's prophecy that Christ would return in 1843 might seem to consign him to a lunatic fringe, but Stauffer assures us that Millerite millennialism was compatible with humanitarian reform. Smith also supported temperance and women's rights as well as abolitionism. In 1846, in one of the most notable acts of philanthropy in American history, he gave 120,000 acres of land in the Adirondacks to three thousand black settlers, thereby establishing the North Elba colony where John Brown later settled. Nevertheless, Smith's mental and ideological collapse after John Brown's raid, as well as some earlier vagaries, reveals a degree of mental and moral instability that make him less than an entirely admirable figure.

James McCune Smith receives the fullest treatment to date in *The Black Hearts of Men*, but, as suggested earlier, many aspects of his life remain obscure. Stauffer contributes relatively little to our factual knowledge of Frederick Douglass and John Brown, both of whom have received extensive biographical treatment in recent years. He is more sympathetic to Brown and his espousal of violence (some might even call it terrorism) than most previous historians. He notes that the attack on Harpers Ferry inspired many slaves in the region to set their masters' property on fire, which suggests that Brown's belief that the slaves could be inspired to rebel was not entirely delusional. He also demonstrates that the common view that Frederick Douglass repudiated Brown's tactics is misleading. Although he declined to participate personally in the raid for prudential reasons, Douglass justified it in retrospect and professed nothing but admiration for Brown himself. More tolerant of Brown than most historians have been, Stauffer seems somewhat less than fair to Frederick Douglass, or at least to Douglass's career after 1863. He represents him as betraying the cause of Radical Abolitionism when he supported Lincoln and the Republican Party after the Emancipation Proclamation. But given the options available, much of his thought and behavior can be justified on pragmatic grounds. As he put it after Reconstruction when some black leaders proposed switching their support to the blatantly racist Democrats, "the Republican Party is the ship and all else is the sea."

The principal contribution of the book to the historiography on the coming of the Civil War is its concept of "Radical Abolitionism," the ideology shared by Smith, Douglass, McCune Smith, and Brown. Up to now, historians of abolitionism have focused on the nonviolent, generally apolitical perfectionism of William Lloyd Garrison, Theodore Weld, and Wendell Phillips. (Phillips, however, might be a candidate for the pantheon of Radical Abolitionism, because he did endorse Brown's raid after the fact.) The political abolitionism that first appeared in the Liberty Party of 1840 has often been viewed as a less radical challenge to slavery and racism than that associated with the Garrisonian advocates of "universal reform." Also, political antislavery is generally seen as growing more conservative as it became devoted to the exclusion of slavery from the territories rather than abolition, first in the Free Soil Party of 1848 and then in the Republican Party of 1855–1856. What Stauffer describes is a form of political abolitionism that becomes revolutionary in its willingness to use violence to overthrow slavery and at the same time embraces an antislavery interpretation of the same Constitution that Garrison burned publicly as "a covenant with hell." An important source for revolutionary political abolitionism was the theory of John Quincy Adams, first promulgated in 1836, that the federal government had the power to abolish slavery if the southern states became "the theatre of war, civil, servile, or foreign" (p. 26). For Radical Abolitionists, according to Stauffer, a massive slave insurrection should be encouraged precisely because it could lead to such federal intervention. (But as the response to John Brown's raid clearly indicated, a more likely reaction would have been the use of federal troops to put down the uprising. It would take southern secession and a civil war to make Adams's theory operative.)

I wonder, however, how much of a role such strategic constitutional thinking really played in the culmination of the Radical Abolitionist project. Stauffer also makes it clear that the principal sanction for Brown's raid was divine revelation, both as experienced by a righteous person and as manifested in the Bible. Brown himself certainly believed that he was acting under direct divine inspiration when he took up arms against slavery. If so, did it really matter very much what the Constitution said or did not say? It was what God said directly to John Brown that mattered. In contemplating Brown's frame of mind, one's historical relativism is put to a severe test. It is possible to accept the justice of Brown's cause and yet be repelled by his apocalyptic self-righteousness. Stauffer expresses some reservations about the ultimate utility of this sanctification of violence, but his main purpose is to portray Brown as an exemplar of the abolition of whiteness rather than as an apostle of holy war. But, troubling as it may be, Brown stood both for the overthrow of slavery and racism and for virtually unrestrained violence in the name of religious conviction.

Whatever judgments one might wish to make about the raid, Stauffer's depiction of Brown's mindset is persuasive. It would also apply reasonably well to Gerrit Smith, at least at those moments in his life when he felt divinely inspired. But I am uncertain how well it describes the mentalities of Douglass and McCune Smith. From the evidence presented it would appear that their religiosity was less intense and was leavened by a strong dose of pragmatic rationality. (At several points in his life Douglass expressed skepticism about enthusiastic religion and biblical literalism; he eventually became a Unitarian.) Supporting the justice of slave rebellion was a way of extending to blacks the same right of revolution against tyranny that white Americans endorsed as central to their national heritage. After the fact, John Brown could serve, and can still serve, as the exemplar or symbol of this principle. But when Douglass chose not to join Brown's raid because he thought it had no chance of success, he was in effect saying that being abstractly right is not everything. One must also calculate whether the means are appropriate to the ends being sought. If he had been asked to participate in Brown's endeavor, I imagine that McCune Smith would have responded in much the same way.

It is nevertheless striking and somewhat troubling that it took a prophetic mentality and sense of being under the direct guidance of God to induce a few antebellum white Americans to escape from their privileged racial identities and empathize fully and effectively with blacks. No stronger evidence could be provided of the depths of American racism. John Stauffer's brilliantly provocative book has looked into the experiences and ideas of four individuals who were able to move across the boundary between white and black. In the process it has provided valuable new insights into the history of racism and antiracism in the United States.

CHAPTER 11

Still Separate and Unequal: The Strange Career of Affirmative Action

This chapter is devoted largely to an evaluation of Ira Katznelson's book, When Affirmative Action Was White: An Untold History of Racial Inequality in Twentieth-Century America *(New York: W. W. Norton, 2005).*

* * *

I.

Affirmative action, the policy of giving preferences for jobs, university admissions, or government contracts to members of designated racial and ethnic groups, has never been popular, and it could soon be abolished. In 2003, the Supreme Court struck down an undergraduate admissions policy at the University of Michigan that provided extra points for minority applicants. At the same time, the Court approved by a single vote the more subjective practice of taking race into account as one factor among several in admissions to the university's law school. The change of one vote would have meant the end of overt affirmative action in higher education. The trend against affirmative action in the states is even more pronounced. In California and Washington, constitutional referendums have banned the government from using affirmative action in any of its activities. Other states have ended or severely limited affirmative action by executive authority.

More remarkable than the current opposition to affirmative action is the fact that it ever came into existence in the first place. On its face, the policy seems to violate one of the most basic American values—the idea that individual merit as manifested in a fair and open competition should be rewarded. A practice that seems to go against the individualistic and meritocratic American ethos is clearly vulnerable to an attack that is likely to be persuasive to many of those who do not stand to benefit from it. Moreover, affirmative action seems contrary to the emphasis on color-blindness that was characteristic of the civil rights movement of the fifties and early sixties, and was expressed in the language of its greatest achievement—the Civil Rights Act of 1964.

Two very different arguments have been advanced for affirmative action. One claims that it is just compensation for historical injustices and disadvantages. In the case of claims by African Americans the emphasis is usually on the wounds inflicted by centuries of slavery, segregation, and discrimination. President Lyndon Johnson made one of the most elegant and influential statements of this position in his Howard University speech of 1965, which is quoted by Ira Katznelson in *When Affirmative Action Was White:*

> You do not take a person who, for years, has been hobbled by chains and liberate him, bring him up to the starting line of a race and then say, "You are free to compete with all the others," and still justly believe that you have been completely fair.... It is not enough just to open the gates of opportunity. All our citizens must have the ability to walk through those gates.... We seek not just legal equity but human ability, not just equality as a right and a theory but equality as a fact and equality as a result.

The other argument, which is reflected in recent Supreme Court decisions and is currently much heard, is based on the assumption that racial and ethnic diversity among "elites"—relatively well-off people who have some degree of responsibility for others, whether private or public—is beneficial to society and its institutions. Prominent among those who defend affirmative action, for example, are spokesmen for the American military who lent conspicuous support to the University of Michigan's side in the 2003 Supreme Court case. Since the enlisted ranks are disproportionately black and Latino, discipline and morale are presumably inspired by having the same groups represented among the officers, including those of the highest rank. Corporations that deal with a multicultural and multiracial clientele, sometimes on an international scale, find obvious advantages in being represented by people who reflect the racial and ethnic diversity of those with whom they are doing business. Many large corporations practice affirmative action voluntarily even when there is no significant pressure from the government.

In higher education the diversity argument takes a slightly different form. Racially and ethnically heterogeneous student bodies are said to create an appropriate educational environment for students who will encounter many different kinds of people when they go out into the world. Faculties, moreover, must be diverse if they are to provide inspiration and suitable "role models" for minority students.

Clearly affirmative action has had its greatest success in producing more diverse elites, particularly in the much-heralded emergence of a substantial

African-American middle class, something that never existed before. But as the sociologist William Julius Wilson has argued for many years, this process of *embourgeoisement* has been accompanied by the equally substantial growth of "the truly disadvantaged," the economically marginal black inhabitants of the urban ghettos. Since the advent of affirmative action in the 1960s, the overall differences between blacks and whites have changed very little with respect to average incomes, property holdings, and levels of educational attainment. What is new is the gulf that has opened in the black community between the middle class and the lower or "under" class.[1]

Affirmative action originated as a pragmatic response by those in the federal government responsible for enforcing the fair employment provisions of the Civil Rights Act of 1964.[2] The Equal Employment Opportunity Commission (EEOC) set up under the act lacked the staff to investigate most individual claims of discrimination in employment. It also lacked legal authority to act effectively on behalf of the complainants. As a result, the only way that the EEOC could begin to do its job was to request government contractors to provide statistics on the racial composition of their labor force. If blacks (and by the 1970s other minorities as well) were underrepresented among the workers relative to their percentage of the local population, the EEOC set numerical goals for minority recruitment sufficient to correct this disproportion. Employers were then required to make "good faith efforts" to meet "quotas" for black workers. If they didn't hire more blacks, they risked losing contracts. The professed aim was equal opportunity, not racial favoritism, but the paradox that bedeviled the program from the start was that it appeared to require preferential means to reach egalitarian ends.

After its fitful beginnings during the Johnson administration, affirmative action took a dramatic turn under Richard Nixon, whose administration put into effect a controversial plan to integrate Philadelphia's construction trades. Historians have concluded that the Philadelphia Plan of 1969–1970, which set firm racial quotas for hiring for one industry in one city, was a political ploy. It was designed by the Nixon Republicans to cause friction between two of the principal constituencies of the Democratic Party—organized labor, which opposed the plan because of the threat it posed to jobs under its control, and African Americans, who had overwhelmingly supported the Democrats since the New Deal.[3] At the same time, Nixon was trying to appeal to southern whites by doing little to enforce desegregation, especially in the schools.

When rising opposition to the war in Vietnam became the critical issue for his administration in 1970 and 1971, and hard hats like the construction workers of Philadelphia were in the forefront of those opposing the antiwar protesters, the Philadelphia Plan was quietly shelved. From then on, Republicans were, for the most part, strongly opposed to affirmative action and benefited from the backlash against it, attacking the Democrats as the "party of quotas" because of their continued support for the policy.

Affirmative action was declared constitutional in 1971 when the Supreme Court ruled in *Griggs* v. *Duke Power Co.* that discrimination in employment could be subject to affirmative action even if it were not intentional or motivated by prejudice. The Court found that the standardized aptitude tests given by the company to employees prevented blacks from moving to higher-paying departments. Such requirements could be "fair in form," the Court said, but they could still be described as "discriminatory in operation" if they had an "adverse impact" on blacks. Hence the EEOC was legally entitled to set goals for increasing minority employment and to require periodic reports on the progress being made on fulfilling such goals by any of the 300,000 firms doing business with the federal government.

In 1978 in *Regents of the University of California v. Bakke,* the Court held by five votes to four that strict numerical quotas, such as those that the medical school of the University of California at Davis had set for minority applicants, could not be permitted. But the concurring opinion of Justice Lewis Powell, who cast the deciding vote, held that race could still be used as a positive factor in considering the qualifications of candidates for admission so long as two criteria were satisfied. If a university were to give preference to blacks, it had to establish a direct connection between the claim to such special consideration and a specific historical injustice such as the exclusion of blacks from professional schools over the years (generalized claims of past racism would not suffice). Racial preferences must also serve a "compelling public interest" or purpose. The constitutional foundation for affirmative action laid by Justice Powell has endured for the past twenty-nine years. The Michigan decisions of 2003 forbid numerical point systems as well as statistical quotas, but it continues to be constitutional to use race among other factors to determine qualifications for university admissions and employment.

II.

Ira Katznelson has made a major contribution to the affirmative action debate in his book *When Affirmative Action Was White.* He accepts Justice Powell's criteria and uses them to justify a much more ambitious governmental attack on racial inequality than currently exists. He presents a new version of the argument that affirmative action is justified as compensation for historical wrongs against black people. Instead of going back to slavery, he maintains that people who are still alive (or have living children or grandchildren) and have been the victims of specific historical injustices can provide strong claims for restitution from the U.S. government, the direct source of these injustices.

Most of Katznelson's book is devoted to showing how the economic and social legislation of the 1930s and 1940s favored whites over blacks. Katznelson is not the first historian to argue that the New Deal and Fair Deal widened the gulf between whites and blacks in the United States, but he is the first to consider such discrimination as the principal justification for an ambitious affirmative action program that would include reparations for blacks.[4]

The undeniable fact is that, by comparison with whites, blacks became relatively worse off during this period. But this relative failure has been obscured by the equally undeniable fact that the material circumstances of African Americans improved and were, on average, significantly better in 1950 than they had been in 1930. What Katznelson shows is that the Democratic social and economic policies of the thirties and forties were rigged so that whites got much more than a fair share of the benefits.

The primary cause of this inequity, Katznelson contends, was the influence of southern segregationists within the Democratic Party. In the 1930s, when the first New Deal policies were being enacted, white southern congressmen provided necessary votes for liberal measures that strengthened the labor movement, set minimum wages, and gave relief or temporary work to the unemployed. But they did so only on the condition that the southern racial order remain insulated against federal actions that might threaten it. The cooperation of New Dealers and segregationists broke down in the 1940s, when a strengthened labor movement began to look south and consider organizing blacks as well as whites. At that point, a new coalition of northern Republicans and southern Democrats succeeded in stopping the advance of organized labor, especially by passing the Taft-Hartley Act of 1947, which put heavy restrictions on union organizing.

In 1948 the Democratic Party, with labor support, took up the cause of civil rights for the first time, and Harry Truman was elected president despite the defection of much of the South to the States' Rights or "Dixiecrat" Party. But this change of heart by the Democrats was, Katznelson points out, less than a complete conversion to the cause of racial justice. He reminds us that the Democrats of the 1950s, trying to keep the South's electoral votes, backtracked on civil rights and made renewed overtures to southern white supremacists. In support of his argument, Katznelson might have noted that Adlai Stevenson's first running mate was a solid segregationist and former Dixiecrat—Senator John J. Sparkman of Alabama.

The New Deal policies that worsened the situation of blacks were not overtly discriminatory. The primary device used by southern white supremacists was to exclude agricultural laborers and domestic servants from coverage under the Social Security Act and National Labor Relations Act of 1935 and the Fair Labor Standards Act of 1938. Since these were the occupations of most southern blacks and of much smaller proportions of southern whites, such exclusions meant that most blacks were being left out of the new welfare state and denied the same chance to escape from poverty that was available to many relatively poor whites. In the South, therefore, the New Deal actually had the effect of strengthening the economic basis of white privilege. It is true that at the height of the Depression, African Americans received some help from the WPA and other emergency measures to provide relief and work, but since southern white supremacists locally administered these programs, racial discrimination continued.

Service in the military during World War II provided blacks with some opportunities for education and for developing valuable skills. But as Katznelson points out, smaller proportions of blacks than whites actually served in the armed forces (more were considered physically or mentally unfit for military service), and the separate but unequal segregation of the armed forces meant that blacks had relatively fewer chances to acquire new skills and advance to higher ranks. Although he mentions it, Katznelson pays little attention to one bright spot in the World War II experience for African Americans—the increased access to industrial jobs, especially in the North, resulting mainly from the tight wartime labor market.

The federal government made a modest contribution to diversifying jobs through the activities of the Fair Employment Practices Committee (FEPC), established in 1941 as the result of protests led by the African-American labor leader E. Philip Randolph. The FEPC, by hearing complaints from blacks and demanding explanations from businesses, allowed more blacks to benefit from the new welfare state and narrowed the difference between the average white and black incomes. Here, for the first time since Reconstruction, the federal government was acting against racial discrimination rather than facilitating it. The federal FEPC did not survive the war but it established an important precedent for later civil rights campaigns.

In the immediate postwar period, Katznelson convincingly argues, the G.I. Bill widened further the economic and social differences between the races. Southern segregation meant that educational opportunities available to whites were withheld from blacks, who were forced to compete for a very limited number of places in all-black institutions. Even in the North many colleges and universities either excluded blacks or admitted only a handful. G.I. loans for buying houses or financing small businesses were very difficult for blacks to obtain because of the discriminatory policies of banks and other lending agencies. Katznelson concludes that most government social policies during the 1930s and 1940s were, in effect, part of a vast affirmative action program for whites that left blacks further behind than they had been at the beginning of the period. He makes a chilling case.

III.

Katznelson is somewhat more effective in describing the problem than in suggesting how to solve it. The general principle behind the kind of affirmative action that he recommends is clear enough: "Under affirmative action," he writes, "[blacks should be] compensated not for being black but only because they were subject to unfair treatment at an earlier moment because they were black."

In an effort to fulfill the requirements that Justice Powell prescribed in the *Bakke* case, Katznelson offers two possible approaches. One would have the government identify all the people, or their immediate descendants, who were injured by exclusions from the various social and economic programs of the 1930s and 1940s. The government would calculate how much they would have gotten had they not been left out, and pay it to them in a lump sum.

Acknowledging that such a program would be "administratively burdensome" (clearly an understatement), he proposes an alternative—an all-out assault on poverty in general, based on the assumption that most of the people who are currently poor have been put at a disadvantage by the unjust policies of the 1930s and 1940s. To some extent, the program he favors would function like the G.I. Bill with "subsidized mortgages, generous grants for education and training, and active job searching and placement." Health insurance and childcare could also be provided.

What is striking and somewhat unexpected is that these proposals do not depend on racial categories. All who suffered from policies of exclusion, whether in education or jobs, including some whites, would be entitled to compensation. It occurs to me that Katznelson's essentially color-blind proposals, especially his second approach, could easily be justified on other grounds than as an antidote to racial inequality. If one simply assumed, as a good social democrat would, that poverty itself is an evil and that wealth should be more equitably distributed, similar policies could be justified. What he may be implying is that white America needs to face up, psychologically as well as materially, to its current as well as its past history of racial oppression, and that basing a color-blind antipoverty program on the need to redress racial discrimination will further this goal. But it remains unclear to me how Katznelson's proposals would differ substantially in practice from those of William Julius Wilson, who distinguishes between affirmative action, which he defines as a way of producing more diversity among elites, and the kind of class-based assault on economic inequality that he believes is needed to raise up what he calls "the truly disadvantaged."[5]

A question that can be raised about the adequacy of Katznelson's historical analysis may also have implications for our understanding of the current prospects for racial equality. Are the South and southern politicians as fully to blame for the increase in white advantages as he contends? Arguably the most important source of the current economic gulf between the races is the vast difference in average net worth or property ownership. Although average black incomes may be around two-thirds those of whites, their average net worth, as Katznelson shows, is only about one-tenth. Much of this difference is explained by the fact that whites own far more homes than blacks and therefore their net worth is higher.

How did this vast inequality come about? It was mainly the result of the greater white access to home mortgages that were insured and subsidized by the federal government. Before the 1930s a home buyer had to put down 50 percent of a house's price and could get only a relatively short-term mortgage, perhaps only ten years. By the 1950s, as a result of a series of federal housing programs, including the G.I. Bill, most Americans could get long-term mortgages—up to thirty years—with a down payment as low as 10 percent. By 1984 seven out of ten whites owned their own homes, worth on average $52,000. But only one in four blacks owned a home, worth, on average, less than $30,000.

Katznelson outlines these facts toward the end of his book, and they illustrate dramatically his general point about the widening economic gulf between the races during the middle decades of the twentieth century. But he makes no effort to explain them as manifestations of southern influence within the Democratic Party. The advantages of whites over blacks that he's describing were more characteristically northern than southern; they manifested themselves in the growth of virtually all-white suburbs outside the major cities and virtually all-black ghettos within them.[6]

This new form of racial segregation was not simply the product of private choices, among them the refusal of white homeowners to sell to blacks, blockbusting and the racial "steering" of home buyers by real estate agents, and the personal prejudice of bankers asked to approve loans for blacks. The urban segregation that has contributed so much to the persistence of black inequality came about in large part because between the 1930s and the 1970s, federal housing agencies refused to approve mortgage loans in neighborhoods that were "redlined," which meant that property values were deemed uncertain because of the presence of blacks.[7]

It is difficult to see the hand of southern segregationists in these policies. It seems that northern politicians were responding more directly to the racist attitudes of northern whites who refused to live close to blacks. They were in effect underwriting the spatial segregation of the metropolitan North. It is not entirely clear how Katznelson's proposal would try to rectify this aspect of affirmative action that benefited whites. Perhaps people could be compensated for the mortgages they were denied; but this would be extraordinarily difficult and would omit those who did not apply for mortgages because they expected they would be turned down.

Also in need of clarification is whether Katznelson's attempt to justify large affirmative action programs for blacks applies to other minorities that are not black. He says virtually nothing about them. Since Mexican Americans in the Southwest during the New Deal era were, like blacks in the South, disproportionately servants and farm laborers, they were similarly excluded from coverage by social security and labor rights legislation. Many of the same factors that make African Americans eligible would thus apply to Chicanos, or at least to those who were in the United States between the 1930s and the 1950s, and to their descendants. But what about more recent Latino immigrants? They cannot claim as forcefully as blacks can that they were historically denied opportunities, such as obtaining mortgages, that were open to non-Hispanic whites.

A case can in fact be made that affirmative action was stretched out of shape and rendered incoherent when it was extended beyond African Americans, Indians, and long-resident Mexican Americans to include recent nonwhite immigrants.[8] Katznelson might agree with this view, but he does not address the question specifically, or even mention Latinos or other nonblack ethnic groups (an omission that will be particularly striking, for example, to readers who live in multicultural California). But Katznelson's book makes as strong a case as I have ever seen made for vigorous action to bring about equal opportunities for African Americans.

PART THREE

Cross-National Comparisons

CHAPTER 12

Race and Racism in Historical Perspective: Comparing the United States, South Africa, and Brazil

For more than fifty years, scholars from various disciplines have been comparing the history of group relations in societies that have traditionally used skin color as a marker of rank or status. None of these societies have attracted more attention than the United States, Brazil, and South Africa. The bulk of this work has compared or contrasted the American case with only one of the others; only rarely have all three been treated at the same time. This scholarship has yielded some significant insights but has also generated much controversy, resulting in periodic revisions and reevaluations.

New historical knowledge and methods have not been the only reasons for the protean nature of the comparisons. Color-coded group relations in all three of these societies have been changing in palpable ways in recent decades, sometimes relatively suddenly, as in the United States in the 1960s and South Africa in the late 1980s and early 1990s. Long-term trajectories, projected on the basis of an understanding of earlier conditions and trends, have often failed to make such changes fully comprehensible and have obliged comparative historians to reevaluate the past in the light of the present. In the case of Brazil, an accumulation of evidence suggesting that there are now significant levels of prejudice and discrimination against people with African ancestry has forced the reconsideration of a past that hitherto had seemed almost idyllic in contrast to the blatant racism that historians had found in South Africa and the southern United States.

Like all history, comparative history is influenced by the location of the historian in time and space. When Americans write about race in Brazil or

South Africa, even if they do not make explicit comparisons with the United States, their work often searches implicitly for analogies or contrasts with the current state of black-white relations in their own country. A similar concern with what is locally relevant is likely to inspire the cross-national work of Brazilians and South Africans. The comparative history of "race" in these societies is clearly not a purely disinterested manifestation of scientific curiosity. To varying degrees, it reflects current interests and ideologies in its search for a "usable past."

To be useful and illuminating, historical comparisons must be based on some fundamental similarities. Juxtaposing radically different entities yields only obvious contrasts rather than the more subtle differences that raise questions of causation that historians and social scientists can fruitfully explore. Comparisons involving the United States, Brazil, and South Africa rest on three pillars. First, all of these societies resulted from the process of European expansion and colonization of the non-Western world that began around 1500. Between the early sixteenth and mid-seventeenth centuries, the Portuguese in Brazil, the English in North America, and the Dutch in South Africa established settler colonies that displaced, marginalized, or subordinated indigenous populations. Second, each of these areas of colonization imported non-European slaves to meet labor needs that the settlers themselves were unable or unwilling to undertake and for which indigenous groups were (at least temporarily) unavailable or deemed unsuitable. Most of these slaves came from Africa, although in the Dutch colony at the Cape of Good Hope, the East Indies and South Asia provided a substantial share of the unfree population. A slaveholding mentality therefore developed in which whiteness or European ancestry meant freedom, and a dark skin, signifying origin outside of Europe, provided a presumption of servitude. (Literal slavery turned out in the long run to be less important as a matrix for race relations in South Africa than in the United States and Brazil, but coercive master-servant relationships between settlers and "natives" provided a similar paradigm.) The third pillar, therefore, is that each society developed at an early stage a color code to determine status. European preeminence and domination were unquestioned assumptions. Some black or brown slaves did become free, but they were relegated by law or custom to an intermediate status between the masters and the slaves—victims of discrimination if not of enforced servitude. Hence an ethnic hierarchy was established by the colonial state and the original white settlers that would persist after these colonial regimes became independent states and after each of them abolished slavery before or after achieving nationhood.

Significant variations—both from place to place and over time in each place—have nevertheless been found in the way racial groups were defined and how their subordination was justified, as well as in the nature and rigidity of the racial order and in the way historical developments or changing conditions have adjusted, weakened, or strengthened the primal hierarchies. If there is one dominant assumption in current comparative studies in race and ethnicity, it is that race is a social and cultural construction and not a fact of nature or a primordial given. But it would be a mistake, in my opinion, to ignore the weight of the past and to assume that race is constantly being reinvented from scratch. The legacy of earlier racial attitudes and hierarchies is difficult, if not impossible, to overcome or fully transcend when racial orders are being reconstructed or reinvented. The burden of history can be lightened, but it would be utopian to think that it can be entirely eliminated.

Serious work on the comparative history of race relations began in the 1940s and 1950s with studies of slavery and its consequences in the United States and Latin America. Frank Tannenbaum's *Slave and Citizen* and Stanley Elkins's *Slavery* contrasted a relatively mild slavery and easy access to freedom in Brazil and other Latin American slave societies with a harsher servitude and more rigid color line in the United States.[1] Their explanation for the difference was based primarily on the implications for slavery and race relations of the cultural antecedents of the European colonists. A relatively tolerant Iberian Catholicism and patrimonialism were pitted against an intensely ethnocentric and exclusionary English Protestantism, which not only set higher standards for conversion and "civilized status," but also unleashed an unfettered capitalism that exposed slaves to more brutal treatment than the allegedly more paternalistic regimes of colonial Latin America.

Revisionists writing in the 1960s and 1970s had little trouble undermining the case for a relatively mild or benign Latin American slavery—the high mortality rates that necessitated a constant influx of new slaves from Africa to Brazil and Cuba could only mean harsh or unhealthy conditions. Some even suggested that in North America, where the slave force more than reproduced itself even before the end of the slave trade, masters normally treated their slaves better, in a physical sense at least, than did slaveholders in Brazil or Cuba—if only because it made good economic sense to do so or because the growing of tobacco and cotton was less lethal to unfree laborers than the production of sugar and coffee.

Critics of the Tannenbaum-Elkins thesis did not deny, however, that emancipation during the slave era was much harder to obtain in the United States and that the form of black-white relations that survived the abolition of slavery was unique in its overt ideological racism and state-sponsored segregationism. The Brazilian state sought to "whiten" its population after the end of slavery by the encouragement of European immigration, but did not extol race purity and seek to promote it by banning intermarriage and regulating interracial social contacts as did many of the North American colonies or states. The two striking peculiarities of race relations in the

United States, scholars continued to affirm, were that there were only two basic racial categories—white and black—and that race was determined on the basis of a strict descent rule, meaning that those with any known African ancestry were considered black. In South America and the Caribbean, there were generally three or more official categories—usually black, mulatto, and white—and those who were of mixed but mostly European descent could, at least in the Iberian societies, hope to be incorporated into the white status group despite acknowledged African ancestry.

To explain the contrast between the rigid race relations in the United States and the more fluid pattern that existed elsewhere in the Americas, the revisionists played down the cultural antecedents of the colonizers and stressed material and demographic factors. According to the anthropologist Marvin Harris in *Patterns of Race in the Americas*, the relative size of the nonslaveholding white population was the critical variable in determining whether mulattos would be routinely emancipated and assigned an intermediate status, as was the case in Brazil by the nineteenth century, or mostly kept in servitude and regarded as outcasts if they somehow gained their freedom, which was apparently what happened in the Old South.[2] Planters needed auxiliaries to provide security against slave resistance and ancillary economic services. If enough lower-class whites were at hand to perform these functions, incentives to grant freedom and intermediate status to mulattos were weak or absent. Harris's thesis was so plausible and persuasive that most subsequent comparativists adopted it to help explain the origins of the seemingly unique black/white dichotomy that emerged in the United States.

Also deemed significant by some revisionists was the sex ratio among whites at the time African slavery became the predominant labor system in a particular colony. Where white women were present in relatively significant numbers, as in colonial Virginia and Maryland, miscegenation was less common, or at least less openly acknowledged, than in colonial Brazil where Portuguese women were in short supply and mixed offspring were more likely to be recognized by their fathers and emancipated. Three-category systems did not mean that race prejudice was nonexistent in Brazil and other parts of Latin America. Whiteness was everywhere privileged over blackness, even if brownness—especially light brownness—was less of a liability than in the United States.

Comparative race relations was also a serious preoccupation of historically oriented sociologists between the 1940s and the 1960s. Unlike historians of the Americas, their work sometimes attempted to incorporate the experience of multiracial societies outside of the Western Hemisphere. Most of them were preoccupied with demonstrating or testing the theories of ethnic conflict and accommodation developed in the 1920s and 1930s by Robert Park at the University of Chicago. According to this theory, racially or ethnically diverse societies went through a predictable series of phases that led ultimately to the assimilation of minorities. Applied to black-white relations in the United States and elsewhere by sociologists like E. Franklin Frazier, this meant an evolution toward the obliteration of group differences through cultural, social, and ultimately biological assimilation (although it was generally recognized that this process could take a long time and was subject to temporary reversals).[3] Frazier and others cited Brazil as an example of a society that was far ahead of the United States in its evolution toward the amalgamation of races. Because of its overwhelming black majority, the model could not readily be applied to South Africa, unless its ultimate destiny was the assimilation of white to black. In some formulations, this optimistic view was linked to the prevailing concept of modernization. When applied to race relations, modernization meant that status based on "ascription" or birth was inevitably replaced by status based on achievement as a society grew more industrialized, urbanized, and interdependent. These sociological studies ranged far and wide and were, for the most part, too general and aprioristic to be applied very fruitfully to individual cases.

The Founding of New Societies, a multi-authored comparative study edited by the political scientist Louis Hartz (who also wrote a lion's share of it), first brought the United States, South Africa, and Latin America (along with Canada and Australia) into juxtaposition.[4] Race relations was not the main theme of this study of settler societies, but its insistence that each of these societies was a "fragment of Europe" that perpetuated cultural characteristics and political tendencies brought by the original settlers had implications for relations with non-Europeans that were compatible with the comparisons of the Tannenbaum-Elkins school. Iberian patrimonialism, Dutch Calvinism, and the incipient liberalism of the middle-class English colonists of North America provided the ideological contexts that put black slaves at the base of a complex status hierarchy in Latin America or at the bottom of a simple white-over-black pattern of dominance in the United States and South Africa. Hartz was the first to argue that the growth of democracy for whites, when combined with a belief in black inferiority, intensified prejudice and discrimination.

More recent studies of patterns of race in the United States, while not explicitly comparative, have suggested that the two-category system and descent rule were not firmly established in the colonial period but became hard-and-fast only in the mid- to late nineteenth century. In the antebellum deep South before the 1850s, mulattos generally occupied a privileged position relative to blacks, especially in Louisiana and South Carolina. Although their status was maintained by custom rather than by law, this three-tiered system had some resemblance to the one that prevailed in the Caribbean plantation societies. Furthermore, some states defined as Negro only those with a black grandparent, making it possible for a few families with known

African ancestry to become white. Discrimination against mulattos surged in the 1850s as a result of the sectional controversy over slavery and the racism that it evoked, but the "one-drop rule" to determine who was black was not legislated until the Jim Crow era around the turn of the century.[5] "Mulatto" persisted as a United States census category until 1920. Furthermore, new studies have shown that some European immigrant groups, especially Irish, Italians, and Jews, were not initially regarded as unambiguously white and had to struggle to obtain full membership in the dominant race.

This new work on the construction of whiteness and blackness means that the stark contrasts posited by the pioneering comparisons between the United States and Brazil will need to be modified somewhat. The assumption that "patterns of race" are fixed early and set in stone now seems ahistorical and essentialist. The current controversy in the United States about the identity of mixed-race people and how they should be enumerated in the census has led to an increased awareness of the contingency and artificiality of racial designations. Systematic comparative work involving the United States and Iberian America has yet to take account of this new understanding of the evolution and reconstruction of racial categories and hierarchies. But the view that there are persistent differences in the precise way race is defined and constructed in the United States and Brazil is likely to survive this reexamination.

A new direction in comparative studies was set in 1967 by a remarkable work that still possesses considerable value. Pierre L. van den Berghe compared the historical evolution of racial orders in the United States, Brazil, South Africa, and Mexico in his book *Race and Racism.*[6] A sociologist who had done his initial work on South Africa, van den Berghe deserves much of the credit for making that country a major reference point in the discourse about comparative race relations. At the same time, he manifested a stronger sense of societal transformation than Hartz and his colleagues and developed a more pessimistic or realistic view of postemancipation black-white relations than had been suggested by comparative sociologists in the Park tradition. He argued that the abolition of slavery occasioned a shift from a "paternalistic" to a "competitive" form of race relations, which meant that racism was likely to be intensified rather than diminished by emancipation. It was the fear of economic and social competition in rapidly modernizing societies that, according to van den Berghe, produced Jim Crow laws in the United States and "native segregation" and apartheid in South Africa. Because they were less modernized and retained strong elements of paternalism in their social attitudes and arrangements, his Latin American cases had not manifested these harsh, exclusionary tendencies. He coined the useful phrase *"herrenvolk* democracies" to distinguish the combination of rigid racial hierarchies with the norm of equal rights and full political participation for all whites, which he believed had developed in the United States and South Africa, from the more traditional social hierarchies based on class and culture that allegedly muted the effect of race per se in Mexico and Brazil. His treatment of Brazil did not challenge the prevailing view that class and culture modified racial attitudes and practices—that money and education could whiten mulattos to an extent that would be inconceivable in the United States. But it did raise the possibility that this paternalistic tolerance would decline as Brazil became more "modern" and competitive.

Since the 1970s, historians and, to a lesser extent, sociologists and political scientists have followed van den Berghe's lead by taking a hard comparative look at South Africa. Ambitious bilateral comparisons of race relations in the United States and South Africa by John Cell, Stanley Greenberg, and myself appeared almost simultaneously in the early 1980s. Following the recent trend in U.S.-Brazilian comparisons, these studies emphasized demographic and material factors more than cultural predispositions inherited from the European past—for example, a Dutch or English Calvinism that drew sharp lines between the saved and the damned that might have reinforced a distinction between white and black. In my own work, *White Supremacy*, I found that differing sex ratios in the seventeenth and eighteenth centuries helped to account for a relatively more permissive attitude toward miscegenation, intermarriage, and the rights of free people of color in the Dutch Cape than in the North American colonies. Race relations in the Cape Colony of the seventeenth and eighteenth centuries were, in some ways, more reminiscent of what historians had found in colonial Brazil than what appeared to be the case in prerevolutionary America. Tracing the evolution from this early permissive pattern to the rigid color line that developed in the twentieth century made me aware of the extent to which racial attitudes and policies can change over time as societies, economies, and polities reorient or reinvent themselves.[7]

Cell and Greenberg concentrated on the late nineteenth and early twentieth centuries and the development of state-imposed segregation and discrimination against blacks. For them, it was clearly the immediate economic and social circumstances, not some ideological or cultural legacy from the past, that was decisive in the emergence of state-supported racism. They found analogous forces at work and similar patterns of development. Cell, in *The Highest Stage of White Supremacy*, argued that segregationist policies in both the deep South and South Africa were essentially rational, modernist responses to urbanization and industrialization. Begging some important questions, he made white supremacy of some sort a given for these societies and then focused on why it took the specific form of segregation, which he argued could not be explained by racism alone but could only have arisen in conjunction with modernization and the triumph of liberal capitalism.[8] Greenberg, in *Race and State in Capitalist Development*, focused on the role of specific "economic actors"—white industrialists, farmers, and workers.

The fate of blacks, he argued, was determined primarily by the conflicts, negotiations, coalitions, and agreements of white interest groups in pursuit of material advantage.[9]

I departed to some extent from this relentless materialism by assuming that cultural racism was a determinant as well as a result of socioeconomic changes and interest group configurations. The sociologist Herbert Blumer's brilliant essay on "Industrialization and Race Relations" (which focused on the United States and South Africa and was published in a volume with the same title edited by Guy Hunter in 1965) pointed me in this direction. Blumer argued that industrial capitalists have adapted to preexisting racial hierarchies more than they have created new ones.[10]

As I have sought, under the influence of Blumer, to distinguish my approach from that of Cell and Greenberg, I have become aware of the extent to which industrialization and urbanization in South Africa and the southern United States may have taken somewhat peculiar forms because of preexisting patterns of white privilege and black subservience. A history of racial subordination and disadvantage had engendered stereotypes in the white mind about the limits of black competence. More concretely, it had left blacks uneducated, low-skilled, lacking in basic rights, and therefore ultra-exploitable. This vulnerability affected how they could be most profitably employed, thus skewing in certain ways the economic development of South Africa and the American South—favoring, for example, labor-intensive, extractive industries over those requiring education, advanced skills, and sophisticated technology. When blacks moved to cities, their low status and ingrained white prejudices against them made it virtually inevitable that they would be segregated in ghettos or peri-urban townships, either by law or by private discrimination (often backed up by violence or the threat of it).

Besides giving greater weight to the culture of racism that preceded the onset of industrialization—the habits of mind arising out of slavery or the exacting of compulsory labor service on white farms from conquered indigenous societies—I also differed from Cell and Greenberg in the degree of variance that I found between the two cases. I contended that the Civil War, Reconstruction, and the promise of equal citizenship in the Fourteenth and Fifteenth Amendments made for significant differences in the long-range prospects and expectations of blacks in the two societies— African Americans had the national Constitution potentially on their side and black South Africans did not. What I did not foresee in 1981—and I was not alone in my pessimism—was that the South African state would be radically transformed into an interracial democracy in the 1990s and that this "miracle" would be accomplished without the drawn-out and bloody conflict that most observers in the 1980s thought would be necessary before fundamental changes could take place.

Taken as a whole, however, the work of Cell, Greenberg, and myself affirmed that the development of race relations is a fluid and variable process that changes over time in response to such developments as class formation and conflict within racial or ethnic communities, economic transformation or restructuring, changes in demography (especially in the relative size of racialized groups), the rise of political parties and leaders among the enfranchised who seek electoral advantage by "playing the race card," and wars or other international developments that conduce states or nations to make adjustments in group relations within their borders.

During the 1980s and 1990s, historians comparing the United States and South Africa shifted some of their attention from structures and ideologies of domination to the ideological and organizational responses of blacks to white supremacy. This reflects a general trend in historical studies away from the study of elites and patterns of domination toward "history from below" and resistance to racial oppression. The recognition that people who were oppressed and discriminated against were not merely victims but also historical agents who creatively and sometimes successfully resisted efforts to deprive them of human dignity has bred a comparative literature focusing on black ideologies and movements. One conclusion that has emerged from this work is the extent to which black protesters in one society have been inspired and influenced by the ideas and actions of those struggling for equal rights or liberation from racial tyranny in the other. The flow has been mostly, but not exclusively, from the United States to South Africa rather than the other way around, and has been variable in its intensity. The work of James Campbell on the African Methodist Episcopal Church in both countries, *Songs of Zion*, is a pioneering effort to explore such linkages in detail.[11]

My own more general study of black ideologies since the 1880s, *Black Liberation*, finds a remarkable parallelism in the way that aspiring black elites, their hopes for equal opportunity having been raised by the ostensibly color-blind liberalism of the mid-Victorian era, responded to the challenge of intensifying white racism and segregationism in the early twentieth century. Since white supremacist ideologues and policymakers in the two societies also shared ideas and programs, it is not really surprising that black elites in the two societies saw similarities in the dangers that they perceived from Jim Crow and "Native Segregation" and in the need they saw to form protest organizations such as the National Association for the Advancement of Colored People and the African National Congress. As the century progressed, they also responded in comparable ways to international developments and movements, such as pan-Africanism and the broader struggle for the decolonization of Africa and Asia that culminated after World War II.[12]

As I attempted to synthesize the scholarship on African-American and black South African affinities and interconnections, I also became aware of the differences in the way similar ideologies were applied and in the degrees of success that they enjoyed. I was particularly struck by divergences in the impact of Garveyism, Marxism, Gandhian nonviolence, and the black identity movements summed up by the slogans "Black Power" and "Black Consciousness." I was left with the question of why black identity politics took firm hold in the United States but was displaced by the African National Congress's "nonracialism" in South Africa. (When Louis Farrakhan tried to bring his brand of black nationalism to South Africa in 1995, he was generally rebuffed.) The answer derives, I suspect, primarily from the difference between a majority coming to power and a minority trying to survive in a hostile environment. The former does not have to be concerned about losing its identity and is less likely to become the pawn of interests other than its own.

Recent work on race and class in Brazil, while not for the most part systematically comparative, has also given us some new perspectives and forced a reevaluation of the standard contrasts between race patterns in the two nations. More specifically, it has raised doubts about the traditional view that color differences are much more benignly interpreted in Brazil than in the United States. A United Nations Educational, Scientific, and Cultural Organization (UNESCO)–sponsored study in the 1950s, which was inspired by the hope that Brazil might serve as a world model for egalitarian race relations, found that nonwhite Brazilians were seriously disadvantaged in comparison to their white compatriots. But this inequality was attributed mainly to the class divisions of a relatively poor and underdeveloped society rather than to color prejudice. The seminal work of the Brazilian sociologist Florestan Fernandes in the 1960s (*Integração do Negro na Sociedade de Classes*, translated as *The Negro in Brazilian Society*) refuted the myth that Brazil was a de facto racial democracy, but attributed black and mulatto disadvantage mainly to the enduring effects of slavery on the competitiveness of Afro-Brazilians in an industrializing society and to the readiness of twentieth-century capitalists to take advantage of their vulnerability to exploitation. He gave little weight to contemporary racial prejudice and discrimination. According to his Marxian analysis, the central problem threatening the democratic possibilities of Brazil was class rather than race.[13]

Carl Degler's major work of comparative history, *Neither Black nor White: Slavery and Race Relations in Brazil and the United States*, took account of the historical persistence of strong prejudices against blacks (*pretos*), but argued that Brazil did differ from the United States because of the existence of a "mulatto escape hatch" that had blurred the color line at its margins by giving people of mixed race (*pardos*) a chance to rise in the world that had normally been denied to the lightest African Americans. But he also noted that the expectation of interracial mobility had the disadvantage of preventing Afro-Brazilians from attaining the group solidarity that would have enabled them to mobilize and fight for equal rights in the way that African Americans did in the 1950s and 1960s. Most of the evidence that Degler provided for mulatto mobility, however, came from the nineteenth century rather than the twentieth, and was anecdotal and impressionistic rather than quantitative.[14]

Subsequent scholars have questioned the notion that modern Brazil really has a "mulatto escape hatch." Something of this sort, it is sometimes conceded, may have existed in the nineteenth century before the wave of European immigrants around the turn of the century established a more "competitive" situation, but thereafter the color line hardened. Although inconclusive, the evidence for significant mulatto opportunity in earlier periods seems generally persuasive. But in the twentieth century, at least in the industrializing regions of the country, the Brazilian elite has apparently whitened itself to the point where current statistical data show that *pardos* are scarcely, if at all, better off than *pretos*. In this situation the myth that Brazil is a "racial democracy" in comparison to the United States serves as an ideological device to conceal the fact that discrimination against virtually all people of acknowledged African ancestry is common and consequential.

The North American scholar who has demonstrated this pattern most effectively is the historian George Reid Andrews. His 1991 study, *Blacks and Whites in São Paulo*, shows that during the century since emancipation, black and brown Paulistas have suffered greatly from palpable discrimination in employment, housing, and access to the ubiquitous social clubs that are central to Brazilian civil society. Aware of the persistence of racism in the United States in the post–civil rights era, Andrews makes a telling comparative point. Brazil has not been analogous to South Africa under apartheid or the South in the age of Jim Crow. But it has been quite similar, he contends, to the American North, where a less clear-cut and rigid form of racial hierarchy has been maintained without the need for legal sanction. "In societies like the American North and Brazil," he writes, "the absence of state-mandated discrimination has made racial injustice significantly more difficult to struggle against."[15]

I suspect that a full-blown comparative study of recent and current race relations in Brazil and the United States would follow the lead of historians like Andrews, who stress similarity or convergence more than difference. In the 1960s, the United States abolished the legalized segregation that constituted an obvious and palpable difference between Brazil and the southern United States. Currently the insistence of some conservatives that racism has ended in the United States, thus making affirmative action unnecessary, may be performing a function similar to the myth of "racial democracy" in Brazil. Denying racial prejudice and discrimination when they in fact exist is sometimes called "the new racism" in the United States. In Brazil, it might be better described as the same old racism. What is apparent in both cases is that racial discrimination and inequality do not require Jim Crow laws and disfranchisement. A combination of institutional patterns and the private acts of individuals can sustain a pattern of inequality quite effectively, unless mass protest movements can force strong governmental action to ensure equal rights and opportunities. And such movements are more difficult to organize when the target is not a blatantly unjust law or government policy but relatively subtle private discrimination, de facto segregation, and the ethnocentric, if technically color-blind, norms or preferences of institutions, organizations, and enterprises to which blacks have previously had very limited access and to which they may often find it difficult to adjust.

Unlike Brazil, the United States has attempted to legislate equality of opportunity through antidiscrimination laws with enforcement provisions, including the controversial affirmative action policies. If affirmative action is attacked in the United States because racism is allegedly dead and buried, enforceable antidiscrimination laws have not been passed in Brazil because of a belief that racism has never existed. Brazil may need affirmative action as much, if not more, than the United States, but opposition to it is likely to be even more intense given the stronger Brazilian tradition of separation between race and state.

But one basic difference remains. More recent comparativists have reinforced Degler's contention that African Americans have a greater proclivity to mobilize in defense of their rights than Afro-Brazilians. This remains true today, despite the emergence of black protest and nationalist groups in Brazil in recent years. It appears that the majority of Afro-Brazilians do not have a very strong sense of racial identity and group interest. Politicized color consciousness had been limited principally to academics and members of an educated elite. What is not clear is whether this lack of racial militancy and assertiveness results from a deep internalization of the myth of racial democracy or can be attributed to the extreme poverty of most Afro-Brazilians—90 percent of all black and brown Brazilians are below the poverty line, a situation that makes day-to-day survival so difficult and time-consuming that it is virtually impossible to concentrate on politics.

Also significant is the fact that a near-majority of white Brazilians are also impoverished—an estimated one-third of the inhabitants of the notorious *favelas* or shantytowns are white. Studies suggest that, contrary to the United States, white prejudice against blacks decreases as you move downward in the socioeconomic hierarchy, which means that a class-based interracial politics that promises to benefit blacks economically is more plausible in Brazil than it would seem to be in the United States, where racism has been endemic in the white working class. The fact that most politically aware Afro-Brazilians support the leftist Workers' Party would seem to bear out the suggestion that those on the bottom can feel a sense of solidarity based on class and economics that would be hard to replicate in the United States.

It also may be the case, although not much work has been done on this issue, that interracial mobility persists in a way that limits the possibility of strong racial identities. Census data show unexplained increases in the number of *pardos* and decreases in the number of *pretos*, along with a growth in those who define themselves as white or *blanco* that cannot be entirely accounted for by natural increase and immigration. Are large numbers of light-skinned people who were formally classified as *pardos* successfully passing for white? It is certainly the case that some Brazilian *blancos* would be considered African-American if they lived in the United States. Although officially the Brazilian population is only 40 to 50 percent of part African ancestry, some demographers suggest that the real figure is closer to 80 percent. Has the historical process of "whitening" light-skinned mulattos persisted, slowed down, or ended? We simply do not know the answer. What is clear enough is that race still does not have exactly the same meaning in Brazil as in the United States.

A very recent study has added a new level of complexity to our understanding of group relations in Brazil and made it more difficult to generalize about the country as a whole. Kim Butler's *Freedoms Given, Freedoms Won*, a comparative study of Afro-Brazilians in São Paulo and Salvador de Bahia during the period since emancipation, argues persuasively that the way racial or ethnic identities are formed differs significantly in the two cities and, by extension, in the regions in which they are located. In São Paulo, where Afro-Brazilians have always been a minority and economic competition with European immigrants was intense in the early twentieth century, the primary distinction has long been between *blancos* and *negros* (Afro-Brazilians of varying pigmentation). The pattern that she finds is therefore similar to the one that George Reid Andrews described. But in Salvador de Bahia, a large city in the less developed northeast where Afro-Brazilians are a substantial majority, group identities have been constructed along a different axis. The key element is not color but culture. In this center of African cultural survivals and adaptations, people of similar physical features may think of themselves as either Afro-Brazilian or Euro-Brazilian, depending on whether their cultural affinities and preferences are thought to be African or European in inspiration. As a result, color is not as clear an indicator of status as in São Paulo. Butler's study implies that Salvadoran *pardos* who adopt a "white" lifestyle and have the resources to sustain it can become *blanco* for most practical purposes. The "mulatto escape hatch" would appear to be alive and well in northeast Brazil, but more as a result of cultural orientations and identifications than of phenotypical characteristics.[16]

Butler's study also suggests to me that efforts to generalize the history about group attitudes and practices in all three of our cases need to take more account than they have of regional variations. Race has not meant exactly the same thing or had the same consequences in the northern and southern parts of the United States or in the Cape of Good Hope and the erstwhile Afrikaner republics of the Transvaal and the Orange Free State. External comparisons need to be supplemented by internal ones. Race relations vary from place to place within the same country, as well as over time. But in this age of political and economic centralization, mass communications, and increased physical mobility the trend is undoubtedly in the direction of homogenization. In the United States today, for example, the North and South differ much less in the character and quality of black-white relations than they did in the past.

Comparisons between race relations in Brazil and South Africa, which might be expected to yield different kinds of insights than juxtaposing either to U.S. patterns, have rarely been attempted. The closest approximation is sociologist Gay Seidman's *Manufacturing Militance: Workers' Movements in Brazil and South Africa, 1970–1985*. As the subtitle suggests, this is a work focusing on class and labor rather than on race relations and might be open to criticism for its limited attention to the role that a consciousness of color differences might play in impeding or advancing the struggles of workers to establish a more egalitarian society. But Seidman does reveal some parallels between South Africa and Brazil that could lay a foundation for comparative studies focusing on race rather than class or, more usefully perhaps, on the relationship between these two interdependent and interacting forms of social inequality. Unlike the United States, she argues, both Brazil and South Africa are late industrializing nations that moved between the 1940s and 1960s toward establishing a manufacturing base under statist and authoritarian auspices. The development of militant unions in both countries during the 1970s can be attributed in part to the opening provided by business opposition to the heavy hand of the state. Confronted with the fact that their living standards were declining due to frozen wages and rising prices in Brazil and changes in the residence patterns of both countries that forced proletarians into peripheral townships or shantytowns far from their places of employment, workers took advantage of dissension among elites to organize themselves and push their demands.[17]

Seidman's work raises important new questions for students of comparative race relations. She compels further attention to a factor emphasized earlier by Stanley Greenberg in his comparative study of South Africa and Alabama—the way that conflicts between business and government can sometimes be exploited by those seeking progressive social change. She also makes us more aware of the crucial role played by black unions in the struggle against apartheid in South Africa and the extent to which their class-based ideology prepared the way for the triumph of "nonracialism" under Nelson Mandela. I paid relatively little attention to labor movements in my comparative study of black ideologies in the United States and South Africa, because there was no American analogue to COSATU (the predominantly black federation of unions that provided much of the muscle behind the struggle for black liberation in the late 1980s and early 1990s). What may make Brazil and South Africa different from the United States is the role that an interracial but predominantly black and brown labor movement has played or could conceivably play in the struggle for racial justice and equality.

The history of race-based movements in Brazil is just beginning to be written. Michael Hanchard's *Orpheus and Power: The Movimento Negro of Rio de Janeiro and São Paulo*, published in 1994, was the first book-length study in English on this subject. It is evident from this work that black consciousness is on the rise among black and brown Brazilians and that efforts to unify them into a single Afro-Brazilian community are not entirely unavailing. But the most significant manifestation of this impulse—the Movimento Negro—has failed to gain mass support. Comparative studies of Afro-Brazilian, African-American, and black South African liberation or identity movements might prove enormously revealing. Hanchard's work shows, for example, that the debates between integrationists and black nationalists in the United States and between nonracialists and Africanists or advocates of "Black Consciousness" in South Africa have their Brazilian analogue in the ongoing Afro-Brazilian argument between the *americanistas* and the *africanistas*.[18]

Hanchard finds that an Afro-Brazilian "culturalism," based on an affirmation of African survivals and identities, has been subject to cooptation by the government and the white establishment. An official willingness to promote and celebrate the African strain in Brazilian national character and culture, which dates back to the 1930s, has served to distract attention from the economic and social plight of Afro-Brazilians and inhibit direct protest against poverty, discrimination, and police brutality. (Could people who seem to have so much fun at Carnival really be victims of oppression?) Butler's comparative study of São Paulo and Salvador provides further evidence that constructing and celebrating a distinctive cultural identity may be an impediment to political mobilization aimed at racial discrimination. It is in São Paulo, where Afro-Brazilians have generally sought inclusion in mainstream Brazilian society, that active and sometimes militant mobilization has occurred. In Salvador, where an Africanist identity thrives, Afro-Brazilians have remained, for the most part, politically passive. The history of black cultural nationalism in the United States and South Africa might also be interpreted to support an argument that black movements seeking justice through inclusion in a common democratic society are normally more militant and ultimately more effective than separatist identity movements, which may encourage escape or evasion rather than a direct confrontation with racism.

Anthony Marx has recently produced the first systematic comparison of how racial orders were constructed in all three countries—*Making Race and Nation* (1998). A political scientist, Marx has focused on the role of the state as the critical variable. His basic argument is that the United States and South Africa developed policies of racial exclusion and oppression primarily because of the imperatives of state or nation building as perceived by political elites that happened to be white. Stability and prosperity—the state's main goals—were threatened by crises resulting from sectional or ethnic divisions among the enfranchised white citizenry, leading in both cases to what amounted to civil wars. The North-South conflict in the United States and the Anglo-Afrikaner struggle in South Africa created a problem for nation builders that had no analogue in Brazil, where the white population has never been seriously split along regional or ethnic lines. Legalized racism, or in the case of the United States, the acquiescence of the federal government to the Jim Crow laws of the southern states, was viewed as the price of national cohesion and a necessary device for building a modern nation-state. In other words, blacks were scapegoated to promote white unity. When, by the 1960s in the United States and by the late 1980s and early 1990s in South Africa, white unity had been firmly established and black resistance had come to constitute a threat to the health or survival of the state, ruling elites in both countries chose to abolish discriminatory laws and fully enfranchise blacks to promote the same goals of national cohesion and prosperity that had earlier led their predecessors to institute the opposite policies.[19]

Marx's work suggests that we need to pay a lot more attention than van den Berghe did to the autonomous role of the state if we want to understand the variable development of race and racism. As I found in my own work on white supremacy in the United States and South Africa, disunity and conflict among whites and efforts to resolve them were a recurring factor that helped to account for changes or adjustments in race policy from the colonial period to the present. But, like any explanation that privileges a single factor, the state-as-actor thesis may risk oversimplifying a complex and multifaceted process. Furthermore, the model applies most directly to government-sanctioned racism, and offers less insight into the de facto prejudice and discrimination that still bedevil all three societies and serve to disadvantage blacks economically and socially.

A fuller and richer comparison of the historical trajectories of race and racism in the three societies would need to deal more fully with two other factors. Max Weber, in his efforts to categorize disparities in social power, pointed to three interacting types of differentiation: class, status, and party. "Party," for Weber, meant access to, and influence over, the state—the factor that Marx stresses. But class—unequal access to the market and the means of production—and status—the culturally constructed norms for the differential apportionment of honor and prestige—act upon the state as well as being influenced by it. Weber's term for what we call race is "ethnic status," the social rank and prestige that come from belonging to a historically dominant ethnic or racial group. Following Weber, I believe that a three-way comparison should take more fully into account the developing economic situation and the kind of class relations to which it gives rise and also the cultural and psychological weight of a status order based on a presumption of white superiority. Another way of advocating this tri-causal model is simply to call for explanations that acknowledge the interaction of the state, the economy, and the prevailing hierarchy of sociocultural identities without giving a priori primacy to any one of them.

Anthony Marx has, with compelling originality, made a case for the state or "party" as an actor in the development and transformations of racial orders in Brazil, South Africa, and the United States, but his contention that racism can be regarded as a constant rather than a variable because it was present in all three cases is debatable. "Ethnic status" in a color-coded form assumed a castelike character in the United States and South Africa that it has never had in Brazil. The banning of interracial marriage in much of the United States from the colonial period to the late 1960s and in twentieth-century South Africa has been unthinkable in Brazil throughout most of its history. In fact, as Thomas Skidmore demonstrated in *Black into White*, twentieth-century Euro-Brazilian intellectuals and political leaders have frequently endorsed intermarriage as another way (along with European immigration) to "whiten" Brazil.[20] A form of racism is clearly involved in this preference for the mostly white over the mostly black, but it is a more tolerant and permissive variety than the fixation with race purity and rigid color lines that characterized U.S. or South African racial thought and policies before and especially during the eras of Jim Crow and apartheid. Unlike Afro-Brazilians, southern African Americans and black South Africans were commonly viewed and treated not merely as social inferiors but as permanent aliens or social outcasts, ineligible even for second-class citizenship. A substantial number of Americans and South Africans of European descent probably still hold this view, consciously or subliminally. American and South African national identities *were* conceived on the basis of a commitment to white racial purity and exclusiveness that has no real analogue in Brazil.

That Brazil followed a trajectory different from that of the United States and South Africa in its postemancipation racial policies can therefore be explained as the product of the special character of its ethnic status hierarchy as well as by the fact that European political unity was never threatened to an extent that impelled nation builders to find a scapegoat. There is, I believe, a measure of truth in the traditional view that Brazil, while still a Portuguese colony or a Luso-tropical empire, and before it aspired to be a modern nation-state, established a pattern of racial classification and interaction that differed significantly from that which developed in the United States and South Africa. The mulatto or *pardo* stereotype was quite dissimilar from that of blacks or *pretos* for a very long time, and to some extent still is, in ways that sanctioned race mixture and offered some mulattos access to many of the advantages of Euro-Brazilian status. The multiplicity of color categories and the permeability of the boundaries between these categories meant that a system of Jim Crow segregation or apartheid would have been virtually impossible to implement in Brazil even if there had been a strong political incentive to do so. It was simply too difficult to determine who was what. South Africa also generated a "colored" middle strata, some of whose members succeeded in passing for white, but this category originated in the intermixture of the white-, brown-, and yellow-skinned peoples resident in the Western Cape in the seventeenth and eighteenth centuries. It was an internally diverse group that was invented by white census takers in the mid-nineteenth century and then left in an ambiguous intermediate position when the confrontation of Europeans and Bantu-speaking Africans became the central theme of South African history. No mulatto category developed out of the frontier interactions that led to white dominance over most of South Africa in the course of the nineteenth century. The offspring of the black-white sexual unions that occurred on the frontier normally became African tribesmen rather than "coloreds."

The sharp black-white dichotomy that, for most practical purposes, came to characterize the U.S. and South African patterns was therefore not replicated in Brazil. If Brazil had been unfortunate enough to have had a sectional civil war in the nineteenth century, it is quite conceivable that the resulting reunion would have unified *blancos* and *pardos* against *pretos*, in a way that might have had some parallels with the black-mulatto division during the Haitian revolution. The state may be an actor in the construction of racial orders, but the raw material it has at hand to construct national citizenship is conditioned by preexisting patterns of stratification or exclusion that may differ significantly.

The independent effect of economic class formation on black-white relations can begin to be assessed by problematizing Anthony Marx's contention that a major goal of national unifications is to foster economic development and prosperity. The obvious question is, prosperity and economic development for whom? The United States, South Africa, and Brazil have at some point in their histories become developing industrial capitalist societies. But they did not all develop at the same time or at the same rate. The United States was the pioneer and South Africa and Brazil came later—in the case of Brazil, much later. One does not have to be a thoroughgoing Marxist to acknowledge that the rise of industrial capitalism creates class divisions between wage earners and the owners of the means of production. If race can serve as a political unifier among white regions or ethnic groups, it can also serve to mitigate class conflict among whites. According to the cruder versions of Marxism, employers encourage racism among white workers in order to prevent proletarians from unifying across the color line. But a more sophisticated class analysis of "split labor markets" acknowledges that white workers may actually benefit from the exclusion of other racial groups from equal opportunity in the labor market. Skilled workers in the United States often excluded blacks or Asians from their trades not merely because they were prejudiced against them but also, and perhaps more important, because it served to protect their wages and increase their bargaining power with employers. In South Africa in 1922, white workers revolted against efforts to increase the proportion of African workers in semiskilled jobs in the gold mines. Their strike was put down by force, but a subsequent government enacted the industrial color bars that made white workers a privileged class with virtually guaranteed access to skilled jobs and high wages. In both the United States and South Africa, capitalists, whose natural inclination was to hire the cheapest labor available, found that the price of peace with class-conscious white workers was an exclusionary policy that privileged white employees. Again, however, as in the case of the political explanation of racism, such job discrimination would have made no sense if a preexisting racial hierarchy had not divided the labor market between those who got there first and were best able to defend their interests and those who arrived later and were deemed to be low-wage menial workers by nature.

Brazil's later industrialization, as Gay Seidman has pointed out, put workers without a tradition of labor organization at the mercy of authoritarian governments and rapacious employers, both of whom wanted economic development that benefited the privileged few at the expense of the many. In this case, however, the unions, which needed all the support they could muster against the powerful forces arrayed against them, did not draw a color line. When the business community and the government split over the specifics of economic development, this fledgling interracial labor movement found some room to operate.

The Great Depression and the New Deal in the United States provided a comparable stimulus for labor organizing in general and made possible the integration of the great Congress of Industrial Organizations' unions. Prejudice among white workers persisted, especially in the South, but the desperate campaign to provide jobs and decent wages in a period of high unemployment and general impoverishment made some key labor leaders aware of the organizational advantages of racial inclusiveness. In South Africa, the white working class declined in size and importance beginning in the 1940s. More and more formerly poor Afrikaners used their state-supported advantage in education, employment, and access to capital to attain a middle-class status and standard of living. Thus the industrial working class became almost exclusively black by the 1960s, making it possible for the African unions that eventually gained legal recognition to become key participants in the struggle against apartheid.

American unions, although they did contribute money and personnel to the civil rights struggles of the 1960s, could not play a similar role. Although most of them were integrated, they remained predominantly white, and their leadership had to take into account the persisting prejudices of many of the white rank and file. Furthermore, the labor movement in general was beginning to decline in membership, militancy, and political clout. Hence militant "workerism" could not play the same role as a counterweight to power and privilege based on class and race that may have been decisive in South Africa and could become so in Brazil.

Even if one takes the existing class structure as a given, the success of the economy has major implications for race relations. Capitalism may foster inequality, but in my view it does not inevitably promote racial inequality (which is not to say that free-market capitalism is capable of rectifying structural inequalities based on a history of racial disadvantage). The production for profit of goods and services to be sold in a free market does not by its nature mandate racial discrimination. If anything, the logic of capitalism is based on a color-blind notion of economic man as entrepreneur, investor, consumer, and worker. As the U.S. experience of the past forty years clearly shows, racial reform is much easier in times of prosperity and rising expectations than in periods of economic decline and scarce resources. Many people believe that South Africa's experiment in nonracial democracy is dependent on whether the economy grows fast enough in the next few years to provide millions of new jobs to currently impoverished and unemployed Africans. The struggles of blacks and other poor Brazilians for a better life obviously requires a vibrant and growing economy, as well as one that distributes the rewards of economic growth much more equitably than it has done in the past.

To fully assess what history can teach us about the prospects for racial equality in the United States, Brazil, and South Africa, one other variable that seems of prime significance to me is the degree to which the prevailing conceptions of national character and identity in the three countries can be used or reconstructed to encourage the incorporation of blacks into the mainstream. Long-standing notions of what a nation stands for, what its highest aspirations are, and what it hopes to achieve are very difficult to change. It is a major element in the dominant belief systems and views of the world that history has bequeathed to the citizens of the countries being compared. Blacks in the United States have benefited historically at certain times—most obviously in the 1860s and the 1960s—from the commitment to individual liberty, equality, and opportunity to be found in the language of the Declaration of Independence (even if the framers of the document can be justly accused of hypocrisy or mental reservations). But does that liberal, individualist tradition still suffice in the circumstances of the late twentieth century—declining mobility for those at the bottom of the economic and educational opportunity structures and increasing cultural diversity? Do we now have to come to terms with the more community-oriented belief systems and practices of those minorities that may eventually become a majority in the United States? It is my personal belief that the best hope we have for a more just society is to continue the struggle to make our reality match our abstract commitment to individual human rights. But we can only do this if we are willing to make cultural and ethnic identity one of the "self-evident" rights that we recognize. Cultural freedom for the individual—the right to be different without being penalized for it—would seem to be as permissible a deduction from the right to "the pursuit of happiness" as are the religious freedom and diversity that are so thoroughly ingrained in American law and political culture.

In Brazil and South Africa, the prevailing racial or ethnic ideologies and conceptions of national purpose are oddly similar to each other in that they both deemphasize race in favor of color-blind democracy and show a greater propensity than seems currently possible in the United States to substitute a conflict between capitalist and socialist or social-democratic ideologies for one that emphasizes racial and ethnic divisions, either openly or covertly. Of course South Africa's racial democracy is proclaimed and enforced by the black majority, while that of Brazil is a myth created and promulgated by a white elite. In the latter case, at least, full exposure of the falsity of the claim could be followed most profitably by efforts to make racial democracy a reality rather than by jettisoning the ideal itself, just as in the United States a struggle based on fulfilling the human rights principles of the Declaration of Independence is likely to be more efficacious than one that rejects them out of hand because of their Euro-American origin.

In South Africa, where a new national identity is being forged, there is a Scylla-and-Charybdis problem. On one side is a fundamentalist version of nonracialism that obscures the reality of ethnic diversity and inhibits efforts to accommodate it. On the other is the danger of accentuating differences to the point where group consciousness and antagonism threaten the precarious unity of this "rainbow" society. Secessionist tendencies among Zulus and Afrikaners remain serious threats to the nationalist project. Furthermore, the failure of an ostensibly class-based nonracialism to deliver the goods to the African majority, at a time when the International Monetary Fund and the World Bank make social-democratic redistributive policies difficult and costly to implement, could easily result in the intensification of racial and ethnic conflict. Africanist and "Black Consciousness" groups are biding their time to see if the African National Congress can really bring white privilege to an end or whether nonracialism is simply a facade for the elevation of black elites into the ruling economic and political circles that were formerly limited to whites.

All these complexities and theoretical speculations do not hide the fact that in all three countries, race matters. By any measure of well-being and opportunity, blacks are still greatly disadvantaged in all three societies.

South Africa has the greatest economic and social inequalities—this is the legacy of apartheid—but has the government with the greatest incentive and commitment to do something about them. In the United States the statistical disparities are much lower than in South Africa and somewhat lower than in Brazil. But the relative deprivation of African Americans may be the greatest because they live in a country in which the majority enjoys one of the highest standards of living in the world, whereas both Brazil and South Africa are among those nations in which the overwhelming majority is desperately poor. In Brazil, blacks are overrepresented among the poor and in South Africa they are virtually all of them. Nevertheless, inequality correlated and associated with race is the common problem, and "affirmative action" of some kind is clearly called for in all three cases.

Precisely what works in one context may not work in the others. Varying circumstances in the United States, Brazil, and South Africa may call for somewhat different strategies to overcome racism. Those concerned with social and political action against racism may get a better sense of what might or might not be effective in a particular context from comparative historical studies. My survey suggests that racism should be combated on two fronts simultaneously. First, attitudes need to be changed through education and the experience of interacting with members of other groups in an atmosphere of equality and trust. Affirmative action programs, properly conceived and implemented, can contribute significantly to the struggle against prejudice as well as enhance the economic opportunities of individuals who would otherwise be denied a chance to reach their potential. Second, economic disparities among historically racialized groups need to be attacked by government policies and voluntary action aimed at the redistribution of wealth and privilege. The most effective of these policies should not be race-specific but would be directed at the eradication or reduction of poverty, whatever the color of its victims. The state, in its efforts to achieve unity, prosperity, and justice, will have to be the central player in these efforts, but the civil society can also make a significant contribution. Comparative historical study cannot hope to provide answers to many of the immediate, practical questions asked by those resisting racism in these differing and constantly changing arenas of group conflict and accommodation. Only those on the ground who wrestle day to day with the current realities of race and racism in Brazil, South Africa, and the United States can hope to do that. But comparative historians can at least point in promising directions that seem to be consistent with past experience. Their work may help policymakers and activists see what they are up against, what untapped material and cultural resources they may possess, and what changes are conceivable if certain initiatives are pursued, assuming that the will exists—or can be created—to sustain the long, hard struggle for racial justice and universal human rights.

CHAPTER 13

Beyond Race? Ideological Color-Blindness in the United States, Brazil, and South Africa

As we enter the twenty-first century, three nations with long histories of racial differentiation and color consciousness—the United States, Brazil, and South Africa—would appear to share a commitment to going beyond race and achieving an egalitarian society in which skin color no longer matters. In South Africa, the African National Congress has come to power under the banner of "nonracialism"; Brazil prides itself on its "racial democracy"; and in the United States the tide seems to have turned against race-based compensatory policies and toward "color-blind" constitutionalism. Superficially these ideologies of race transcendence are similar, and the abstract proposition that phenotype and ancestry should not affect rights or status in an egalitarian society is unchallengeable. Yet the relation to reality and the programmatic adequacy of each of these conceptions is debatable. There is good reason to pay critical attention to the role played by ideological color-blindness in these societies, given their long histories of white advantage and black disadvantage. The denial of race may be a denial of those histories.

Comparative study of South Africa, the United States, and Brazil has noted major differences in historic patterns of race relations, but has also detected a recent convergence.[1] The end of legalized segregation in the American South and of apartheid in South Africa has brought these nations into line with Brazil as places where racial inequality is no longer sustained by law in an explicit way. The powerful and respectable in all these societies now claim to be opposed to racism and affirm that the policies they advocate are the best way to eliminate it (if, in fact, they concede that it still exists). Open espousals of white supremacy are limited to fringe groups like the Ku Klux Klan in the United States and the Afrikaner Resistance movement in South Africa.

But what is "racism," and how can we be so sure that it has been eliminated or contained? Critics of the dominant or emerging theories of what
constitutes racial equality are challenging the assumption that racism is
present only when its proponents affirm the existence of innate biological
differences among physically distinguishable population groups. Those
who have uncovered a "new racism" also deny that state sanction and legal
inequality are necessary to the maintenance of white supremacy. A broadened
conception of racism draws attention to the ways that culture can serve as
a surrogate for biology. According to the British sociologist and cultural
critic Paul Gilroy, "where culture or subculture is defined as a fixed and
impermeable quality of human life," the shift from genetics to culture is "a
difference of degree rather than any fundamental divergence."[2] Racism based
on reified and essentialized views of culture, often in the form of stereotypes
about "national" or ethnic character, predated the scientific racism of the
nineteenth century and the first half of the twentieth, and has survived its
decline in cogency and respectability.[3] Even if group culture is regarded as
changeable, the belief that some cultures are superior to others can offer
out-groups a Hobson's choice between assimilation and subordination that
denies their right to cultural self-determination. It is from this perspective
that the antidote to racism is seen as some form of multiculturalism rather
than assimilation, amalgamation, or integration.[4]

Critics of the adequacy of official color-blindness also point to the persistence of relatively subtle and illusive patterns of discrimination by individuals, organizations, and institutions that require race-conscious remedies.
The recognition that unfairness may result from customary behaviors and
procedures, even in the absence of conscious prejudice or bigotry, is central
to the case for affirmative action—various forms of extra effort and special
consideration that conflict with the notion that racial equality requires absolute color-blindness in law and public policy. Debates about the meaning
of racism and antiracism have occurred in all three countries with which
we are concerned, but they have played out differently in each. The United
States, Brazil, and South Africa have differing histories, cultural patterns, and
racial and ethnic demographics. Hence the convergences, while undeniable
and significant, should not be overstated. Similar ideologies and policies
may have varying, even contrasting, meanings depending on the context.
Looking at the meaning of race and racism in each case will reveal critical
differences as well as similarities.

In his famous dissent in *Plessy v. Ferguson* (1896), the Supreme Court
decision that gave legal sanction to racial segregation in the United States,
Justice John Harlan affirmed that "our constitution is color-blind and neither knows nor tolerates classes among citizens"—meaning that it does not
permit the kind of invidious distinctions between whites and blacks that he
believed were implicit in the Jim Crow laws being passed at that time in the

southern states. In his view, these laws were "conceived in hostility to, and enacted for the purpose of humiliating, citizens of a particular race," and as such were "inconsistent not only with the equality of rights that pertains to citizenship but with the personal liberty enjoyed by every one within the United States."[5] The black struggle for equality that led to the Civil Rights Acts of 1964 and 1965 was viewed by many of its supporters as a campaign for the total separation of law and race. Equal access to public facilities and the ballot box meant that race should not be used, either overtly, as in the case of the Jim Crow laws, or implicitly, as in the case of suffrage restrictions, to prevent a class of citizens from exercising their constitutional rights.

Nevertheless, Martin Luther King, Jr., the most prominent black civil rights leader, and Lyndon B. Johnson, the president who was responsible for getting the Civil Rights Acts of 1964 and 1965 through Congress, both understood that substantive equality required more than outlawing official racism. King's book, *Why We Can't Wait*, published in 1964, and Johnson's 1965 speech at Howard University both argued that it is not yet a fair race when some of the contestants come to the starting line with injuries and disabilities resulting from centuries of slavery and state-enforced racial discrimination.[6] Out of a sense of the burdens imposed by a history of oppression of African Americans came the affirmative action programs requiring categorization by race and the setting of goals and timetables for the greater inclusion of blacks among those endowed with opportunities for social and economic mobility. "In order to get beyond racism," argued Supreme Court Justice Harry Blackmun in 1978, "we must first take account of race. There is no other way. And in order to treat some persons equally, we must treat them differently. We cannot—we dare not—let the Equal Protection Clause perpetuate racial supremacy."[7]

Recognizing race for the purpose of combating the legacy and persistence of racism has always been controversial, but affirmative action did not encounter substantial popular opposition until the 1990s. The Republican Party, which had previously supported most affirmative action policies and had even initiated some of them during the Nixon administration, was the principal fount of the assault. The decision of Republicans like Governor Pete Wilson of California to use "racial preferences" as a wedge issue against the Democrats helped turn public opinion against affirmative action.

Although this political opposition was emerging, the Supreme Court and other federal courts persisted in a trend that began in the late 1970s to limit the application of affirmative action and other race-conscious policies to circumstances that were defined more and more narrowly. First, the *Bakke* decision of 1978 outlawed numerical quotas for admissions to higher education, but permitted race to be taken into account if the aim was a diverse student body rather than the rectification of past injustices. Then, a series of decisions limited affirmative action or federal intervention in state and local election arrangements to cases where past discrimination could be clearly demonstrated. In the *Hopwood v. Texas* decision of 1996, a circuit court overruled *Bakke* and forbade the use of race as one criterion among many for university admission. If the Supreme Court had sustained this principle, affirmative action in public higher education would have been a thing of the past.[8] The Michigan decisions of 2003 did allow race to be considered as one factor in individual cases but not to be utilized on any statistical basis. More generally, any government action that makes explicit use of race, even as a means of overcoming disadvantage, is currently under the gun. The assault on affirmative action, which has achieved victory by popular referenda in California and Washington, is justified in one of two ways: either affirmative action has served its purposes and is no longer needed (because blacks no longer suffer from racial discrimination) or it was never justified in the first place because it violated the nonracial or color-blind character of America's laws or basic principles.[9]

Both propositions are dubious. Innumerable books and studies, ranging from careful journalism to quantitative social science, document beyond the shadow of a doubt that African Americans are still disadvantaged when they seek opportunities or amenities comparable to those routinely enjoyed by whites. Racism, defined here simply as unfair treatment resulting from a perception of physical difference, is alive and well, and true equality of opportunity remains an elusive goal.[10]

It is also misleading to say that the Constitution is inherently a nonracial or color-blind document. Before the Reconstruction era, the Constitution sanctioned racial slavery and official discrimination against those defined as nonwhite. The Thirteenth, Fourteenth, and Fifteenth Amendments respectively outlawed slavery, extended citizenship to anyone born in the United States, and made it unlawful to deny the vote to anyone because of "race, color, or previous condition of servitude." Although the Thirteenth and Fourteenth Amendments, unlike the Fifteenth, made no mention of race, their primary purpose was to free blacks from racial slavery and provide them with the substantive rights of American citizenship. The specificity of the Fourteenth Amendment was revealed in its exclusion from citizenship of Indians born in the United States but not taxed. The Fifteenth Amendment was explicitly targeted at blacks in ways that had unfortunate consequences, for the vote was later denied to blacks through the discriminatory application of seemingly nonracial qualifications. Yet the implicit or explicit focus on the citizenship rights of blacks in particular in the Reconstruction amendments— and, more importantly, the enforcement clauses that went with them—gave to Congress the power to pass legislation that goes beyond enunciating a general egalitarianism and addresses specific and practical obstacles to the attainment of equal rights for African Americans. In contrast to the Civil Rights Act of 1964, which extended its umbrella beyond African Americans to women and other minorities, the Voting Rights Act of 1965 and its reinforcement by subsequent legislation were more group-specific, and clearly sanctioned the recognition of racial demography and the history of black exclusion from the suffrage in determining whether the voting arrangements of states and localities gave substantive political equality to African Americans.[11]

Affirmative action, like careful scrutiny of electoral districts and procedures, is a way of taking account of race in order to combat racial discrimination and disadvantage. Two leading civil rights enforcers of the Kennedy-Johnson era, Attorney General Nicholas Katzenbach and Assistant Attorney General Burke Marshall, argued eloquently in the *New York Times Magazine* in February 1998 that affirmative action is well within the bounds of the Constitution. Here is their response to the argument that special consideration based on race violates the Fourteenth Amendment by discriminating against whites: "For racial bias to be a problem, it must be accompanied by power. Affirmative action programs are race-based not to show preference of one race over another but to resolve that problem."[12] In other words, one does not discriminate against an empowered majority when one gives a leg up to members of minority groups who have long been denied access to a fair share of power and opportunity. It is difficult to resist the conclusion that the current epidemic of constitutional color-blindness in the United States provides camouflage for an insidious new racism that, if unchecked, will thwart further progress toward racial equality.

Unlike the United States and South Africa, Brazil does not have a history of segregation laws or officially mandated discriminatory practices. It is also evident that color lines have been less rigid, as reflected in a more tolerant attitude toward miscegenation and a greater fluidity of racial identity. Mulattos have been viewed as part white, rather than as simply black, and there has been the possibility of changing one's color classification and rising in the chromatic hierarchy—as crudely reflected in the claim that "money whitens." Hence wealth and education have turned some blacks (*pretos*) into browns (*pardos*) and some light browns (*morenos*) into whites (*blancos*).[13]

Yet there is another side to the Afro-Brazilian story that brings out the positive aspects of what happened to African Americans after emancipation. The abolition of slavery in Brazil in 1888 left the mass of ex-slaves without the kind of constitutional rights and protections authorized (if not made immune from judicial nullification) by the Reconstruction amendments in the United States. There was no legalized segregation, but there was also no Freedmen's Bureau and no effort to secure access to suffrage. A simple literacy requirement prevented most Afro-Brazilians from voting for several generations after emancipation. Recent studies show clearly that black and brown Brazilians have been, and remain to this day, severely disadvantaged relative to their white fellow citizens—in income, living conditions, educational attainment, access to employment, and political power.[14]

One especially telling indication of the denial of equal opportunity is the incredible disparity between the proportion of the total population that is of acknowledged African descent—about 45 percent—and their minuscule representation among university students—only 1 percent at the University of São Paulo, for example. Brazilian sociologists have calculated that whites have an 8.5 times better chance than blacks of ever becoming university students, and a 5.0 times better chance than browns. This compares with the 1.4 times advantage of Euro-Americans over African Americans.[15] One reason Brazil may seem less racially stratified than the United States or South Africa is that poverty is more obviously multiracial. According to the 1980 census, 91.6 percent of Afro-Brazilians were at or below the poverty line, but no less than 41 percent of those deemed poor on the basis of their earnings were classified as white.[16] Economic inequality and race do correlate strongly, but in Brazil it is more difficult than in South Africa or the United States to distinguish the effects of deliberate racial discrimination and oppression from the disparities produced by a dominant class's normal inclination to neglect the welfare of the poor and disfranchised, whatever color they happen to be.

The history of racial ideologies in Brazil is more variable and complicated than most observers have realized. As Thomas Skidmore has shown, scientific racism had a vogue in Brazil in the late nineteenth and early twentieth centuries that was reflected in immigration policies designed to attract Europeans and thus "whiten" the country.[17] The recently emancipated Afro-Brazilians were regarded as a superfluous and expendable population. Limitation of suffrage to the literate and a lack of provision for the education of the freed people made Afro-Brazilians as politically voiceless (and thus as weakly positioned to influence the distribution of public resources) as blacks in South Africa before 1994 or southern African Americans before 1965. The eugenics movement, with its advocacy of public policies aimed at "race improvement," spread to Brazil, but the sheer size of the black and brown population there encouraged deviation from the Anglo-American preference for "pure" races. Most Brazilian eugenists eventually concluded that a mixed race was more adaptable to the climate and conditions of their country than was a purely white one.[18]

Brazilian conceptions of race relations changed in the period between the 1920s and the 1940s, as European immigration declined and Afro-Brazilians received symbolic recognition as contributors to a distinctive Brazilian culture that synthesized Portuguese and West African ingredients. In the fertile imaginations of intellectuals like Gilberto Freyre, Brazil contrasted sharply with the United States because of its encouragement of the cultural cross-fertilization and even biological mixing of Europeans and Africans. Thus was born the myth of Brazil as a "racial democracy" free of North American–style prejudice and discrimination. Yet the literary and artistic celebration of black and brown Brazil did not lead to political and economic empowerment. For the most part, Brazilians of distinguishable African ancestry remained impoverished, illiterate, and powerless.[19]

The post–World War II period brought these inequalities to the surface and exposed them to the light of day. Yet the sociological research of Florestan Fernandes and others in the 1950s and 1960s blamed Afro-Brazilian disadvantage almost exclusively on the legacy of slavery and the normal tendency of capitalism to grind down the poor. The possibility that the racial prejudices and discriminatory practices of contemporary white Brazilians played a substantial role was not seriously entertained.[20] It was not until the 1980s and 1990s that the myth of Brazil as a "racial democracy"—in spirit and intention, if not in results—was seriously challenged. Social scientists and historians demonstrated that racial prejudice was alive and well in Brazil and was directed as much, or almost as much, at mulattos (*pardos*) as at blacks (*pretos*). They also found that patterns of economic and social discrimination were pervasive and effective, although they differed in character and intensity by region, with São Paulo showing more resemblance to North America's hierarchical biracialism than did Salvador, for example. The weight of the evidence makes it clear that the characterization of Brazil as a "racial democracy" is a myth that obscures the fact that substantial inequalities correlated with race persist and that Afro-Brazilians remain second-class citizens, from the perspective of economic, social, and political power, if not in the eyes of the law.[21] That Brazil has a race problem has been difficult for elites to acknowledge, but they have done so to the extent of enacting antidiscrimination legislation. Enforcement has been feeble, however, and affirmative action remains unthinkable because of the entrenched belief that North American– or South African–style white supremacy, the legacies of which may justify policies, has never existed—and could never exist—in Brazil.

In the United States the claim that prejudice and discrimination are no longer serious obstacles to African-American opportunity and equality is called by its critics "the new racism," or "color-blind racism." In Brazil the continued affirmation that Brazil has a deeply rooted "racial democracy" might be described as the same old racism that has long obscured the realities of racial privilege and subordination. What is new is a growing realization, at least among social scientists and intellectuals, that such terms as "racism" and "white supremacy" might be applicable after all.

What is called "nonracialism" in South Africa is abstractly similar to America's color-blind constitutionalism and Brazil's ideal of racial democracy. Yet there is a critical difference in the origins and function of the African National Congress's conception of a nonracist state and the conceptual analogues in the United States and Brazil. Whites in South Africa never claimed, as it would have been patently absurd to do so, that the constitution that was in effect between 1910 and 1993 was color-blind. This constitution specifically denied non-Europeans the right to sit in parliament and countenanced their exclusion from the voting rolls in three of the four provinces of the Union. The doctrine of apartheid, as elaborated after the coming of the Afrikaner Nationalists to power in 1948, ruled out any prospect of interracial democracy by closing loopholes allowing a relatively small fraction of the nonwhite population to take part in the political process. The relegation of black politics to the dependent Homelands or Bantustans reflected a belief that representative government could succeed only in polities that were ethnically and racially homogeneous. If there is a sense in which South Africa before the 1990s was a democracy, it was, like the American South under slavery and segregation, a "Herrenvolk democracy"—a form of government in which one racial or ethnic group endows its own members with full citizenship and the right to political participation while denying these to the subordinated "Others," whether conquered indigenes or former slaves, who are treated like rightless aliens in the land of their birth.[22]

"Nonracialism" in South Africa was a revolutionary slogan of the oppressed. It was asserted by blacks in their long struggle against a blatantly discriminatory form of minority rule that presented itself as opening the way to ethnic or national self-fulfillment for all segments of the South African population. It is important to recognize that apartheid was more often rationalized in terms of cultural essentialism (*volkgeists*) than in the idiom of biological determinism or genetics. The biblical literalism of Afrikaner Calvinism limited the impact of eugenics and the kind of racialized Darwinism that served white supremacists well in the United States and even, for a time, in Brazil. An adherence to its own conception of cultural diversity and group self-determination was central to the propaganda of apartheid, which helps to explain why American multiculturalism has not traveled very well to South Africa.[23]

In South Africa, therefore, nonracialism became the banner of the oppressed rather than a myth to conceal the persistence of inequality, as it has long been in Brazil and has recently become in the United States. The belief affirmed in the ANC's Freedom Charter of 1955 that "South Africa belongs to all who live in it, white and black" has been controversial. After all, South Africa might well be considered a land that the whites stole from the blacks. Nonracialism, which meant that equal rights and full recognition of South African national identity should be accorded to all the groups separated under apartheid—Africans, "Coloreds," Indians, and whites—was challenged by Africanists in the 1950s on the grounds that an ANC-sponsored alliance of group-specific antiapartheid organizations gave disproportionate influence to whites and Indians.[24]

The rival Pan Africanist Congress, formed in 1959, demanded priority for black African culture, identity, and claims to the soil, but the PAC's black nationalist definition of the cause did not prevail. In the 1970s, the Black Consciousness movement mounted a similar but somewhat more inclusive challenge to the ANC's nonracialist ideology. Indians and Coloreds were invited to affirm their "blackness" and join the struggle, but whites, even the most radical and antiracist among them, were excluded. Nevertheless, when resistance culminated in the domestic upheavals and international pressures of the 1980s, it was the United Democratic Front, which endorsed the Freedom Charter and served as the domestic surrogate for the banned ANC, that stood in the forefront, relegating Black Consciousness groups like the Azanian People's Organization (AZAPO) and the National Forum to the margins of the struggle.[25] When Nelson Mandela emerged from twenty-seven years of captivity in 1990 to lead South Africa to liberation, he did so with an undiminished commitment to the nonracialism that he had espoused in the 1950s and early 1960s. As he told the U.S. Congress a few months after his release from prison, his aim was to transform "this complex South African society, which has known nothing but racism for three centuries ... into an oasis of good race relations, where the black shall to the white be sister and brother, a fellow South African, an equal human being—both citizens of the world."[26]

The durability and success of the ideology of nonracialism were due to a number of factors. One was the direct antithesis it offered to the philosophy of apartheid and the appeal that it had for believers in universalist ideals of human rights and human solidarity, both within South Africa and throughout the world. Christianity and Marxism, the most influential belief systems of the educated African elite that led the struggle against apartheid, both affirmed a nonracialist ideal. Furthermore, significant ethnic divisions among Africans, as well as between Africans and the Colored and Indian minorities, made identity politics among the oppressed a luxury that the movement could ill afford, even if it failed to weaken the oppressors by garnering significant white support. Yet imported Western ideologies and the strategic requirements of the struggle may not be the whole story behind the triumph of nonracialism. Historian Shula Marks has called attention to the probable influence of indigenous African cultures, with their tendency to favor exogamy over endogamy and their openness to the assimilation of ethnic strangers into their tribal communities. Such cultural traditions, she argues, may have predisposed Africans to accept what she calls "non-racism."[27]

What is the future of nonracialism in South Africa? Will it go down in history as an effective slogan for the overthrow of apartheid that proved unworkable in a more pluralistic and democratic setting? Nonracialism has proved difficult to implement consistently for two quite distinct reasons. First and most obvious is the sheer fact of ethnic and racial diversity in a country that has as great a variety of colors and cultures as any in the world. Cultural diversity is well reflected in the fact that South Africa now has eleven official languages. Denying the existence of multiculturalism in the name of a common South African identity will not make ethnic particularism or ethnic politics go away. The ANC-dominated government elected in 1994 and reelected in 1999 has had to make some pragmatic concessions to the subnationalism of Zulus and Afrikaners. A growing emphasis on distinctive Indian and Colored identities and interests, as might well have been expected from insecure minorities that are unlikely to disappear in the foreseeable future, may also require some accommodation on the part of the African majority. The Constitution and Bill of Rights protect individuals in their adherence to particular cultural traditions and practices. Will this be enough, or will rights have to be accorded to groups as well as individuals? In fact, Kwazulu still represents a kind of nation within the nation, the quasi-autonomous preserve of Gatsha Buthelezi and the Inkatha Party. Formal group representation under some form of ethnic federalism is out of the question because of the resemblance any such policy would have to efforts made by the white minority government in the 1980s to reform apartheid without abolishing it. The politicization of ethnicity is obviously a great potential threat to the unity of the new South Africa, but what North American multiculturalists call a "politics of recognition" is unavoidable, and the question of how to make it compatible with national cohesion and domestic tranquility is one of the greatest challenges that South Africa faces.

A second problematic aspect of nonracialism stems from an interpretation of it that inhibits efforts to challenge the economic and social position of the relatively affluent and well-situated white minority. The transition from white minority rule to black majority power in the early 1990s was accomplished relatively peacefully because the whites understood nonracialism to mean that they would not be divested of their property, economic leverage, or social amenities. Even the predominantly white civil service was granted tenure. As a result, no real revolution has occurred except in the realm of racial or ethnic status. South Africans of European origin still hold the lion's share of the country's wealth, natural resources, educational advantages, and career opportunities, while the mass of Africans remain impoverished and lacking in opportunities that most whites take for granted. Rectifying the legacy of apartheid would seem to call for a substantial redistribution of wealth and privilege, or at the very least some kind of affirmative action program. After years of seeking to influence corporate hiring policies by informal pressure (especially by favoring in the awarding of contracts firms that were black-owned or that practiced affirmative action), the government enacted an Employment Equities Act in 1998, prescribing American-style affirmative action for all firms with fifty or more employees. Quite predictably, many whites have protested that the government has violated its own professed principle of "nonracialism." Leading the charge are the white liberals in the Democratic Party, which, because of its successes in the recent election, has become the official opposition. White anger against affirmative action inspires antiwhite feeling among blacks, who are likely to feel that whites have gotten off much too easily as it is.[28]

Nonracialism, if interpreted as the denial of special consideration under the law or in public policy for any racially defined group, renders impossible the redistribution of wealth and opportunity that justice for black South Africans would seem to require. The problem with a literal-minded application of nonracialism, as with color-blind constitutionalism and the myth of racial democracy, is (in the words of Justice Blackmun) that it is likely to "perpetuate racial supremacy." It precludes official discrimination in the present but does not compensate adequately for the toll that three centuries or more of race-based oppression have taken on its surviving victims.

In my opinion, substantive racial equality in the United States, Brazil, and South Africa can be achieved only if a combination of strong affirmative action policies and antipoverty measures creates a much more equitable distribution of wealth and opportunity. South Africa and Brazil lead the world in the maldistribution of wealth, while the United States outranks other Western industrial nations in its degree of economic inequality. Although affirmative action is necessary to make the dominant institutions and enterprises of these societies reflect the diversity of their populations, social democratic or class-based reforms are needed to reduce significantly the gaps between the "haves," who are predominantly white, and the "have nots," who are disproportionately black and brown. Yet, whether such a tilt to the left in individual nations is possible in today's world economy—dominated as it is by multinational corporations and their agents in the World Bank and the International Monetary Fund—is a sobering question. Hope is always more efficacious than despair, but optimism would be unwarranted. It is consoling to remember, however, that past struggles for racial justice have achieved much against great odds. Martin Luther King, Jr. and Nelson Mandela never succumbed to discouragement, even in the face of what others thought were insuperable obstacles. We should follow their example.

CHAPTER 14

Diverse Republics: French and American Responses to Racial Pluralism

At first glance, a comparison of French and American responses to ethnic and racial diversity may seem arbitrary and unproductive. One response emerges from an old European country with more than a thousand years of continuous existence, the other from a country formed by European settlement and then constituted as a nation scarcely two centuries ago. To avoid turning a historical comparison between France and the United States into a mere set of contrasts, it will be useful to begin with four salient similarities.

First and most obviously, both France and the United States revolted against kingly rule to establish republics in the late eighteenth century.[1] In the process, they became the world's first nation-states of substantial size based on popular sovereignty and government by consent. By abolishing or prohibiting nobility as well as monarchy, they created a presumption of legal and political equality for all citizens. The Declaration of Independence and the *Declaration des droits de l'homme et du citoyen* set forth the principle that merely being human entitles individuals to basic natural rights. The kind of nationalism that developed to defend this radical political project is usually categorized as "civic" or "territorial," as opposed to the "ethnic" or "organic" type that developed in nineteenth-century Europe, especially in Germany.[2] The civic type meant that, in theory at least, one belonged to the nation simply by being there; by contrast, membership according to the ethnic type required the right ancestry.

As Anthony D. Smith has pointed out, all nations—including France and the United States—have combined "ethnic solidarity" and "political citizenship," albeit in differing proportions.[3] Still, whatever ethnoracial identities were implicitly or explicitly privileged in the two societies, the theory promulgated to justify the revolutions was a universalistic conception of citizenship as one embodiment of human rights. At the same time, citizenship in both France and the United States was also a bounded concept. The resulting need to establish qualifications for full membership in the nation-state enabled both societies to limit civil rights according to particularistic standards involving age, gender, place of birth, and (sometimes) parentage or racial ancestry.

A second common feature—in sharp contrast with the shared commitment, however abstract, to universal human rights—was the involvement of both France and the United States in the enslavement of Africans on the plantations of the Caribbean and the American South.

In the period just before the revolutions of the 1790s in France and Haiti, plantation slavery and the transatlantic trade associated with it constituted the most profitable and dynamic sector of the French economy. After the loss of Haiti, it declined in significance, but the planters of Martinique, Guadeloupe, and Bourbon (La Réunion) were able to resist significant reform until the revolution of 1848 unexpectedly put opponents of slavery into power.

North American slavery appeared to be in economic trouble at the time of the American Revolution because of the collapse of the tobacco market upon which the profitability of slavery in the Chesapeake region depended. But the relatively prosperous growers of rice and long-staple cotton in South Carolina and Georgia would not have joined the Union had their interests been unacknowledged and unprotected. Subsequently, the rise in the production of short-staple cotton in the expanding deep South of the early nineteenth century made the planter class so affluent and politically powerful that it took a bloody civil war to bring about the abolition of slavery. The long association of black people with a form of servitude never imposed on whites would encourage the belief in both countries that blacks were servile by nature and therefore incapable of being the self-governing citizens of a republic. One result of this belief was the long-lasting conflict in both societies between the universalism of the republican ideology and popular opinion about the natural incapacity of blacks.

A third common element is immigration. Unlike other European nations, France has been a country of immigration rather than emigration, and has at times resembled the United States in the proportion of its population recruited from foreign countries.

An estimated one-third of the current French population is of second-, third-, or fourth-generation foreign ancestry. (The U.S. proportion is quite similar.) Because of low birthrates and the extent to which the peasantry remained rooted to the soil, France in the late nineteenth and early twentieth centuries had to recruit much of the labor for its industrial revolution from other countries. As with American immigration of the same period, the principal sources were Southern and Eastern Europe, especially Italy and Poland.

The time of greatest influx was not exactly the same, however. American immigration from Europe peaked between 1900 and 1910, whereas the high point for France was the 1920s. The French manpower losses in World War I created an acute labor shortage, and America's new policy of immigration restriction made France a more feasible destination than the United States for work-seeking Poles and Italians.[4] In the period since the 1960s, both countries have seen new waves of immigration (mostly from non-European countries), and both have engaged in similar debates on how best to integrate the recent arrivals. Meanwhile, hostility to immigrants has been a recurring phenomenon in both countries. This hostility has in large part been the result of nativism, an attitude usually based more on cultural intolerance than on biological racism.[5]

The fourth salient element shared by France and the United States is a history of expansionism involving the conquest, subjugation, and (in some instances) assimilation of other peoples. The last stage of this expansionism was the establishment of overseas colonies that eventually became independent.

The creation of modern France through expansion goes back to the establishment of a small kingdom in the area around Paris in the late tenth century. The existing hexagon that took shape was the result of a long series of wars and conquests involving the triumph of French language and culture over what were once autonomous and culturally distinctive communities.[6] The assimilation of Gascons, Savoyards, Occitans, Basques, and others helped to sustain the myth that French overseas expansionism in the nineteenth century, especially to North and West Africa, was a continuation of the same project. But a variety of circumstances, including the cultural and racial prejudices of the colonizers, impeded the transformation of Arabs and Africans into Frenchmen and put these groups on the path to national independence.

American expansionism before the end of the nineteenth century took the form of a westward movement that, despite some rhetorical gestures in the direction of assimilation, displaced rather than incorporated the indigenous Indian populations. The Spanish-speaking inhabitants of the territories wrested by force from Mexico in the 1840s were granted citizenship under the treaty that ended the Mexican-American War, but were excluded from effective power even in the areas where they predominated. With the acquisition of Puerto Rico and the Philippines after the Spanish-American War, the United States acquired its first overseas colonies, thus following the example of France and other European powers. As in the case of France, a prior history of conquering contiguous territories to enlarge the national domain influenced the character and ideology of the new imperialism.

Having established the broad commonalities on which a comparison can be based, we will now look for the differences that appear when we move from the general themes to their specific applications. Both nations have proclaimed themselves to be republics, but their conceptions of republicanism have differed significantly.

From the tradition of absolute monarchy the French revolutionaries inherited the concept of a centralized unitary state, with the critical difference that it should now reflect the general will as manifested in an elective national assembly rather than the particular will of the ruler. The belief that there should be no intermediaries between the individual and the sovereign state was basic to French revolutionary thought.

The American republic, on the other hand, began as the cooperative struggle of thirteen British colonies, each with a distinctive history and relationship to the Crown, for independence from the mother country. During and immediately after the Revolutionary War, the states, as they were now called, functioned as a loose confederation. Although the Constitution of 1787 established a stronger central authority, it divided sovereignty between the federal government and the states in a manner that made no more sense to the French than French centralization and *étatism* made to the Americans.

John Adams found Turgot's classic dictum that "all power should be one, namely that of [a single] nation" to be "as mysterious as the Athanasian creed."[7] In the American republican ideology, a strong central state was viewed as a threat to liberty because it could fall into the hands of corrupt or power-hungry men. For French revolutionaries, who were seeking to destroy strong pre-existing hierarchies based on birth and to obliterate the remnants of feudalism, the prime objective was the guarantee of individual equality that could only be provided by a powerful state acting uniformly on all citizens. Although liberty and equality were affirmed in both revolutions, the priority was given to the former in the American case and to the latter in the French.[8] A second difference that was there from the beginning and that has persisted to the present day was the role that religion was expected to play in the public life of the nation. The French Revolution was animated by a fierce anticlericalism directed at the association of the Catholic Church with the *ancien régime*. The revolution bequeathed to future republicans the principle of *laïcité*, which forbids the display of religious identities and symbols in what is considered public space. This tradition of official secularism can be understood in part as a defensive reaction to the Catholic Church's long-standing opposition to the republic and its support for a monarchical restoration—dispositions that lasted well into the twentieth century. That a powerful, centralized, and internationally supported religious body could retain the adherence of a French majority and still be at odds with the political principles of French republicanism created a contentious situation with no American analogue.

The American separation of church and state developed in the context of a basically Protestant religious pluralism. Since no single denomination could claim national predominance, and movements for disestablishment and religious tolerance were developing in several states, it is not surprising that the Founding Fathers of 1787 decreed a separation of church and state that implied no hostility to religion. Consequently, expressions of a generalized, nondenominational theism (originally Protestant in inspiration but later broadened to cover the beliefs of Catholics and Jews) have a place in public discourse and patriotic ritual in the United States that they clearly do not have in France.

Paradoxically, however, a need to come to terms with the power and popularity of the Catholic Church has forced French republican regimes to associate with the church in ways that would violate American conceptions of church-state separation. Between the creation of the officially secular Third Republic in 1870 and the disestablishment of religion in 1905, the Third Republic paid the salaries of Catholic priests and held title to church property. Religious neutrality was maintained by also paying the salaries of Protestant ministers and rabbis. Even after the formal separation of church and state in 1905, the government continued to hold title to previously existing religious structures and was responsible for their physical maintenance. Currently, the French state provides direct aid to religious schools on a contractual basis, and official, government-subsidized bodies negotiate with the state on behalf of religious communities.[9] Last year, Muslims gained the right to elect a council empowered to make representations to the state, a privilege previously granted only to Catholics, Protestants, and Jews.[10]

America's tradition of religious tolerance and pluralism has for the most part precluded direct government support of particular denominations or churches (except in the form of tax exemptions), while French laïcité has found a place for the official recognition and empowerment of religious communities, which the French state regards as corporate entities over which it must exercise a measure of control. A full analysis of this surprising anomaly is beyond the scope of this essay, but it needs to be borne in mind whenever claims are made that cultural pluralism or diversity is institutionalized in the United States but not in France. In the realm of religion, the reverse would actually seem to be the case. If American law and public policy recognize ethnoracial identities for some purposes, France makes an analogous accommodation in the realm of religion.

Comparison of the two forms of republicanism is of course complicated by the fact that there have been five republics in France and, in a formal sense at least, only one in the United States. France did not become permanently committed to democratic forms of republicanism until the establishment of the Third Republic in the late nineteenth century. The American Revolution, on the other hand, created a durable national consensus behind republican principles. The basic structure established by the Constitution of 1787 remains in effect to this day, although an argument could be made that the North's victory in the Civil War and the resulting Reconstruction-era amendments to the Constitution ushered in a *de facto* second republic.

What needs emphasis here is that the French Revolution was a much more internally divisive event than the American. It produced two nations— revolutionary, republican France with its commitment to the rights of man, and traditional, Catholic France with its lingering dedication to the institutions and values of the *ancien régime*. The latter allegiance, although only a minority persuasion, came to the surface spectacularly in the hysteria surrounding the Dreyfus Affair at the turn of the century and in the rhetoric and policies of the Vichy government during World War II. Anti-Semitism and nativism were among its hallmarks, and its legacy can be found today in the anti-immigrant agitation of Jean-Marie Le Pen and the *Front National*.[11]

If the precarious and episodic character of French republicanism stemmed from the Revolution's failure to eradicate the conservatism of the old order, the American experiment faced its greatest threat when the division of sovereignty between the states and the federal government became of crucial importance in the contest for national power between slave and free states in the period 1846–1861. The resulting civil war was far bloodier than the revolutionary upheavals that occurred in France in 1830, 1848, and 1871. The Union victory in the war ended claims of state sovereignty, but the retention of federalism and some states' rights left the postbellum United States far less centralized than the Third Republic. One consequence was that the citizenship rights for African Americans proclaimed in the Fourteenth and Fifteenth Amendments could not be effectively enforced in the southern states after white supremacists regained control there in the 1870s.

The issue upon which the Union broke apart—the future of black slavery—was also an issue in France, both during the Revolution and in the 1830s and 1840s. But the relation of slavery to the dominant political and social values clearly loomed larger in the United States; for the French, slavery before the Revolution had been mostly confined to distant Caribbean colonies. As Sue Peabody has shown, there were concerted efforts throughout the eighteenth century to prevent the growth of slavery and of the black population in metropolitan France.[12] Under a 1777 law, for example, West Indian planters visiting the metropole could be attended by their slaves during the voyage but then had to deposit them in special detention centers in the port cities, from which they would be sent back on the next available ship.[13] It is hard to determine how much of this exclusionary policy was based on the belief that slavery as an institution was contrary to French values, and how much of it was based on the prejudicial desire to ensure that France remained virtually all white. But the result in any case was to prevent both slavery and a black presence from developing in metropolitan France. As Robin Blackburn has suggested for both France and England, the confinement of slavery and of most blacks to distant colonies

may have put limits on the growth of "popular racism."[14] Certainly there
was less fertile ground in France than in the United States for the development of such racism.

Before the American Revolution, slavery had been established everywhere
in the North American colonies; afterward it was phased out in the northern
states, although cities like New York and Philadelphia retained substantial
black populations. The Constitution negotiated the slavery issue by making
provision for the future abolition of the international slave trade, but also
rendering it virtually impossible for the federal government to take action
against slavery where it was authorized under state law. As previously suggested, such a compromise was necessary to appease the planter-dominated
states of the deep South.

Meanwhile, the French National Assembly, where West Indian planters
were virtually unrepresented, voted to abolish slavery in 1794, the first time
any nation had taken such action. Historians debate the extent to which this
decision was motivated by principled adherence to the rights of man, as opposed to pragmatic calculations arising from the Haitian revolution and the
competition with the British for control of the Caribbean. But clearly there
was a more efficacious sense of the incompatibility of republican values and
chattel slavery in the Paris of 1794 than in the Philadelphia of 1787. French
revolutionary emancipation was short-lived, however, except in Haiti. In
1803, at a time when gradual emancipation was proceeding in the American North, Napoleon reinstated slavery in France's remaining plantation
colonies. By the 1830s and 1840s, antislavery movements had developed in
both metropolitan France and the northern United States.

The French movement, which scrupulously avoided mass meetings and
popular agitation, was much more cautious and elitist than the American
one. It succeeded in 1848 only because of a special opportunity created by
the revolution of that year.[15] American abolitionism, like that of Britain,
appealed to the moral and religious sentiments aroused by an evangelical
revival that scarcely touched France, a country where Protestants were a
small minority. But the American antislavery movement, unlike the British
one, aroused massive internal opposition. Until 1860, the slaveholding South
was able to dominate the national political arena and thwart antislavery
reform and action against the expansion of slavery. Consequently, it took a
sectional civil war to bring about a reform that occurred much more easily
in mid-nineteenth-century France, where the institution under attack had
come to be viewed as a marginal and mainly colonial interest.

Black slavery left significantly different legacies in the two countries
because the cultural and social weight of slavery as an institution was so
much greater in one case than in the other. Post-1848 France did not have
a domestic color line for the simple reason that no significant black population had been allowed to develop there. That France had ever been seriously

implicated in African slavery was virtually wiped from the national memory. The history texts used in French schools before the 1980s condemned slavery in general but contained no acknowledgment whatever that French slave colonies had ever existed or that slavery had been abolished, reinstituted, and then abolished again.[16]

In the United States, on the other hand, slavery left behind a domestic heritage of racial division and inequality that has remained a central feature of the national experience. African Americans have remembered slavery as the brutal oppression of their ancestors and as a source of their enduring stigmatization. Many whites, consciously or subconsciously, have used the memory of blacks as slaves and whites as masters to buttress their sense of priority and supremacy over a race stereotyped as inherently servile. Emancipation did not destroy a status order based on pigmentation and ancestry. Indeed, the color line was most clearly and fully articulated in the Jim Crow system that developed in the South in the late nineteenth and early twentieth centuries. Reformist efforts to make the relationship between blacks and whites more egalitarian or competitive (such as those made by Reconstruction-era radicals and the interracial progressives who formed the NAACP in 1910) kept hopes for racial justice alive but also intensified the reactive racism of many whites. The French were not color-blind, but their sense of identity was far less dependent on whiteness than was that of many Euro-Americans. "Otherness" for them would be construed somewhat differently.

As we have seen, both the United States and France were immigrant-receiving societies that required massive importation of foreign labor for industrialization in the late nineteenth and early twentieth centuries. But they did not manage immigration in the same way. Immigration to the United States was primarily an individual matter, especially after the 1885 ban on the importation of contract labor. Before the 1920s, the most salient restriction on the admission of foreigners to American shores was the exclusion of most Asians, beginning with Chinese laborers in 1882. Most French immigration in the period 1900–1930 involved groups of workers whose recruitment was coordinated through state cooperation with labor-hungry industries, and whose terms of employment were negotiated with the countries of origin.[17]

For European immigrants to America, citizenship through naturalization was relatively easy to secure, but this right was denied to Asians until the mid-twentieth century. France made naturalization much more difficult for everyone by establishing stringent cultural and linguistic requirements. In 1930, 55 percent of the foreign-born in the United States had become citizens, as compared to only 11 percent in France.[18] Under the American system of *jus soli*, all American-born children of immigrants are automatically citizens. In France there has been an elaborate set of compromises between *jus soli* and *jus sanguinis* (descent-based citizenship). Under *double jus soli*, the system that has prevailed from 1889 to the present, birthright citizenship is granted only to the children of foreigners who were themselves born in France. Until recently, French-born children of immigrants could become citizens only through a process of naturalization when they reached maturity. Although the full naturalization process is no longer required, children of the second generation do not officially become citizens until they have reached maturity and met a residence requirement.

Bars to immigration and naturalization in the United States have tended to be based on ethnoracial categorizations, going back all the way to the first law governing the naturalization of immigrants, passed in 1790, which limited the right to "free white person[s]." The establishment of quotas for European nationalities in 1924 responded not only to cultural nativism, but also to the belief that old-stock Nordic or Anglo-Saxon Americans were innately superior to the new immigrants from Southern and Eastern Europe. In France an immigrant's right of entry has been based primarily on the needs of the economy, and his or her access to citizenship has been more dependent on perceptions of cultural difference or distance than on the kind of broad racial categories that were traditionally applied in the American case.

The relation of immigration to national identity has played itself out quite differently in the two contexts. Inhabitants of a country populated mainly by settlers and immigrants (voluntary or involuntary), Americans have often viewed some form of immigration as central to the meaning of the national experience. As citizens of an old nation with a long past that predated substantial immigration by several centuries, the French have tended to see newcomers simply as candidates for assimilation into the existing cultural crucible. Although the subject has not been extensively investigated, it appears that the immigration to France from other parts of Europe that occurred between the 1880s and the 1930s did not inspire the kind of fervent assimilationism that has developed more recently. It was simply taken for granted that foreigners who desired citizenship would become culturally French. And to a considerable extent they did.

Two factors promoted rapid cultural assimilation, particularly of the second generation. One was a uniform, centralized, and compulsory educational system that effectively inculcated French language and culture. The other was the strength of class consciousness. Most immigrants were laborers. Foreigners brought in to work in mines and factories were sometimes objects of intense hostility from French workers who saw them as competition, especially during periods of high unemployment. But when these immigrants or their offspring gained citizenship rights, they were likely to be integrated into the institutions and subculture of the French working class, and subsequently they often substituted a class-based identity and ideology (socialism or communism) for one based on national origins. Those of the second generation who had middle-class origins or did particularly well in school could benefit from the meritocratic quality of French higher education and public bureaucracies.

In the late nineteenth and early twentieth centuries, individual Jews may have had readier access to French elites than Jewish immigrants and their children had to the equivalent inner circles in the United States. But in France they also encountered more public anti-Semitism and found that the price of success was often the self-suppression of their ethnoreligious identity. A delegate to the National Assembly during the Revolution expressed an enduring French republican attitude toward Jews (and toward ethnicity in general): "To the Jews as a nation, one must refuse everything; but to Jews as men, one must grant everything . . . , there cannot be a nation within the nation."[19]

American schools, like those of France, played a major role in acculturating immigrants. But the decentralized American educational system also allowed for local control, which meant that in areas where one ethnic group predominated, public education often included instruction in a foreign language. World War I brought an end to this form of multiculturalism, which included German-medium schools in the Midwest.

More powerful and lasting as sustainers of the ethnic identities of Americans of recent immigrant background were the comparatively nonpolitical character of the American labor movement and the pervasive national belief in upward social mobility. Politics, especially local urban politics, did not normally revolve around class interests and ideologies, but around a struggle for ethnic influence in the allocation of public jobs and resources, as between the Irish and the old-stock Americans in many cities in the late nineteenth century. Whereas French centralization and class-based politics left little scope for mobilizing around ethnic identities, American localism and interest-group politics provided fertile ground for this kind of pluralism.

In the job market and other areas of American life, immigrants often benefited from being able to claim a white identity. Doing so put them on the right side of the great ethnoracial cleavage in American society, providing economic opportunities unavailable to blacks and simultaneously bolstering their self-esteem and sense of belonging. It also acted as a further inhibition to class consciousness.

The French, lacking a domestic color line, defined otherness primarily in terms of nationality. The major distinction was, and continues to be, between foreigners and French citizens of whatever ancestry. The question of the moment is whether some foreigners are more likely than others to become French. Before World War II, most immigrants to France came from other European nations, and their descendants are now regarded as thoroughly French. But the recent immigration from outside of Europe and especially from North and West Africa has raised serious questions about the current and future viability of the assimilationist model. Many Algerians have gained French citizenship by virtue of having been born in Algeria when it was still considered part of France. But in this case, recognition of citizenship has not led to assimilation.

Understanding the situation of Algerians and other North African Muslims in contemporary France requires attention to our last comparative theme: the growth of the national domain and the establishment of new settlements and colonies. As we have seen, both the United States and France had a history of geographical expansionism even before they acquired overseas colonies. The creation of the French hexagon by conquests and annexations established an ideological precedent for the "civilizing mission" that served as a rationale for French colonialism. A long history of turning peasants and culturally exogenous provincials into Frenchmen seemed to raise the possibility that the same could be done for colonized peoples in Africa and Asia. The universalism of the Revolution and the republican tradition could provide a blueprint for liberating and civilizing the world. The sense of mission that accompanied American expansionism also invoked universalist principles. Westward expansionism under the banner of Manifest Destiny was meant to extend "the area of freedom," and the acquisition of the Philippines in 1899 was proclaimed as an opportunity to bring civilization to what William Howard Taft called "our little brown brothers."

But proto-colonialist expansionism in the two cases differed in the degree to which indigenous populations were actually assimilated. Occitans, Savoyards, and Bretons became French to a fuller extent than American Indians, or even the Latino inhabitants of the formerly Mexican Southwest, have become Americans. The greater role of "race" in white American thinking is part of the explanation, but not all of it. The cultural proximity of the peoples involved and the demographics of their relationship also have to be taken into account. Efforts to "civilize" and assimilate American Indians were notably ineffectual (when not hypocritical), partly because of the sheer volume of white settlement in what had been their homeland, and partly because of cultural differences and antagonisms. Not only were whites contemptuous of what they took to be Indian savagery, but many Indians vigorously resisted the demands of missionaries and government agents that they abandon their traditional way of life. By contrast, those groups that were assimilated into France over the centuries were already part of the broader European (and Christian) civilization, and were usually not displaced by settlers from France.

These contrasts are obvious. Less self-evident and more intriguing were the consequences for subsequent colonialism of the earlier histories of expansion into contiguous areas. As in the case of nonwhite immigration, America's melting-pot assimilationism once again ran up against barriers of race and color. Elevating Filipinos and other nonwhites to citizenship was unthinkable at the end of the nineteenth century, both to the proponents of the new colonialism and to those who opposed it. Since these peoples could not become full citizens, they had to be granted independence or a peculiar "commonwealth" status. French colonialism, on the other hand, was compatible, at least in theory and rhetoric, with a color-blind assimilationism.

But theory and rhetoric are not reality, and it would be unrealistic to conclude that the "civilizing mission" of French imperialism was genuinely egalitarian in purpose and effect. The presumption that French republican civilization was the universal norm to which all humanity should aspire can of course be seen as covertly ethnocentric. And quite apart from contemporary doubts about the truth claims of Enlightenment universalism, the assimilationist ideal could not be successfully implemented because of two principal factors. One was racial prejudice. Although generally less susceptible to color-coded racism than white Americans, the French were not immune to it. In 1778, intermarriage between blacks and whites was formally prohibited in metropolitan France. Although the ban was not enforced and disappeared with the Revolution, it was indicative of a residual tendency to stereotype blacks as inferior, buffoonish creatures beyond the pale of respectable society.[20] Attitudes of this kind were most salient and openly avowed, it would seem, among traditionalists who retained serious reservations about republican ideals and values. Some in France believed that imperialist militarism might release the French from the dead weight of bourgeois egalitarianism and individualism.

A second and weightier factor impeding the assimilation of non-Europeans into a greater France was a sense of difference or otherness that was rooted in culture and religion rather than in race as marked and determined by physical characteristics or ancestry. Even those genuinely committed to a universalist civilizing mission had to confront the immediate and practical challenges of ruling colonies with cultures vastly different from that of France. Given the limited manpower and resources available, colonial administration in many places would have been impossible without establishing a dual system of laws and rights. In their North and West African colonies, the French generally made a distinction between the many indigenes who wished to adhere to their traditional way of life and those few who were willing to give up that way in order to become French. In practice this meant that most people were granted a dispensation to follow Islamic or other non-Christian laws and customs (polygamy, for example), but that the rights associated with French citizenship were withheld from them so long as they continued to do so.

The idea that colonized people could exercise citizenship within a greater France was always limited to those who would or could become culturally French, a qualification that paralleled the French concept of immigrant assimilation. When Algeria became a colony of European settlement with its own representative institutions in the late nineteenth century, members of the indigenous Muslim majority were in effect required to give up their religiously based customs and become apostates in order to vote and have full civil rights. (Very few were willing to do so.) If a color bar operated to limit the American civilizing and assimilating mission, a culture bar directed particularly at Islam had a similar effect in some French colonies.

Indicative of the dualistic character of the French response to ethnic *différence* was the open-door inclusiveness of eligibility for membership in French Algeria. Not only were the majority of settlers recruited from Southern European countries other than France itself, but also the resident Jews were granted naturalized French citizenship in 1870. (This decision from the metropole sparked hostile reactions from many of the European settlers and made Algeria a hotbed of anti-Semitism at the time of the Dreyfus Affair.[21]) After 1889, the descendants of non-French European settlers in Algeria could gain citizenship on the basis of the *double jus soli* that applied to the offspring of immigrants to France itself.

A somewhat different pattern prevailed in Senegal, where an original French enclave dating back to the slave trade of the seventeenth century had produced a class of African or mixed-race *assimilés* who were granted French citizenship in 1833, saw these rights suspended in 1851 under the Second Empire, and then had them restored by the Third Republic in 1871.[22] As the colony expanded in the nineteenth century through the conquest of traditional societies, the ideal of assimilation continued to be proclaimed, and a few Africans took advantage of the opportunity to acculturate and gain French citizenship. But most did not and were ruled under a separate set of laws. During the early twentieth century, the ideology of the colonizers vacillated between assimilationism and "associationism," a doctrine that acknowledged cultural pluralism and sanctioned indirect rule through the agency of cooperative chiefs or other traditional authorities.[23]

Appreciating the tangled and ambiguous heritage of French colonialism is essential to an understanding of current French attitudes toward race and ethnicity, even though its influence, like that of the heritage of slavery, is rarely acknowledged. Currently the United States and France would appear to have sharply contrasting conceptions of how to manage ethnoracial diversity. Recognizing the role that race has played in producing group inequalities, the United States in the 1970s and 1980s adopted race-specific policies such as affirmative action and electoral reforms designed to promote greater representation for minorities. After a brief experiment with multiculturalism in the 1980s, France has decisively rejected what it takes to be the American model and has resolutely returned to an assimilationist approach to the diversity created by the new wave of immigration.[24]

In recent years there has been much acerbic French commentary on American multiculturalism and similarly critical American complaints about the French refusal to acknowledge and confront forms of ethnoracial discrimination. Both sides in the debate have failed to give sufficient attention to differences in the two situations as they have developed historically. Group-specific policies in the United States were originally justified as a response to the peculiar disadvantages and castelike status of African Americans. They were later extended to other groups, especially Latinos, on the grounds that they had also suffered historical injustices. The emphasis on cultural diversity as valuable in itself is a fairly recent development.

Elites in the United States are apparently more comfortable with understanding affirmative action as an effort to achieve diversity, loosely defined, rather than as a direct, redistributive attack on the structural inequalities bequeathed by a long history of slavery, segregation, and discrimination. The fact that there is no domestic population group in France with a history of oppression and disadvantage equivalent to that of African Americans must be constantly borne in mind when comparing the two situations. Policies that may seem warranted in one context might be more problematic or difficult to justify in the other.

The differences are subtler when it comes to comparing the responses to recent immigration from outside the developed West. In my view, France has a more serious problem with nativism and xenophobia than does the United States, where antiblack racism continues to affect group relations in a decisive way. In France, North Africans and especially Algerians experience the greatest hostility; blacks of slave ancestry from the French Antilles encounter less prejudice and discrimination. The colonial experience and the immense trauma of the Algerian war help to explain these attitudes. The long-standing view (going back to the early nineteenth century) that Muslims are the ultimate "Other" and therefore difficult if not impossible to assimilate, along with the fallout from the traumatic failure to create an *Algérie Française*, is a major historical source of current prejudice.[25] The alleged incompatibility between a strong Islamic identity and the French concept of *laïcité*—as reflected most dramatically in the headscarf ban of 2004—stimulates current fears about the growth of the Muslim population in France, and legitimates fervent appeals to the heritage of universalistic assimilationism.

Before 9/11 at least, and arguably up to the present, the United States has had less of a problem accommodating immigrants of Islamic faith because of its stronger tradition of religious pluralism and toleration. American concerns about the diversity created by recent immigration have tended to focus on Latinos and especially Mexicans. The sheer size of the influx, and the close ties immigrants maintain with their friends and relatives across the border, have engendered a concern for the survival of Anglo-American culture in some parts of the nation. But the reaction has been muted by a thirst for the low-wage, unskilled labor these immigrants provide, and also by the increasing acceptance of cultural pluralism as a general principle.

It seems to me that the United States and France can learn from each other. French universalism is a powerful weapon against any form of racism that is based on the belief in innate unalterable differences among human groups. A stronger awareness of such human commonality may be needed in the United States at a time when emphasis on diversity and ethnic particularism threatens to deprive us of any compelling vision of the larger national community and to impede cooperation in the pursuit of a free and just society. On the other hand, the identification of such universalism with a particular national identity and with specific cultural traits that go beyond essential human rights can lead to an intolerance of the Other that approaches color-coded racism in its harmful effects.

CHAPTER 15

Mulattoes and *Métis*: Attitudes toward Miscegenation in the United States and France since the Seventeenth Century

The English word "miscegenation" is a loaded term that should not be used without implicit quotation marks. It was coined during the American election of 1864 as the title of a pamphlet purportedly advocating intermarriage between blacks and whites. (The earlier American term for this kind of race mixture was "amalgamation.") The pamphlet appeared to have been issued by the Republican Party but was actually a Democratic ruse designed to embarrass the Republicans. It failed to accomplish its objective because almost no one took seriously the notion that the Republican Party would advocate or even condone miscegenation.[1] The equivalent but less pejorative French term is *métissage*.

Both terms depend on there being a concept of race, meaning that human beings can be classified on the basis of physical appearance and/or ancestry into groups that are thought to differ innately in temperament and capabilities. It is not essential to the concept of race that one group be considered superior to another. But if hierarchy is assumed, we have passed beyond race or racialism per se and into the realm of racism as an ideology that uses a deep sense of difference to justify inequality of treatment.[2] A concept of miscegenation or *métissage* does not necessarily imply racism in this hierarchical sense. It can be, and sometimes has been, viewed as a desirable form of hybridity that improves both of the original stocks or at least one of them. Much more often, however, it is seen as a form of degeneration that weakens the allegedly higher race by polluting its blood and undermining its capabilities. The classic exponent of the idea that race mixture of any kind equaled degeneration was Joseph-Arthur de Gobineau, the mid-nineteenth-century French racial theorist who thought that European *métissage* had already passed the point of no return and that civilization was doomed.[3] His Nazi disciples would make heroic efforts to try to prove him wrong by seeking to isolate and protect an allegedly pure Aryan stock.

There are, schematically speaking, four possible responses to the practice or prospect of miscegenation that can be found in the legal, political, and social history of modern nations that have had a socially salient conception of race.

1. Law, as in apartheid South Africa after 1950 and in Nazi Germany after 1935, prohibits both interracial marriage and extramarital sex between the designated groups in a generally effective way.

2. Marriage between the races is outlawed, but concubinage and casual sex between men of the dominant group and women of the subordinated group are tacitly condoned, despite the existence in some cases of special penalties for interracial fornication. Such laws, if they exist at all, are weakly enforced on men of the dominant group and do not prevent them from sexually exploiting women of the lower racial caste. On the other hand, sex between women of the dominant group and men of the subordinated one is strongly discouraged and likely to be severely punished. This was the pattern in the American South in the nineteenth century, especially during the slave era when black women were at the mercy of their owners and other whites.[4]

3. Intermarriage is legal but socially frowned upon and entails a loss of status for the upper-caste spouse and any children resulting from the union. This was the situation in most nineteenth- and early twentieth-century European colonies in Africa and Asia. So far as I have been able to determine, only German Southwest Africa actually banned marriage between colonists and indigenes.[5]

4. Intermarriage under certain prescribed conditions is actually promoted or encouraged as a way of providing a loyal colonial population in the absence of substantial migration, especially female migration, from the metropole. The clearest examples of this orientation can be found in the history of Portuguese and Dutch colonization of the East Indies and parts of Africa during the sixteenth and seventeenth centuries, and to a lesser degree thereafter. In these cases common religion and culture could trump differences in ancestry and physical appearance, or what we would call race.[6]

It follows from this typology that the statuses of the offspring of interracial unions will also vary.

1. They can be assigned to the same group as the lower-caste parent. In the United States the mixed-race products of miscegenation between those designated as black and white have generally been considered simply black or Negro. This system of "hypodescent," which eventually became, in theory at least, the notorious "one-drop rule" for defining blackness, was a unique American phenomenon.[7]

2. More common has been the practice of assigning mixed offspring to an intermediate category of mulatto, mestizo, or *métis* that ranks below the dominant settler or slaveholding group but above the unmixed indigenous, slave, or ex-slave populations. The best examples are the three-category societies that developed in the plantation colonies of the Caribbean with their white/brown/black hierarchies. But there have been significant variations in the rigidity of the line between the groups, especially between white and brown or mulatto. In the Iberian colonies, such as Brazil and Cuba, the line has usually been more permeable than in the three-category colonies of French or English origin[8]—although as we shall see, the French story is quite complicated.

Now let us focus directly on the development of attitudes toward miscegenation in the English colonies that became the United States and in France, including its colonial possessions, in the seventeenth and eighteenth centuries.

In English North America we find a very restrictive attitude toward miscegenation developing quite early, certainly by the end of the seventeenth century. In 1662, Virginia doubled the normal fine for fornication when the perpetrators were of different races. In 1691, Virginia effectively criminalized intermarriage, and Maryland did the same the following year. They did not make such unions null and void, as would be the later practice, but simply banished the offending couple from the colony. By the middle of the eighteenth century, six of the thirteen colonies, including Massachusetts and Pennsylvania, had legislated against the intermarriage of blacks and whites.[9]

The interracial marriages that occurred before they were banned, which were most often between white female indentured servants and black male slaves, as well as the illicit miscegenation involving white men and black slave women that continued to take place afterwards, resulted in a substantial mixed-race population. Since the offspring followed the status of the mother, mulattoes could be either free or slave at birth. Hence they did not come to constitute a distinctive social category, as happened in the British West Indies, but were treated in much the same way as those of pure African descent, some of whom also managed to obtain their freedom. Thus originated the unique two-category system with the single color line between white and black that predominated in most of the United States by the beginning of the nineteenth century. Partial and increasingly tenuous exceptions to this rule have been found in South Carolina and Louisiana, where a de facto three-category system of Caribbean origin persisted until the 1850s. It is also important to note, lest we consider racial categorizations as facts rather than constructions, that the strict definition of whiteness that would later become the one-drop rule had not been codified. Those with less than one-fourth or one-eighth black ancestry were, depending on the state, legally white in the Old South although not always treated as such. (In fact some of them were slaves, like the children of Thomas Jefferson and his mulatto concubine, Sally Hemings.) But nowhere in the antebellum United States were mulattoes granted a separate legal status (except as a census category between 1850 and 1920), and a majority of them remained enslaved. They were nevertheless overrepresented in the "free Negro" population either because of the tendency of some slave owners to emancipate their own offspring or, more rarely, because of white maternal ancestry.[10]

Attitudes toward intermarriage of whites with the third of America's original "three races"—the Indians—were less restrictive, as the celebrated marriage between John Rolfe and Pocahontas in 1614 might suggest. No hypodescent or "one-drop rule" was applied to the descendants of Indian-white sexual relations, although it is also true that no separate mestizo or *métis* category really developed. "Mixed bloods" either identified with the indigenous or tribal side of their ancestry or, if light-skinned and acculturated to white ways, passed over into the Euro-American community. In the case of black-Indian intermarriage the descent rule normally kicked in to make the children black, but some Indian tribes absorbed substantial numbers of African Americans.[11]

The French confrontation with race and race mixture in the seventeenth and eighteenth centuries was more ambiguous and complicated. It is well known that in Canada, French missionaries and representatives of the Crown positively encouraged intermarriage between French men and Indian women, both to help spread the Gospel and to encourage the fur trade. (The paucity of French female colonists was also a factor.) Consequently an intermediate *métis* group developed that might have been absorbed into the European population had not the French surrendered Canada to the British, who imposed a narrower conception of what it meant to be white or European. (Being half-French was not enough.)

In the seventeenth- and eighteenth-century French plantation colonies of the West Indies—Saint-Domingue, Guadeloupe, and Martinique— intermarriage between whites and blacks was not officially encouraged, but neither was it prohibited. The early settlers on these islands were virtually all male and, unsurprisingly, they took up with slave concubines, routinely freeing their mixed-race offspring and thus laying the foundation for a free colored class. *Le Code Noir*, promulgated in 1685 for the French Antilles, attempted to formalize and Christianize these relationships. Masters with slave concubines (still a common situation since, as in Canada, few women could be induced to leave France and settle in the colonies) were enjoined to enter into Christian marriage with these de facto spouses, after which they and all children resulting from the union would be emancipated. Those who lived in open concubinage but failed to make such marriages were subject to fines and confiscation of their slaves. As in the case of Franco-Indian marriages in Canada, the influence of the Catholic Church, with its usual tendency to value piety and morality over racial or ethnic purity, can be detected here. By encouraging the manumission of mulattoes but making the freeing of pure-blooded Africans, especially males, quite difficult, the authorities in the French West Indies laid the foundation for a three-category system of racial classification in which, generally speaking, pigmentation and status corresponded closely.[12]

In the United States in the late colonial period and early nineteenth century, manumissions in the upper South and gradual emancipation in the North created a "free Negro" population that was not exclusively or even predominantly mulatto and a slave population that included a substantial mulatto minority. By contrast, the free people of color in Saint-Domingue, Guadeloupe, and Martinique in the late eighteenth century were mostly of mixed race. What developed however, especially after 1765, was a relatively rigid color line between mulattoes and whites. Although some people of color prospered and even became substantial planters and slave owners, they increasingly found themselves objects of discrimination and social segregation (separate seating in theaters, for example), as the colonists of putatively pure white ancestry attempted to fashion themselves into an aristocracy or quasi-nobility. In Saint-Domingue a virtual one-drop rule differentiated free people of color from whites by the time of the revolution of the 1790s. A consequence of this exclusivity was that the desperate efforts of whites to enlist free mulattoes in their struggles against the rebellious slaves had little chance of success. In fact it was the free *gens de couleur* who first rose in rebellion, when the island's white elite refused to acknowledge the equal rights granted to them by the revolutionary French National Assembly.[13]

In metropolitan France, a heightened concern developed during the mid- to late eighteenth century about the relatively small number of blacks that had been brought from the colonies by their West Indian masters. Part of the problem was that slavery as a legal status did not exist in France itself, a situation that gave these slaves a claim to freedom if they could get their cases into the courts, as some managed to do. By the 1770s the royal authorities became so concerned that unruly blacks would mix too freely with disorderly lower-class whites that they were making concerted efforts to reduce or even eliminate the domestic black population. Under a law of 1777, for example, planters from the Antilles visiting the metropole could be attended by their slaves during the voyage but then had to deposit them in special detention centers in the port cities, from which they could be sent back on the next available ship. At about the same time, the government enacted special police regulations to control the behavior of the blacks already in France, and in 1778 it banned interracial marriage. Anticipating the opposition of the Church, which continued to favor the marriage of Catholics with those of any color who had been converted, the law was justified in terms of religion rather than biological race—as a new application of the Church-sanctioned ban on unions with Protestants, Jews, or Moslems. In any case the ban was not enforced and died with the Revolution.[14]

The subject of race entered mainstream French intellectual discourse in the eighteenth century not primarily as a black/white question but mainly in the form of an inquisition into the ancestry of the French themselves. What we might consider ideological racism emerged first as a claim by some who considered themselves blue bloods that the nobility was descended from the racially superior Franks, a Germanic people who had conquered the Gauls, an inferior and impure Celtic/Mediterranean race, at the end of the Roman era.[15] At the time of the Revolution some champions of the common people (the "Third Estate") accepted this ethnology and turned it on its head by making the descendants of the Gauls the true French, who needed to be liberated from an alien aristocracy. Such a racialized conception of social class and its association with liberation from tyranny was put to use by French colonial expansionists of the early to mid-nineteenth century, beginning with Napoleon's Egyptian expedition of 1798–1801 and coming to fruition with the colonization of Algeria in the 1830s and 1840s. According to Jean-Loup Amselle, a historian of French anthropology, the standard justification for such imperialist adventures was that one race—Ottoman Turks or Mamelukes as the case might be—were oppressing an Arab majority that needed to be liberated by the French.[16]

Out of such racialism came a qualified endorsement of miscegenation or *métissage*. Now that the aristocracy had lost its castelike privileges, it became possible in the nineteenth century to associate French national identity with the fusion or amalgamation of originally diverse racial or ethnic groups through intermarriage. The concept of the French as a mixed race whose Latin, Celtic, and Germanic elements were being blended to make a greater whole came into common currency and can of course be contrasted with the German concept of a single-strain, blood-based nationalism that was emerging during the same period.[17]

Such a positive evaluation of *métissage* was at times also used as a rationalization for French colonial expansionism. In its original form at least, the "assimilationism" that was touted as the philosophy of the French empire was sometimes thought of as being a process of biological as well as cultural amalgamation. The belief that it was possible and desirable to assimilate indigenous populations through intermarriage drew on both strains of French universalism—the Counter-Reformation Catholicism that had inspired the Jesuit missionaries in Canada and the Enlightenment or revolutionary assertion of human equality and fraternity. The Abbé Grégoire, the pious priest who supported the Revolution and was a notable champion of racial equality, managed to synthesize both strains in his fervent advocacy of intermarriage.[18] Such universalistic endorsements of *métissage* became less common during the late nineteenth- and early twentieth-century heyday of Western racism and imperialism. But while it lasted, such an emphasis on the positive effects of miscegenation served to distinguish French attitudes quite sharply from those that predominated in the United States at the same time.

The closest equivalent would be those few abolitionists of the Civil War era whose ideology of "romantic racialism" led them to view the biological union of blacks and whites as a desirable amalgam of human qualities.[19] Such an idealization of the results of a specifically black and white miscegenation can also be found in France in the early to mid-nineteenth century, but it is unclear how widespread it was.[20] Intra-European conceptions of racial fusion were clearly easier to accept than those involving groups that differed more conspicuously in physical appearance and culture.

The rise to prominence and respectability of a harder-edged, more authoritative racial determinism, one that drew credibility from the latest thinking in the natural sciences, affected attitudes toward miscegenation in both countries during the mid- to late nineteenth century. By the 1840s and 1850s, advanced ethnological thinkers in France and the United States were embracing "polygenism"—the belief that the great color-coded races were distinct species that, contrary to the biblical narrative of Adam and Eve, lacked a common origin and had been created (or had evolved independently) within different climatic zones or continents. In the United States the polygenism of that period became associated with the ideological defense of slavery against egalitarian conceptions of a common humanity. This "American School of Ethnology" regarded miscegenation as the unnatural union of incompatible species and claimed that mulattoes were less fertile than people of pure race, becoming, as the proslavery ethnologist Josiah Nott argued, sterile by the third generation.[21]

In France polygenists also tended to look askance at *métissage*, but they could make exceptions for closely related or compatible races and certainly did not decry all forms of human hybridity. For example, Paul Broca, the founder of French anthropology, was a polygenist who argued in the 1850s that cross-breeding resulted in varying degrees of infertility and that some hybrids were not only as fecund as their parent species, but might be superior in other ways. Broca also attributed the greatness of the French to the fact that they were a good mixture of originally diverse races. He thus disputed the views of Josiah Nott and those of his own countryman Joseph-Arthur de Gobineau (who, as suggested earlier, ended up having more influence in Germany than in France) that race mixture inevitably led to degeneration.[22]

Although the division of humanity into separate species clearly raised doubts about the desirability or viability of at least some mixed-race populations, French polygenists, quite unlike their American counterparts, were capable of advocating the intermarriage of blacks and whites under certain circumstances. The belief that whites were innately superior to blacks and mulattoes was generally accepted, a consensus that would seem to point to the conclusion that intermarriage should be prohibited, as it was generally in the United States, or at least strongly discouraged. Yet a surprising number of French adherents of mid-nineteenth-century scientific racism advocated black-white unions as appropriate and desirable in colonial settings where whites were a seemingly permanent minority. It would, they maintained, have an elevating effect on the quality of the general population.[23] Contrary to the common American notion that mulattoes combined the worst of both races, or that the bad blood overwhelmed the good, French scientific racists often concluded, somewhat more consistently than their American counterparts, that the superior white blood would win the contest, making mulattoes closer in temperament and capability to the white rather than the black side of their ancestry. Nineteenth-century ethnologists and race theorists in both countries believed in biogenetic determinism and innate differences among "the types of mankind." But only in the United States did scientific racists generally conclude that their beliefs mandated racial purity through hypodescent and the absolute prohibition of intermarriage.

A belief in the permanent and fixed character of races as separate species of the genus *Homo* was challenged in the late nineteenth century by the ascendancy of evolutionism. In the United States the Darwinist conception that differing species had evolved over a vast period of time through a process of natural selection proved compatible with naturalistic concepts of racial hierarchy. Even if humankind had a common origin a million years ago, evolution had, according to the new breed of scientific racists, created such great divergences that the end result was hierarchical speciation. Racial Darwinism could make as strong a case against miscegenation as the older polygenetic racism by arguing that miscegenation weakened a population in its "struggle for existence." It also had more persuasive scientific credentials.[24]

In France, the Darwinian mechanism of natural selection was not accepted until well into the twentieth century, but Lamarckianism, the homegrown variety of evolutionism that permitted the inheritance of acquired characteristics, could also be used to sanction racial hierarchies, if not necessarily forever at least for a long time to come. It could also raise serious doubts about the desirability of miscegenation and intermarriage.

By the 1870s, according to historian Alice Conkin, the once-prevalent idea that intermarriage with indigenous populations would facilitate France's mission to extend civilization to other parts of the world had largely disappeared from imperialist discourse. The belief that *métis* were monsters seemed to have taken hold.[25] But the growing opposition to miscegenation in French ethnological thought did not prevent or even discourage many of the French men who went out to the colonies from establishing public liaisons with native women and siring mixed-race children. During the same period, interracial concubinage was condoned or even encouraged much more than in the British colonies. Mixed marriages themselves were not prohibited, and a few actually took place (along with some polygamous unions sanctioned by local custom rather than French law), but many of these male empire builders already had wives in France to whom they returned after their colonial service. In some French colonies (West Africa for example) separate schools were established for the *métis* children they left behind and opportunities were provided for graduates in the colonial administration.[26] In 1902 a published guide for French men about to embark on African service explicitly advised them to take native mistresses and have children by them, for "it is by creating mulatto children that we most easily Gallicize West Africa." Similarly candid views about the positive role that this kind of *métissage* could play in the French civilizing mission were being expressed as late as 1938.[27]

It would be too much to say, however, that the Lamarckian evolutionism that predominated in French racial thought in the late nineteenth and early twentieth centuries made race mixture an essential or prominent feature of the civilizing mission as it was then defined. On the contrary, such thinking more often led to the discouragement of intermarriage and miscegenation, at least until subject peoples climbed higher on the ladder of evolution. But if acquired characteristics could be inherited, enlightened governance and education might by themselves improve the innate biological characteristics of colonized peoples to the point where, sometime in the future, they could become fully civilized and thereby unambiguously eligible for intermarriage and biological assimilation. France's history of absorbing a variety of Europeans, through both the annexation of territory and immigration, might serve as a precedent for the eventual incorporation of African and Asian peoples into a greater France. Such, at least, was what much of the rhetoric associated with "the civilizing mission" implied. It would be absurd, however, to claim that such rhetoric made the French immune to prejudice based on color or other physical characteristics.[28]

What made American imperialist discourse of the early twentieth century different from the French was the absence of assimilationist rhetoric, even of a kind that may seem to us evasive and insincere. Biologically incorporating African Americans, even in the remote future, was clearly not on the white agenda. When the United States acquired and pacified the Philippines and Puerto Rico at the turn of the century, no one seriously contemplated the full assimilation—even in some remote future—of these people of color who now lived under the American flag. The United States at that time was being defined more insistently than ever before as a white man's nation.[29]

America's restrictive attitude toward race mixture did not begin to change significantly until the last half of the twentieth century. As recently as 1950 a substantial majority of the American states (thirty of forty-eight) outlawed interracial marriage of one kind or another. A few of these laws banned the intermarriage of whites with Asians or Indians, but all of them prohibited unions of whites and blacks.[30] In the southern states prior to the 1930s and 1940s accusations against black men for sexually assaulting white women, or even showing signs of thinking about it, often resulted in the brutal lynching of the alleged perpetrators. In 1912, southerners and others from states with antimiscegenation laws mounted a serious campaign to pass a constitutional amendment banning white-black intermarriage everywhere in the United States. The amendment failed to pass, but the situation remained basically unchanged for the next half-century.

Even the beginnings of the civil rights movement in the 1950s and early 1960s did not result in a direct assault on laws banning intermarriage. In a controversial essay of 1959, the émigré German-Jewish philosopher Hannah Arendt found it remarkable that efforts were being made to end segregation in the public schools, while a more fundamental and Nazi-like form of legalized discrimination—the laws against intermarriage—did not seem to be under attack.[31] The Civil Rights Acts of 1964 and 1965, which ended other forms of Jim Crow segregation, did not touch on the subject of marriage. In its 1967 decision in the case of *Loving v. Virginia*, the Supreme Court did finally rule that state antimiscegenation laws were a violation of the equal protection clause of the Fourteenth Amendment and were therefore null and void. But historians of the period generally treat this decision as an almost incidental afterthought coming in the wake of the more fundamental reforms that gave blacks voting rights and equal access to public facilities.

The end of legal obstacles did not result in a massive increase in black-white marriages. To this day, whites are much less likely to marry blacks than members of other groups considered to be nonwhite, such as Asians, Indians, or Latinos.[32] Joel Perlmann reveals that among the age group 25–34 who married in 1990, two-fifths of the Hispanics and fully half of the Asian Americans married members of other ethnoracial groups, but fewer than one-tenth of African Americans did so.[33] As recently as 1996 an attitude survey showed that only 45 percent of whites approved of white-black marriages in principle, and 16 percent thought they should be against the law. The actual rate of black-white intermarriage is suggested by the fact that of all the marital unions involving blacks in 1996, only 8.6 percent were with whites.[34] Although the number of such marriages has been slowly increasing in recent years, it would appear that America's peculiarly intense miscegenation taboo has not been fully overcome.

Metropolitan France has passed no laws against intermarriage since the short-lived decree of 1778. It is true that some French colonies with substantial black populations did have such laws for limited periods—Louisiana from 1724 to 1763 (when the Spanish took over) and what remained of the French Antilles—mainly Guadeloupe and Martinique—in the period after

Napoleon reestablished slavery there in 1802.[35] In France itself the subject has occasioned little attention or concern partly because of the sheer weight of demography. Relatively few blacks or other non-Europeans lived in the metropole before the post–World War II period, and intermarriages were therefore infrequent and inconspicuous. Another form of intermarriage, between Jews and gentiles, aroused more concern, especially after the Dreyfus Affair of the 1890s brought to the surface a virulently racist strain of anti-Semitism. But no serious proposals to ban such unions were forthcoming. Even under the fascist Vichy regime of 1940 to 1944, which did not hesitate to denaturalize many Jewish immigrants and turn them over to the Nazis, marriage between Jews and gentiles was never banned as it was in the Third Reich under the Nuremberg laws of 1935.

The French have not been immune to racism in some of its forms, but they have not generally idealized race purity and at times have been receptive to positive assessments of *métissage*. Indeed they have had a tendency to define themselves as a mixed race, a kind of Gallic stew composed of delicious ingredients perfectly blended. In the late nineteenth and early twentieth centuries they often compared themselves favorably to the allegedly pure Aryans of Germany and took great pride in the vigor and creativity that they associated with their hybridity.

Throughout most of its history the United States has manifested a restrictive and hostile attitude toward the intermarriage of populations defined as racially different. But the primary focus of concern has always been the white-black relationship, and the greatest taboo was always the kind of intermarriage that produced mulattoes and thus threatened to blur the color line. American racial ideologies have generally adhered to an ideal of race purity. Unlike German Aryanism, however, it was eventually extended to the entire white or Caucasian race and not to just one subdivision of it. To explain why the American attitude differed from the French, we have to take into account the long history of slavery and segregation within the heartland of the American nation-state. Color-coded French racism, on the other hand, was rooted mainly in distant colonies and not in the metropole. There has been no equivalent in metropolitan France for the American color line. Currently there is a rising tide of xenophobic hostility to North African Muslims, who now constitute a percentage of the population similar to that of African Americans in the United States. But it would appear that North Africans intermarry with French people of European antecedents at a substantially higher rate than blacks do with whites in the United States.[36] Jean-Philippe Mathy cites a 1992 study by the National Demographic Institute showing "that among Algerian men who had arrived in France after age fifteen, 20 percent had a French spouse or partner (excluding daughters of parents born in Algeria)." These and other figures provided by Mathy suggest that the rate of intermarriage between Algerians and those considered natives of

France is more than twice as high as that between blacks and whites in the United States. And no one, not even Jean-Marie Le Pen and others on the far reaches of the right wing, has proposed banning such marriages.

Our special problem in the United States has been, and still is, the product of a tragic history of color-coded slavery, segregation, and discrimination that is close to the center of the national experience. It is not therefore simply one more manifestation of the virtually universal propensity to reject or mistreat the ethnic or racial "other." France has its own special problems resulting from a history of colonial expansionism that hid its ethnocentric character under a cloak of enlightened universalism. Juxtaposing and comparing the two experiences might provide useful perspectives to the citizens of both republics as they confront the mounting challenge of ethnoracial diversity in the twenty-first century.

NOTES

Chapter 1

Originally published in Deborah A. Prentice and Dale T. Miller, eds., *Cultural Divides: Understanding and Overcoming Group Conflict* (New York: Russell Sage Foundation, 1999), pp. 23–34.

1. See, for example, Dinesh D'Souza, *The End of Racism: Principles for a Multi-racial Society* (New York: Free Press, 1995).

2. George M. Fredrickson, *The Comparative Imagination: On the History of Racism, Nationalism, and Social Movements* (Berkeley: University of California Press, 1997), ch. 5.

3. James Axtell, *The European and the Indian: Essays in the Ethnohistory of Colonial North America* (New York: Oxford University Press, 1981); Winthrop D. Jordan, *White over Black: American Attitudes toward the Negro, 1550–1812* (Chapel Hill: University of North Carolina Press, 1968).

4. John Higham, *Strangers in the Land: Patterns of American Nativism, 1860–1925* (New York: Atheneum, 1968); Stuart Creighton Miller, *The Unwelcome Immigrant: The American Image of the Chinese, 1785–1882* (Berkeley: University of California Press, 1969).

5. Dale T. Knobel, *Paddy and the Republic: Ethnicity and Nationality in Antebellum America* (Middletown, CT: Wesleyan University Press, 1986).

6. Higham, *Strangers.*

7. Milton M. Gordon, *Assimilation in American Life: The Role of Race, Religion, and National Origins* (New York: Oxford University Press, 1964), ch. 4.

8. George M. Fredrickson, *The Black Image in the White Mind: The Debate on Afro-American Character and Destiny, 1817–1914* (Middletown, CT: Wesleyan University Press, 1987), ch. 1.

9. Knobel, *Paddy.*

10. Adrienne Koch and William Peden, eds., *The Life and Selected Writings of Thomas Jefferson* (New York: Modern Library, 1944), pp. 210–11.

11. Robert F. Berkhofer, Jr., *The White Man's Indian: Images of the American Indian from Columbus to the Present* (New York: Alfred A. Knopf, 1978); Frederick E. Hoxie, *A Final Promise: The Campaign to Assimilate the Indians, 1880–1920* (Lincoln: University of Nebraska Press, 1984); Robert W. Mardock, *The Reformers and the American Indian* (Columbia: University of Missouri Press, 1971).

12. Gordon, *Assimilation*, ch. 5.

13. Gunnar Myrdal, *An American Dilemma* (New York: Harper and Row, 1944).

14. Manning Marable, *Race, Reform, and Rebellion: The Second Reconstruction in Black America* (Jackson: University of Mississippi Press, 1991); William L. Van Deburg, *New Day in Babylon: The Black Power Movement and American Culture, 1965–1975* (Chicago: University of Chicago Press, 1992).

15. Wilson Jeremiah Moses, *The Golden Age of Black Nationalism, 1850–1925* (Hamden, CT: Archon Books, 1978).

16. Randolph S. Bourne, *War and the Intellectuals: Collected Essays, 1915–1919* (New York: Harper Torch, 1964), ch. 8.

17. John Higham, *Send These to Me: Jews and Other Immigrants in Urban America* (Baltimore: Johns Hopkins University Press, 1984), ch. 9; Horace Kallen, *Culture and Democracy in the United States: Studies in the Group Psychology of American Peoples* (New York: Boni and Liveright, 1924).

18. David Levering Lewis, *W. E. B. DuBois: Biography of a Race, 1868–1919* (New York: Henry Holt, 1933).

19. Will Herberg, *Protestant-Catholic-Jew: An Essay in American Religious Sociology* (Garden City, NY: Anchor Books, 1960).

20. Arthur M. Schlesinger, Jr. *The Disuniting of America* (New York: Norton, 1992).

21. David Hollinger, *Postethnic America: Beyond Multiculturalism* (New York: Basic Books, 1995).

22. George M. Fredrickson, *Black Liberation: A Comparative History of Black Ideologies in the United States and South Africa* (New York: Oxford University Press, 1995), chs. 2, 4, 7.

23. David Gutierrez, *Walls and Mirrors: Mexican Americans, Mexican Immigrants, and the Politics of Ethnicity* (Berkeley: University of California Press, 1995), pp. 184–85).

Chapter 2

Originally presented as a paper at the U.N. conference on racism in Durban, South Africa, in September 2001 and later published in Yusuf Bangura and Rodolfo Stavenhagan, eds., *Racism and Public Policy* (Basingstoke, UK: Palgrave Macmillan, 2005), pp. 25–47.

1. Anthony D. Smith, *The Ethnic Origins of Nations* (Oxford: Blackwell, 1984).

2. Such as federal responsibility to assist in the return of fugitive slaves and to come to the aid of state authorities in times of domestic insurrection.

3. On the English background of American conceptions of citizenship, see James H. Kettner, *Development of American Citizenship, 1608–1870* (Chapel Hill: University of North Carolina Press, 1978), pp. 13–61.

4. Linda K. Kerber, "The Meanings of Citizenship," *Journal of American History* 84, no. 3 (1997), p. 841; Rogers M. Smith, *Civic Ideals: Conflicting Visions of Citizenship in U.S. History* (New Haven, CT: Yale University Press, 1997), pp. 159–60.

5. Marshall's decision in the 1831 case of *Worcester v. Georgia* was meant to protect the Cherokees against the extension of state law over territories assigned to them by treaties with the federal government. It was not, however, enforced by

the administration of Andrew Jackson, which was committed to the removal of the Indians from the southeastern states to designated areas west of the Mississippi.

6. Kettner, *Development*, pp. 214–16.

7. The standard work on the development of anti-black prejudices in early American history is Winthrop D. Jordan, *White over Black: American Attitudes toward the Negro, 1550–1812* (Chapel Hill: University of North Carolina Press, 1968).

8. George M. Fredrickson, "Social Origins of American Racism," in *The Arrogance of Race: Historical Perspectives on Slavery, Racism, and Social Inequality* (Middletown, CT: Wesleyan University Press, 1988), pp. 189–205.

9. Kettner, *Development*, p. 259; emphasis added.

10. George M. Fredrickson, *The Black Image in the White Mind: The Debate on Afro-American Character and Destiny, 1817–1914* (Middletown, CT: Wesleyan University Press, 1987; orig. pub. 1971), pp. 61–64, 90–96.

11. Kenneth L. Karst, *Belonging to America: Equal Citizenship and the Constitution* (New Haven, CT: Yale University Press, 1989), pp. 48–49; Leon F. Litwack, *North of Slavery: The Negro in the Free States, 1790–1860* (Chicago: Chicago University Press, 1961).

12. Fredrickson, *Black Image*, and "America's Diversity in Comparative Perspective," *Journal of American History* 85 (1998), pp. 859–87.

13. Linda K. Kerber, *No Constitutional Right to Be Ladies: Women and the Obligations of Citizenship* (New York: Hill and Wang, 1998), p. 243.

14. Charles J. McClain, *In Search of Equality: The Chinese Struggle against Discrimination in Nineteenth-Century America* (Berkeley: University of California Press, 1994).

15. Stuart Creighton Miller, *The Unwelcome Immigrant: The American Image of the Chinese, 1775–1882* (Berkeley: University of California Press, 1969); Alexander Saxton, *The Indispensable Enemy: The Anti-Chinese Movement in California* (Berkeley: University of California Press, 1971).

16. Smith, *Civic Ideals*.

17. Leon F. Litwack, *Trouble in Mind: Black Southerners in the Age of Jim Crow* (New York: Alfred A. Knopf, 1998).

18. Matthew Frye Jacobson, *Whiteness of a Different Color: European Immigrants and the Alchemy of Race* (Cambridge, MA: Harvard University Press, 1998).

19. The classic expression in an American context of this form of racism is Madison Grant, *The Passing of the Great Race* (New York: Charles Scribner's Sons, 1916).

20. Leo Frank was lynched by a Georgia mob in 1915, after he had been accused of murdering a white Christian woman who worked in the factory that he managed.

21. John Higham, *Send These to Me: Immigrants in Urban America*, rev. ed. (Baltimore: Johns Hopkins University Press, 1984), pp. 95–174.

22. David Montgomery, *The Fall of the House of Labor: The Workplace, the State, and Labor Activism, 1865–1925* (Cambridge: Cambridge University Press, 1987), pp. 25, 46, 81–87.

23. W. E. B. Du Bois, *Black Reconstruction in America, 1860–1880* (New York: Atheneum, 1970; orig. pub. 1935), p. 700.

24. Joel Williamson, *The Crucible of Race: Black-White Relations in the American South since Emancipation* (New York: Oxford University Press, 1984).

25. Barbara Miller Solomon, *Ancestors and Immigrants* (Chicago: University of Chicago Press, 1956).

26. J. R. Barrett and David R. Roediger, "Inbetween Peoples: Race, Nationality and the 'New Immigrant' Working Class," *Journal of American Ethnic History* 16 (1997), pp. 3–43.

27. In 1931 the nomination of Judge John Parker was rejected by the Senate in part because he had once declared that blacks should not have the right to vote.

28. Harvard Sitkoff, *A New Deal for Blacks: The Emergence of Civil Rights as a National Issue: The Depression Decade* (New York: Oxford University Press, 1978); John B. Kirby, *Black Americans in the Roosevelt Era* (Knoxville: University of Tennessee Press, 1980).

29. George W. Stocking, Jr., *Race, Culture, and Evolution: Essays in the History of Anthropology* (New York: Free Press, 1968); Elazar Barkan, *The Retreat of Scientific Racism* (Cambridge: Cambridge University Press, 1992).

30. Gunnar Myrdal, *An American Dilemma* (New York: Harper and Row, 1944).

31. The impact of the Cold War is demonstrated in Mary L. Dudziak, *Cold War Civil Rights: Race and the Image of American Democracy* (Princeton, NJ: Princeton University Press, 2000), and in Philip A. Klinkner and Rogers M. Smith, *The Unsteady March: The Rise and Decline of Racial Equality in America* (Chicago: University of Chicago Press, 1999).

32. Valuable summaries of the current status and condition of African Americans include Andrew Hacker, *Two Nations: Black and White, Separate, Hostile, Unequal* (New York: Scribner, 1992); Douglas S. Massey and Nancy Denton, *American Apartheid: Segregation and the Making of the Underclass* (Cambridge, MA: Harvard University Press, 1993); Orlando Patterson, *The Ordeal of Integration: Progress and Resentment in America's "Racial" Crisis* (Washington, DC: Civitas Counterpoint, 1997); Melvin L. Oliver and Thomas M. Shapiro, *Black Wealth/White Wealth: A New Perspective on Racial Inequality* (New York: Routledge, 1995); and David K. Shipler, *A Country of Strangers: Blacks and Whites in America* (New York: Alfred A. Knopf, 1997).

33. William Julius Wilson, *The Declining Significance of Race: Blacks and Changing American Institutions* (Chicago: University of Chicago Press, 1978); William Julius Wilson, *The Truly Disadvantaged: The Inner City, the Underclass and Public Policy* (Chicago: University of Chicago Press, 1987).

34. William V. Flores and Rina Benmayor, eds., *Latino Cultural Citizenship: Claiming Identity, Space, and Rights* (Boston: Beacon Press, 1997).

35. For some figures on the extent of intermarriage among Asians, see S. B. Gall and T. L. Gall, eds., *Statistical Record of Asian Americans* (Detroit: Gale Research, 1993), p. 144.

36. Fredrickson, "America's Diversity in Comparative Perspective."

37. Liah Greenfeld, *Nationalism: Five Roads to Modernity* (Cambridge, MA: Harvard University Press, 1992).

38. Rogers Brubaker, *Citizenship and Nationhood in France and Germany* (Cambridge, MA: Harvard University Press, 1992); P. Weil, "Nationalities and Citizenship: The Lessons of the French Experience for Germany and Europe," in David Cesarini and Mary Fulbrook, eds., *Citizenship, Nationality and Migration in Europe* (London: Routledge, 1996).

39. Asked which category of immigrants constituted the greatest difficulty for integration, 50 percent of French respondents named North Africans and only 19

percent specified black Africans. Also see Donald L. Horowitz, "Immigration and Group Relations in France and America," in *Immigrants in Two Democracies: The French and American Experiences*, ed. Donald L. Horowitz and Gérard Noiriel (New York: New York University Press, 1992).

40. Brubaker, *Citizenship*.

41. Brubaker, *Citizenship*, p. 149; Cesarini and Fulbrook, eds., *Citizenship*, pp. 88–105.

42. Cesarini and Fulbrook, eds., *Citizenship*, p. 78; Riva Kastoryano, *La France, l'Allemagne, et leurs immigrés; Negocier l'identité* (Paris: Armand Colin, 1996), pp. 133–57; C. Wilpert, "Les Fondements institutionnels et idéologiques du racisme dans la République Fédérale d'Allemagne," in *Racisme et modernité*, ed. Michel Wieviorka (Paris: La Découverte, 1993), pp. 225–35.

43. The comparison made here between German and American racism is developed more fully in George M. Fredrickson, *Racism: A Short History* (Princeton, NJ: Princeton University Press, 2002).

Chapter 3

This chapter, with slight variations, was delivered as the presidential address to the annual meeting of the Organization of American Historians in Indianapolis on April 3, 1998. It was originally published in the *Journal of American History* 85, no. 3 (Dec. 1998), pp. 859–75.

1. For a selection from the literature on the construction of "whiteness," see Richard Delgado and Jean Stefanic, eds., *Critical White Studies: Looking behind the Mirror* (Philadelphia: Temple University Press, 1997). A groundbreaking work in this vein is David Roediger, *The Wages of Whiteness: Race and the Making of the American Working Class* (London: Verso, 1991).

2. See John Higham, *Send These to Me: Immigrants in Urban America* (1975; Baltimore: Johns Hopkins University Press, 1984), pp. 198–232; David Hollinger, *Postethnic America: Beyond Multiculturalism* (New York, 1995), pp. 88–98; and Will Herberg, *Protestant-Catholic-Jew: An Essay in American Religious Sociology* (Garden City, NY: Doubleday, 1955).

3. See, for example, Arthur M. Schlesinger, *The Disuniting of America: Reflections on a Multicultural Society* (New York: Norton, 1992).

4. Todd Gitlin, *The Twilight of Common Dreams: Why America Is Wracked by Culture Wars* (New York: Henry Holt, 1996).

5. Daniel Bell, "Ethnicity and Social Change," in *Ethnicity: Theory and Experience*, ed. Nathan Glazer and Daniel P. Moynihan (Cambridge, MA: Harvard University Press, 1975), pp. 160–71.

6. Nathan Glazer, *We Are All Multiculturalists Now* (Cambridge, MA: Harvard University Press, 1997).

7. William Julius Wilson, *The Truly Disadvantaged: The Inner City, the Underclass, and Public Policy* (Chicago: University of Chicago Press, 1987); and William Julius Wilson, *When Work Disappears: The World of the New Urban Poor* (New York: Knopf, 1996).

8. For a critique of the African-American elite, see Manning Marable, *Beyond Black and White: Transforming African-American Politics* (London: Verso, 1995).

9. K. Anthony Appiah, "The Multiculturalist Misunderstanding," *New York Review of Books*, Oct. 9, 1997, pp. 30–36.

10. See Michael W. Doyle, *Empires* (Ithaca, NY: Cornell University Press, 1986), and D. K. Fieldhouse, *The Colonial Empires: A Comparative Survey from the Eighteenth Century* (New York: Delacorte Press, 1965).

11. See Frederick Merk, *Manifest Destiny and Mission in American History* (New York: Vintage Books, 1963), pp. 180–201.

12. Will Kymlicka, *Multicultural Citizenship: A Liberal Theory of Minority Rights* (Oxford: Clarendon Press, 1995), pp. 11, 56, 183.

13. See Frederick E. Hoxie, *A Final Promise: The Campaign to Assimilate the Indians, 1880–1920* (Lincoln: University of Nebraska Press, 1984).

14. Kymlicka, *Multicultural Citizenship*, pp. 10–33.

15. According to the constitution of New Mexico, none of the rights of citizenship can be "restricted, abridged or impaired on account of … inability to speak, read or write the English or Spanish languages" (N.M. Const. art. VII, sec. 3). It also requires that all teachers in public schools be "proficient in both the English and Spanish languages" (N.M. Const. art. XII, sec. 8).

16. Immigrants from the Caribbean and Africa sometimes testify that they do not encounter as much prejudice as African Americans, apparently because their exotic accents give them a partial immunity from white hostility.

17. Jeffrey G. Reitz and Raymond Breton, *The Illusion of Difference: Realities of Ethnicity in Canada and the United States* (Toronto: C.D. Howe Institute, 1994).

18. On the current debate on affirmative action, see George M. Fredrickson, "America's Caste System: Will It Change?" *New York Review of Books*, Oct. 23, 1997, pp. 68–75.

19. Reitz and Breton, *Illusion of Difference*, pp. 10, 14–16.

20. A general account of the development of British race policy in comparison with that of the United States that has influenced my thinking on this subject is John Stone and Howard Lasus, "Two Societies Divided by a Common Language: Immigration and Ethnic Relations in Britain and America," a paper presented at the annual meeting of the American Sociological Association, Washington, DC, Aug. 19, 1995 (in George M. Fredrickson's possession).

21. Paul Gilroy, *"There Ain't No Black in the Union Jack": The Cultural Politics of Race and Nation* (Chicago: University of Chicago Press, 1991).

22. See Tariq Modood, "The Limits of America: Rethinking Equality in the Changing Context of British Race Relations," in *The Making of Martin Luther King and the Civil Rights Movement*, ed. Brian Ward and Tony Badger (Basingstoke, Hampshire: Macmillan, 1996), pp. 181–93.

23. Anne Phillips, "Why Worry about Multiculturalism?" *Dissent* (Winter 1997), p. 59; Modood, "Limits of America."

24. For a critical view of the current situation, see Philomena Essed, *Diversity: Gender, Color, and Culture* (Amherst: University of Massachusetts Press, 1996). Hans van Amersfoort finds that the response to nonwhite immigrants was relatively tolerant during the period covered in his study: Hans van Amersfoort, *Immigration and the Formation of Minority Groups: The Dutch Experience, 1945–1975* (Cambridge: Cambridge University Press, 1982).

25. Riva Kastoryano, *La France, l'Allemagne, et leurs immigrés: Négocier l'identité* (Paris: Armand Colin/Masson, 1996), pp. 133–57; William Rogers Brubaker, *Citizenship and Nationhood in France and Germany* (Cambridge, MA: Harvard University Press, 1992), pp. x, 78, and passim; Czarina Wilpert, "Les Fondements institutionels et idéologiques du racisme dans la République Fédérale d'Allemagne," in *Racisme et Modernité*, ed. Michel Wieviorka (Paris, 1993), pp. 225–35.

26. See Linda Kerber, "The Meanings of Citizenship," *Journal of American History* 84 (Dec. 1997), pp. 833–54. For comparative studies of what citizenship means, see William Rogers Brubaker, ed., *Immigration and the Politics of Citizenship in Europe and North America* (Lanham, MD: University Press of America, 1989).

27. Kastoryano, *La France, l'Allemagne, et leurs immigrés*, pp. 113–32. See also Brubaker, *Citizenship and Nationhood in France and Germany*, and Maxim Silverman, *Deconstructing the Nation: Immigration, Racism, and Citizenship in Modern France* (London: Routledge, 1992).

28. Donald L. Horowitz, "Immigration and Group Relations in France and America," in *Immigrants in Two Democracies: French and American Experience*, ed. Donald L. Horowitz and Gérard Noriel (New York: New York University Press, 1992), p. 335, esp. 15. For a full and up-to-date account of the headscarf affair, see John R. Bowen, *Why the French Don't Like Headscarves: Islam, the State, and Public Space* (Princeton, NJ: Princeton University Press, 2007).

29. Michael Walzer, *On Toleration* (New Haven, CT: Yale University Press, 1997), pp. 73–74.

30. "Asked in a survey which category of immigrants poses the greatest difficulty for integration, 50 percent of French respondents identified North Africans, far more than the 19 percent who named Black Africans": Horowitz, "Immigration and Group Relations," p. 19.

31. See Richard J. Jensen, *The Winning of the Middle West: Social and Political Conflict, 1888–1896* (Chicago: University of Chicago Press, 1971); Aryeh Neier, "Language and Minorities," *Dissent* (Summer 1996), pp. 31–35.

32. Amy Gutmann, "Introduction," in Charles Taylor et al., *Multiculturalism: Examining the Politics of Recognition*, ed. Amy Gutmann (Princeton, NJ: Princeton University Press, 1994), p. 8; Jürgen Habermas, "Struggles for Recognition in the Democratic Constitutional State," ibid., p. 113.

33. Habermas, "Struggles for Recognition in the Democratic Constitutional State," p. 135; Martin E. Marty, *The One and the Many: America's Struggle for the Common Good* (Cambridge, MA: Harvard University Press, 1997).

34. Jennifer Hochschild, *Facing Up to the American Dream: Race, Class, and the Soul of the Nation* (Princeton, NJ: Princeton University Press, 1995), pp. 247–48 and passim.

35. This is the general conclusion one draws from the most authoritative overview of immigration: John E. Bodnar, *The Transplanted: A History of Immigrants in Urban America* (Bloomington: Indiana University Press, 1985).

36. Kymlicka, *Multicultural Citizenship*, pp. 11–48.

37. For a discussion and analysis of this debate, see George M. Fredrickson, *Black Liberation: A Comparative History of Black Ideologies in the United States and South Africa* (New York: Oxford University Press, 1995).

38. John Ogbu, *Minority Education and Caste: The American System in Cross-Cultural Perspective* (New York: Academic Press, 1978). My attention was first drawn to Ogbu's comparative perspectives on race and caste by Benjamin DeMott, *The Trouble with Friendship: Why Americans Can't Think Straight about Race* (New York: Atlantic Monthly Press, 1995).

39. Vernon Williams, *From a Caste to a Minority: Changing Attitudes of American Sociologists toward Afro-Americans, 1896–1945* (New York: Greenwood Press, 1989).

40. Of the total number of existing marital unions that involved blacks in 1996, 9.6 percent were interracial (blacks with any other race), and 8.6 percent resulted from blacks having married whites. These figures represent a substantial increase in recent years, more than a doubling of the absolute numbers of black-white couples since 1980. But the rate of involvement in mixed marriages among Hispanics has remained roughly triple that of blacks since 1980. In 1996, 27.4 percent of all existing marital unions involving Hispanics resulted from out-marriages. These calculations are based on United States, Bureau of the Census, *The Statistical Abstract of the United States, 1997* (Washington, DC: U.S. Department of Commerce, Economics, and Statistics Administration, 1997), Population Table 62, "Married Couples of Same or Mixed Races and Origins, 1980–1996," p. 57. The out-marriage rates of Asian Americans, especially Japanese, have been even higher than those of Hispanics. In 1985 in Los Angeles, for example, 51.2 percent of Japanese marriages and 30 percent of Chinese marriages were with members of other ethnic groups. See table 183 in Susan B. Gall and Timothy L. Gall, eds., *Statistical Record of Asian Americans* (Detroit: Gale Research, 1993), p. 144. Even though an increasing number of African Americans are marrying whites, less than 1 percent (0.7) of all existing marital unions involving whites in 1996 were the result of black-white intermarriages, and a majority of whites remain opposed in principle to marriage across the color line. In 1994, polls revealed that only 45 percent of whites approved of marriages between blacks and whites, and 16 percent thought they should be made illegal. This contrasted with the 68 percent of blacks (down from 76 percent in 1983) who approved of such marriages, and the minuscule 3 percent who believed they should be banned. See table 2 of Stephan Thernstrom and Abigail Thernstrom, *America in Black and White: One Nation Indivisible* (New York: Simon and Schuster 1997), p. 524.

Chapter 4

This chapter was originally published with the title "Wise Man" in the *New York Review of Books*, Feb. 28, 2002.

1. For biographical information on Higham, see Lewis A. Erenberg's introduction to *A Tribute to John Higham: Historian as Moral Critic*, a special issue of *Mid-America: An Historical Review* 82 (2000), pp. 7–20.

2. *Strangers in the Land: Patterns of American Nativism, 1860–1925* has gone through four editions, the first (1955) and the most recent (1988) by Rutgers University Press.

3. See John Higham, *Writing American History: Essays on Modern Scholarship* (Bloomington: Indiana University Press, 1970).

4. C. Vann Woodward, *Origins of the New South, 1877–1913* (Baton Rouge: Louisiana State University Press, 1951); *The Strange Career of Jim Crow* (New York: Oxford University Press, 1955). *Strange Career* would be revised several times, most recently in 1974.

5. Kenneth Stampp, *The Peculiar Institution: Slavery in the Ante-Bellum South* (New York: Knopf, 1956).

6. John Higham, "Immigration," in *The Comparative Approach to American History*, ed. C. Vann Woodward (New York: Basic Books, 1968), pp. 91–105.

7. John Higham, *Send These to Me: Jews and Other Immigrants in Urban America* (New York: Atheneum, 1975). Johns Hopkins University Press published the revised edition in 1984.

8. Arthur M. Schlesinger, *The Disuniting of America* (New York: Norton, 1992).

Chapter 5

Originally published in the *New York Review of Books*, Nov. 2, 2000.

1. I discussed some of this work in the *New York Review of Books*, Sept. 30, 1976. The essay appears in slightly revised form in my collection *The Arrogance of Race: Historical Perspectives on Slavery, Racism, and Social Inequality* (Middletown, CT: Wesleyan University Press, 1988). The most significant books are Herbert G. Gutman, *The Black Family in Slavery and Freedom, 1750–1925* (New York: Pantheon, 1976), which occasioned the review; John W. Blassingame, *The Slave Community: Plantation Life in the Antebellum South* (New York: Oxford University Press, 1972); Eugene D. Genovese, *Roll, Jordan, Roll: The World the Slaves Made* (New York: Pantheon, 1974); and Robert William Fogel and Stanley L. Engerman, *Time on the Cross: The Economics of American Negro Slavery* (Boston: Little, Brown, 1974).

2. Elkins compared the effect of slavery to that of the concentration camp, which, according to psychological studies then in vogue, reduced its victims to an equivalent of the grinning, shuffling "Sambos" of proslavery lore. He therefore proposed a nonracist explanation for this stereotype. See *Slavery: A Problem in American Institutional and Intellectual Life* (Chicago: University of Chicago Press, 1959). Kenneth M. Stampp's *The Peculiar Institution: Slavery in the Ante-Bellum South* (New York: Knopf, 1956) had represented slaves as discontented and resistant to the master's authority but nevertheless living in a state of "cultural chaos" without strong ties of family or community.

3. These were the views that became influential in the study of slavery. The one that did not was the claim of Robert Fogel and Stanley Engerman that the slaves were the willing collaborators in and beneficiaries of a rational and efficient form of production.

4. Gutman did acknowledge family breakup, and in fact found some of his strongest evidence for the strength of family ties in the heroic efforts slaves made after emancipation to reconstitute families earlier dissolved by sale. But the focus of his attention was on the stability and durability of many slave unions despite the persistent danger of forced separations.

5. See Michael Tadman, *Speculators and Slaves: Masters, Traders, and Slaves in the Old South* (Madison: University of Wisconsin Press, 1989); Norrece T. Jones, *Born a Child of Freedom, Yet a Slave: Mechanisms of Control and Strategies of Resistance in Antebellum South Carolina* (Middletown, CT: Wesleyan University Press, 1990); and Wilma King, *Stolen Childhood: Slave Youth in Nineteenth-Century America* (Bloomington: Indiana University Press, 1995).

6. Tadman, *Speculators and Slaves*, p. 219.

7. John Hope Franklin and Loren Schweninger, *Runaway Slaves: Rebels on the Plantation* (New York: Oxford University Press, 1999). See the review in the June 10, 1999, issue of the *New York Review of Books* by Edmund S. Morgan. John Hope Franklin is, of course, the much-honored dean of African-American and southern historians. See my essay on some of his work in the *New York Review of Books*, Sept. 23, 1993.

8. The selections made by Andrews and Gates might be questioned. Three especially powerful and frequently cited narratives, those of Solomon Northrup, Charles Ball, and John Brown, were not included. Of less value, in my opinion, are those by James Albert Ukawsaw Gronniosaw, Sojourner Truth, and Jacob D. Green, which are in the book. Sojourner Truth is, of course, a major figure in African-American history, but the narrative that she told to a white abolitionist mainly concerns her religious experiences combined with some recollection of being a slave in New York before she was emancipated in 1827. It records aspects of her life before she became a leading abolitionist and feminist. It is thus only a filtered and truncated Sojourner Truth who is revealed in the narrative. For a full understanding of her remarkable career and what she has come to represent, see Nell Irvin Painter's brilliant biography, *Sojourner Truth: A Life, a Symbol* (New York: Norton, 1996).

9. See *Remembering Slavery: African Americans Talk about Their Personal Experiences of Slavery and Emancipation*. The original edition, published by the New Press in 1998, was reviewed by Edmund S. Morgan in the *New York Review of Books*, Dec. 3, 1998. The paperback edition was issued by the New Press in 2002.

10. The historiography on this issue up to 1988 is discussed in several of the essays in my collection *The Arrogance of Race*.

Chapter 6

Originally published as "They'll Take Their Stand," in the *New York Review of Books*, May 25, 2006.

1. David Brion Davis, *The Problem of Slavery in Western Culture* (Ithaca, NY: Cornell University Press, 1966); *The Problem of Slavery in the Age of Revolution, 1770–1823* (Ithaca, NY: Cornell University Press, 1975). I reviewed the latter in the *New York Review of Books*, Oct. 16, 1975.

2. Eugene D. Genovese, *Roll, Jordan, Roll: The World the Slaves Made* (New York: Pantheon, 1974).

3. Elizabeth Fox-Genovese, *Within the Plantation Household: Black and White Women of the Old South* (Chapel Hill: University of North Carolina Press, 1988).

4. Eugene D. Genovese, *The World the Slaveholders Made: Two Essays in Interpretation* (New York: Pantheon, 1969).

5. Elizabeth Fox-Genovese and Eugene D. Genovese, *Fruits of Merchant Capital: Slavery and Bourgeois Property in the Rise and Expansion of Capitalism* (New York: Oxford University Press, 1983), reviewed by me in the *New York Review of Books*, Jan. 19, 1984.

6. Twelve Southerners, *I'll Take My Stand: The South and the Agrarian Tradition* (1930; Baton Rouge: Louisiana State University Press, 1977), pp. 166, 168.

Chapter 7

Originally published in the *New York Review of Books*, Mar. 25, 2004.

1. Ira Berlin, *Many Thousands Gone: The First Two Centuries of Slavery in North America* (Cambridge, MA: Belknap Press/Harvard University Press, 1998).

2. See Anthony S. Parent, *Foul Means: The Formation of a Slave Society in Virginia, 1660–1740* (Chapel Hill: University of North Carolina Press, 2003), for a thorough discussion of this transition.

3. Here I find myself in some disagreement with Garry Wills's book, *Negro President: Jefferson and the Slave Power* (Boston: Houghton Mifflin, 2003). Unlike Fehrenbacher, Wills views the three-fifths clause as a southern power grab rather than as a genuine compromise.

4. Fehrenbacher's *Prelude to Greatness: Lincoln in the 1850s* (Stanford, CA: Stanford University Press, 1962) remains the classic study of Lincoln's emergence as a national political figure and his influence on the ideological development of the Republican Party.

5. Lincoln's racial views changed significantly during the last two years of the war. By then the military contribution of black troops to the Union cause and the public response that it evoked made him more hopeful that racial equality could be achieved. See my book *Big Enough to Be Inconsistent: Abraham Lincoln Confronts Slavery and Race* (Cambridge, MA: Harvard University Press, 2008).

6. See my review of *The Black Family in Slavery and Freedom, 1750–1925* (New York: Pantheon, 1976) in the *New York Review of Books*, Sept. 30, 1976. Another new work that follows in this tradition and enlarges upon it by showing the relationship between the familialism of African Americans and their conceptions of property is Dylan C. Penningroth, *The Claims of Kinfolk: African American Property and Community in the Nineteenth-Century South* (Chapel Hill: University of North Carolina Press, 2003).

7. A critique of the dominant conception or "paradigm" of the black family, and the emphasis on "agency" to which it has given rise, can be found in a new book by a sociologist who specializes in the demographic history of Appalachia. See Wilma A. Dunaway, *The African-American Family in Slavery and Emancipation* (New York: Cambridge University Press, 2003), especially pp. 4–5, 268–74, 285. An earlier effort to redress the balance between agency and coerciveness was Norrece T. Jones, *Born a Child of Freedom Yet a Slave: Mechanisms of Control and Strategies of Resistance in Antebellum South Carolina* (Middletown, CT: Wesleyan University Press, 1990).

8. For a good example of this tendency, see the monumental and in many ways very impressive book by Steven Hahn, *A Nation under Our Feet: Black Political*

Struggles in the Rural South from Slavery to the Great Migration (Cambridge, MA: Belknap Press/Harvard University Press, 2003).

Chapter 8

Originally published in the *New York Review of Books*, July 14, 2005.

1. On France see Sue Peabody, *"There Are No Slaves in France": The Political Culture of Race and Slavery in the Ancien Régime* (New York: Oxford University Press, 1996).

2. On the Moravians see two excellent studies by Jon F. Sensbach, *A Separate Canaan: The Making of an Afro-Moravian World in North Carolina, 1763–1840* (Chapel Hill: University of North Carolina Press, 1998) and *Rebecca's Revival: Creating Black Christianity in the Atlantic World* (Cambridge, MA: Harvard University Press, 2005).

3. For a full account of this campaign see Adam Hochschild's narrative history, *Bury the Chains: Prophets and Rebels in the Fight to Free an Empire's Slaves* (Boston: Houghton Mifflin, 2005).

4. See James M. McPherson's review of three books on Brown in the *New York Review of Books*, May 12, 2005.

5. David S. Reynolds, *John Brown, Abolitionist: The Man Who Killed Slavery, Sparked the Civil War, and Seeded Civil Rights* (New York: Knopf, 2005), pp. 500–503.

Chapter 9

Originally published in the *New York Review of Books*, Aug. 10, 2006.

1. On the Mansfield decision, see Steven M. Wise, *Though the Heavens May Fall: The Landmark Trial That Led to the End of Human Slavery* (Cambridge, MA: Da Capo, 2005).

2. This is the conclusion that one is likely to reach from a reading of Adam Hochschild's recent and authoritative history of British antislavery, *Bury the Chains: Prophets and Rebels in the Fight to Free an Empire's Slaves* (Boston: Houghton Mifflin, 2005). The movement to abolish the slave trade did not really get off the ground until the mid- to late 1780s, when Thomas Clarkson and William Wilberforce assumed positions of leadership.

3. I am indebted for this suggestion to Jill Lepore's review of Pybus and Schama in the *New Yorker*, May 8, 2006, p. 78.

4. On Carter, see Andrew Levy, *The First Emancipator: The Forgotten Story of Robert Carter, the Founding Father Who Freed His Slaves* (New York: Random House, 2005).

Chapter 10

Originally published in *Modern Intellectual History* 1, no. 1 (2004), pp. 123–33.

1. This interest in McCune Smith was anticipated almost twenty years ago in a little-noticed article by David A. Blight, "In Search of Learning, Liberty, and

Self-Definition: James McCune Smith and the Ordeal of the Antebellum Black Intellectual," *Afro-Americans in New York Life and History* 9, no. 2 (July 1985), pp. 7–26.

2. See Stuckey's *Slave Culture: Nationalist Theory and the Foundations of Black America* (New York: Oxford University Press, 1987), and the introduction to his edited volume, *The Ideological Origins of Black Nationalism* (Boston: Beacon Press, 1972).

3. For uses of such a concept of racism for historical analysis, see George M. Fredrickson, *Racism: A Short History* (Princeton, NJ: Princeton University Press, 2002).

4. See Kwame Anthony Appiah, "Racisms," in *Anatomy of Racism*, ed. David Theo Goldberg (Minneapolis: University of Minnesota Press, 1990), pp. 4–5.

5. Leslie M. Harris, *In the Shadow of Slavery: African Americans in New York City, 1626–1863* (Chicago: University of Chicago Press, 2003), p. 206 and passim.

6. David R. Roediger, *The Wages of Whiteness: Race in the Making of the American Working Class* (London: Verso, 1991); Matthew Frye Jacobson, *Whiteness of a Different Color: European Immigrants and the Alchemy of Race* (Cambridge, MA: Harvard University Press, 1998).

Chapter 11

Originally published as "Still Separate and Unequal" in the *New York Review of Books,* Nov. 17, 2005.

1. See William Julius Wilson, *The Truly Disadvantaged: The Inner City, the Underclass, and Public Policy* (Chicago: University of Chicago Press, 1987), and *The Declining Significance of Race: Blacks and Changing American Institutions* (Chicago: University of Chicago Press, 1978).

2. The following historical survey is based on the book under review, supplemented by Terry H. Anderson, *The Pursuit of Fairness: A History of Affirmative Action* (New York: Oxford University Press, 2004).

3. For descriptions and assessments of the Philadelphia Plan, see John David Skrentny, *The Ironies of Affirmative Action: Politics, Culture and Justice in America* (Chicago: University of Chicago Press, 1996), pp. 193–211, and Anderson, *The Pursuit of Fairness*, pp. 111–40.

4. Philip F. Rubio makes this point in *A History of Affirmative Action, 1619–2000* (Jackson: University Press of Mississippi, 2001). But as his title indicates, he presents the New Deal's inequities as one of a series of episodes going back to the introduction of African slavery that collectively constituted affirmative action for whites, rather than giving the 1930s and 1940s the kind of unique and self-sufficient importance that Katznelson does.

5. See the works cited above by Wilson and also his *When Work Disappears: The World of the New Urban Poor* (New York: Knopf, 1996).

6. The best account of this development is Douglas S. Massey and Nancy A. Denton, *American Apartheid: Segregation and the Making of the Underclass* (Cambridge, MA: Harvard University Press, 1993).

7. According to Michael B. Katz, Mark J. Stern, and Jamie J. Fader, "The underwriting practices of federal agencies that insured mortgages introduced redlining, that

is, the refusal to lend to buyers in certain neighborhoods, which virtually destroyed central-city housing markets, froze blacks out of mortgages, and encouraged white flight to suburbs." See "The New African-American Inequality," *Journal of American History* 92, no. 1 (June 2005), p. 79.

8. This is the view of Hugh Davis Graham in *Collision Course: The Strange Convergence of Affirmative Action and Immigration Policy in America* (New York: Oxford University Press, 2002).

Chapter 12

Originally published in Charles V. Hamilton et al., eds., *Beyond Racism: Race and Inequality in Brazil, South Africa, and the United States* (Boulder, CO: Lynne Rienner Publishers, 2001), pp. 1–26.

1. Frank Tannenbaum, *Slave and Citizen: The Negro in the Americas* (New York: Alfred A. Knopf, 1946); Stanley M. Elkins, *Slavery: A Problem in American Institutional and Intellectual Life* (Chicago: University of Chicago Press, 1959).

2. Marvin Harris, *Patterns of Race in the Americas* (Westport, CT: Greenwood Press, 1964).

3. E. Franklin Frazier, *Race and Culture Contacts in the Modern World* (Boston: Beacon Press, 1957).

4. Louis Hartz, *The Founding of New Societies: Studies in the History of the United States, Latin America, South Africa, Canada, and Australia* (New York: Harcourt, Brace and World, 1964).

5. Joel Williamson, *New People: Miscegenation and Mulattoes in the United States* (New York: Free Press, 1980).

6. Pierre L. van den Berghe, *Race and Racism: A Comparative Perspective* (New York: Wiley, 1967).

7. George M. Fredrickson, *White Supremacy: A Comparative Study in American and South African History* (New York: Oxford University Press, 1981).

8. John Whitson Cell, *The Highest Stage of White Supremacy: The Origins of Segregation in South Africa and the American South* (New York: Cambridge University Press, 1982).

9. Stanley Greenberg, *Race and State in Capitalist Development: Comparative Perspectives* (New Haven: Yale University Press. 1980).

10. Herbert Blumer, "Industrialization and Race Relations," in *Industrialization and Race Relations: A Symposium*, ed. Guy Hunter (Oxford: Oxford University Press, 1965), pp. 228–53.

11. James T. Campbell, *Songs of Zion: The African Methodist Episcopal Church in the United States and South Africa* (New York: Oxford University Press, 1995).

12. George M. Fredrickson, *Black Liberation: A Comparative History of Black Ideologies in the United States and South Africa* (New York: Oxford University Press, 1995).

13. Florestan Fernandes, *Integração do negro na sociedade de classes* (1965); trans. Jacqueline D. Skiles, A. Brunel, and Arthur Rothwell, *The Negro in Brazilian Society* (New York: Columbia University Press, 1969).

14. Carl N. Degler, *Neither Black nor White: Slavery and Race Relations in Brazil and the United States* (New York: Macmillan, 1971).

15. George Reid Andrews, *Blacks and Whites in São Paulo, Brazil, 1888–1988* (Madison: University of Wisconsin Press, 1991), p. 4.

16. Kim Butler, *Freedoms Given, Freedoms Won: Afro-Brazilians in Post Abolition São Paulo and Salvador* (New Brunswick, NJ: Rutgers University Press, 1998).

17. Gay W. Seidman, *Manufacturing Militance: Workers' Movements in Brazil and South Africa, 1970–1985* (Berkeley: University of California Press, 1994).

18. Michael George Hanchard, *Orpheus and Power: The Movimento Negro of Rio de Janeiro and São Paulo, Brazil, 1945–1988* (Princeton, NJ: Princeton University Press, 1994).

19. Anthony W. Marx, *Making Race and Nation: A Comparison of South Africa, the United States, and Brazil* (Cambridge: Cambridge University Press, 1998).

20. Thomas E. Skidmore, *Black into White: Race and Nationality in Brazilian Thought* (New York: Oxford University Press, 1974).

Chapter 13

Originally published in Curtis Stokes et al., eds., *Race in 21st Century America* (East Lansing: Michigan State University Press, 2001), pp. 59–72.

1. Anthony W. Marx, *Making Race and Nation: A Comparison of the United States, South Africa and Brazil* (Cambridge: Cambridge University Press, 1998), pp. 269–74; Thomas E. Skidmore, "Bi-racial U.S.A. vs. Multi-racial Brazil: Is the Contrast Still Valid?" *Journal of Latin American Studies* 25 (1993), pp. 373–86; George M. Fredrickson, *Black Liberation: A Comparative Study of Black Ideologies in the United States and South Africa* (New York: Oxford University Press, 1995), pp. 319–23.

2. Paul Gilroy, *"There Ain't No Black in the Union Jack": The Cultural Politics of State and Nation* (Chicago: University of Chicago Press, 1988), p. 110.

3. See David Theo Goldberg, *Racist Culture: Philosophy and the Politics of Meaning* (Cambridge, MA: Blackwell, 1993), pp. 70–80 and passim, for an incisive analysis of "cultural race."

4. See Charles Taylor, *Multiculturalism: Examining the Politics of Recognition*, ed. and intro. Amy Gutman (Princeton, NJ: Princeton University Press, 1994).

5. Quoted in Stephan Thernstrom and Abigail Thernstrom, *America in Black and White: One Nation, Indivisible* (New York: Simon and Schuster, 1997), p. 33.

6. Martin Luther King, Jr., *Why We Can't Wait* (New York: Signet Books, 1964), p. 134. Johnson's speech is quoted in George M. Fredrickson, *The Comparative Imagination: On the History of Racism, Nationalism, and Social Movements* (Berkeley: University of California Press, 1997), p. 171.

7. Quoted in Thernstrom and Thernstrom, *America in Black and White*, p. 414.

8. Ibid., pp. 412–20, summarizes these cases.

9. Ibid. Thernstrom and Thernstrom argue strongly for the latter position.

10. See, for example, Andrew Hacker, *Two Nations: Black and White, Separate, Hostile, and Unequal* (New York: Scribner, 1992); Douglas S. Massey and Nancy A. Denton, *American Apartheid: Segregation and the Making of the Underclass* (Cambridge, MA: Harvard University Press, 1993); and David K. Shipler, *A Country of Strangers: Blacks and Whites in America* (New York: Alfred A. Knopf, 1997).

11. See J. Morgan Kousser, *Colorblind Injustice: Minority Voting Rights and the Undoing of the Second Reconstruction* (Chapel Hill: University of North Carolina Press, 1999).

12. Nicholas deB. Katzenbach and Burke Marshall, "Not Color Blind Just Blind," *New York Times Magazine*, Feb. 22, 1998, pp. 42–45. This essay argues convincingly, in my opinion, for the constitutionality of race-based policies.

13. The classical historical account and analysis of the contrast between Brazil's fluid three-category system of race relations and the rigid black-white dichotomy found in the United States is Carl N. Degler, *Neither Black nor White: Slavery and Race Relations in Brazil and the United States* (New York: Macmillan, 1971).

14. Evidence of these disadvantages can be found in a number of recent works. See especially France Winddance Twine, *Racism in a Racial Democracy: The Maintenance of White Supremacy in Brazil* (New Brunswick, NJ: Rutgers University Press, 1998); George Reid Andrews, *Blacks and Whites in São Paulo, Brazil, 1888–1988* (Madison: University of Wisconsin Press, 1991); and Pierre Michel Fontaine, ed., *Race, Class, and Power in Brazil* (Los Angeles: University of California Press, 1985).

15. Twine, *Racism in a Racial Democracy*, pp. 1, 60.

16. I. K. Sundiata, "Late Twentieth Century Patterns of Race Relations in Brazil and the United States," *Phylon* 68, no. 1 (1987), pp. 70, 74.

17. Thomas E. Skidmore, *Black into White: Race and Nationality in Brazilian Thought* (New York: Oxford University Press, 1974).

18. See Nancy Stepan, *"The Hour of Eugenics": Race, Gender, and Nation in Latin America* (Ithaca, NY: Cornell University Press, 1991), pp. 153–69.

19. Skidmore, *Black into White*, pp. 173–205; Twine, *Racism in a Racial Democracy*, pp. 6–9, 112–13.

20. Skidmore, "Bi-racial U.S.A. vs. Multi-racial Brazil," pp. 375–76; Florestan Fernandes, *The Negro in Brazilian Society*, trans. Jacqueline D. Skiles, A. Brunel, and Arthur Rothwell (New York: Atheneum, 1971).

21. See note 14 above. For evidence of the lack of a strong mulatto advantage over blacks, see appendix B of Andrews, *Blacks and Whites*, pp. 249–58. Several of the essays in Fontaine, ed., *Race, Class and Power*, offer data that contradict the racial democracy myth, as does Twine, *Racism in a Racial Democracy*. On regional differences, see Kim D. Butler, *Freedoms Given, Freedoms Won: Afro-Brazilians in Post-Abolition São Paulo and Salvador* (New Brunswick, NJ: Rutgers University Press, 1998).

22. See Pierre L. van den Berghe's pioneering *Race and Racism: A Comparative Perspective* (New York: John Wiley, 1967), which compares the United States and South Africa with Brazil and Mexico; and George M. Fredrickson, *White Supremacy: A Comparative Study in American and South African History* (New York: Oxford University Press, 1981).

23. See Saul DuBow, *Scientific Racism in Modern South Africa* (Cambridge: Cambridge University Press, 1995), pp. 246–83.

24. These developments are described and analyzed in Fredrickson, *Black Liberation*, pp. 237–52 and 277–86.

25. Ibid., pp. 297–313.

26. Quoted in ibid., p. 312.

27. Shula Marks, *The Tradition of Non-Racism in South Africa*, Eleanor Rathbone Memorial Lecture, Somerville College, Oxford, 1994 (Liverpool: Liverpool University Press, 1995).

28. An incisive analysis of the South African situation at the time of the election of June 2, 1999, is Mark Gevisser, "Seeking South Africa's Dream," *The Nation* 268 (June 7, 1999), pp. 19–22. See also Suzanne Daley, "South Africa: The Voters Realign the Opposition," *New York Times*, June 6, 1999, p. 14.

Chapter 14

Originally published in *Daedalus* 134, no. 1 (Winter 2005), pp. 88–101.

1. For a comparison of the two revolutions, see Patrice Higonnet, *Sister Republics: The Origins of French and American Republicanism* (Cambridge, MA: Harvard University Press, 1988).

2. See especially Liah Greenfeld, *Nationalism: Five Roads to Modernity* (Cambridge, MA: Harvard University Press, 1992).

3. Anthony D. Smith, *The Ethnic Origins of Nations* (Oxford: Blackwell, 1986), p. 149.

4. Gary S. Cross, *Immigrant Workers in Industrial France: The Making of a New Laboring Class* (Philadelphia: Temple University Press, 1983). On French immigration more generally, see Gérard Noiriel, *The French Melting Pot: Immigration, Citizenship, and National Identity* (Minneapolis: University of Minnesota Press, 1996).

5. John Higham employed the term "nativism" in his classic study of anti-immigrant movements in the United States, *Strangers in the Land: Patterns of American Nativism, 1860–1925*, rev. ed. (New Brunswick, NJ: Rutgers University Press, 1988). Miriam Feldblum applies the term to France in *Reconstructing Citizenship: The Politics of Nationality Reform and Immigration in Contemporary France* (Albany: State University Press of New York, 1999), pp. 52–53. The closest French equivalent is *xénophobie* (xenophobia). What Americans might call "nativism" is often subsumed by the French under a loose conception of "racism."

6. See Suzanne Citron, *Le Mythe national: L'Histoire de France en question* (Paris: Edition Ouvriéres, 1987).

7. Quoted in Higonnet, *Sister Republics*, pp. 166–67.

8. David Brion Davis makes this point in *Revolutions: Reflections on American Equality and Foreign Liberations* (Cambridge, MA: Harvard University Press, 1990), p. 11.

9. See Jean-Louis Ormières, *Politique et religion en France* (Brussels: Complexe, 2002), and Guy Coq, *Laïcité et république: Le Lien nécessaire* (Paris: Editions du Félin, 1995).

10. Elaine Sciolino, "French Islam Wins Officially Recognized Voice," *New York Times*, Apr. 14, 2003.

11. See Michel Winock, *Nationalism, Anti-Semitism, and Fascism in France* (Stanford, CA: Stanford University Press, 1998).

12. Sue Peabody, *There Are No Slaves in France: The Political Culture of Race and Slavery in the Ancien Régime* (New York: Oxford University Press, 1996).

13. Ibid., pp. 116–18.

14. Robin Blackburn, *The Overthrow of Colonial Slavery, 1776–1848* (London: Verso, 1988), pp. 528–29.

15. Lawrence C. Jennings, *French Anti-Slavery: The Movement for the Abolition of Slavery in France, 1802–1848* (Cambridge: Cambridge University Press, 2000), pp. 278–84.

16. Citron, *Mythe national*, pp. 62–63.

17. See Cross, *Immigrant Workers in Industrial France*.

18. Noiriel, *The French Melting Pot*, p. 259.

19. Quoted in Winock, *Nationalism, Anti-Semitism, and Fascism in France*, p. 133. See also Frederic Cople Jaher, *The Jews and the Nation: Revolution, Emancipation, State Formation, and the Liberal Paradigm in America and France* (Princeton, NJ: Princeton University Press, 2002).

20. Peabody, *There Are No Slaves in France*, pp. 128–31. For a variety of perspectives on French attitudes toward color and race, see also Peabody and Tyler Stovall, eds., *The Color of Liberty: Histories of Race in France* (Durham, NC: Duke University Press, 2003).

21. Jonathan K. Gosnell, The *Politics of Frenchness in Colonial Algeria, 1930–1954* (Rochester, NY: Rochester University Press, 2005), pp. 24, 160ff.

22. Alice L. Conklin, *A Mission to Civilize: The Republican Idea of Empire in France and West Africa, 1895–1930* (Stanford, CA: Stanford University Press, 1997), pp. 76–77.

23. Ibid., passim.

24. On how and why this occurred, see especially Feldblum, *Reconstructing Citizenship*.

25. See Patricia M. E. Lorcin, *Imperial Identities: Stereotyping Prejudice and Race in Colonial Algeria* (London: I. B. Tauris, 1995).

Chapter 15

Originally published in the *International Social Science Journal* 57, no. 183 (March 2005), pp. 103–12.

1. S. Kaplan, "The Miscegenation Issue in the Election of 1864," *Journal of Negro History* 34 (1949), pp. 274–343.

2. Kwame Anthony Appiah, "Racisms," in *Anatomy of Racism*, ed. David Theo Goldberg (Minneapolis: University of Minnesota Press, 1990), pp. 4–5; George M. Fredrickson, *Racism: A Short History* (Princeton, NJ: Princeton University Press, 2002), pp. 153–56.

3. On Gobineau, see Tzvetan Todorov, *Nous et les autres: La Réflexion française sur la diversité humaine* (Paris: Seuil, 1989), pp. 129–40. [*On Human Diversity: Nationalism, Racism, and Exoticism in French Thought* (Cambridge, MA: Harvard University Press, 1993).]

4. This pattern is well described in Joel Williamson, *New People: Mulattoes and Miscegenation in the United States* (New York: Free Press, 1980), and in several of the selections in Werner Sollors, ed., *Interracialism: Black-White Intermarriage in American History, Literature, and Law* (New York: Oxford University Press, 2000).

5. See Fredrickson, *Racism*, pp. 102, 112.

6. George M. Fredrickson, *White Supremacy: A Comparative Study in American and South African History* (New York: Oxford University Press, 1981), pp. 108–10.

7. Williamson, *New People*.

8. The classic study is H. Hoetink, *The Two Variants of Caribbean Race Relations: A Contribution to the Sociology of Segmented Societies* (Oxford: Oxford University Press, 1967).

9. Fredrickson, *White Supremacy*, pp. 99–108.

10. Fredrickson, *White Supremacy*; Williamson, *New People*.

11. Fredrickson, *White Supremacy*, pp. 110–12.

12. The fullest account of the legal position of people of color and intermarriage during the slave era in the French Antilles is Y. Debbasch, *Couleur et liberté: Le Jeu du critère ethnique dans un ordre juridique esclavagiste* (Paris, 1967), especially pp. 44–49, 72–73. For a brief account of the racial situation in Saint-Domingue before the revolution, see John Garrigus, "Race, Gender, and Virtue in Haiti's Failed Foundation Fiction," in *The Color of Liberty: Histories of Race in France*, ed. Sue Peabody and Tyler Stovall (Durham, NC: Duke University Press, 2003).

13. Debbasch, *Couleur et liberté*, pp. 53–105; Garrigus, "Race," pp. 75–79. A contemporary reflection of the hardening of racial attitudes among the white elite in Haiti just before the revolution is M. L. E. Moreau de Saint-Méry in *A Civilization That Perished: The Last Years of Colonial Rule in Haiti*, ed. Ivor D. Spencer (Lanham, MD: University Press of America, 1985).

14. Sue Peabody, *"There Are No Slaves in France": The Political Culture of Race and Slavery in the Ancien Régime* (New York: Oxford University Press, 1996), pp. 74–76, 111–20, 128–31.

15. The fullest account of eighteenth-century French thought on racial differences among the domestic population continues to be Jacques Barzun, *The French Race* (1932; Port Washington, NY: Kennikat Press, 1966). See also Jean-Loup Amselle, *Vers un multiculturalisme français: L'Empire de la coutume* (Paris: Aubier, 1996). [*Affirmative Exclusion: Cultural Pluralism and the Rule of Custom in France* (Ithaca, NY: Cornell University Press, 2003).]

16. Amselle, *Vers un multiculturalisme français*, pp. 32–76.

17. For evidence of such a conception in the writings of thinkers like Renan and Michelet, see Todorov, *Nous et les autres*.

18. Amselle, *Vers un multiculturalisme français*, pp. 33–34; Alyssa Goldstein Sepinwall, "Eliminating Race, Eliminating Difference: Blacks, Jews, and the Abbé Grégoire," in *The Color of Liberty*, ed. Peabody and Stovall, pp. 28–41.

19. George M. Fredrickson, *The Black Image in the White Mind: The Debate on Afro-American Character and Destiny, 1817–1914* (Middletown, CT: Wesleyan University Press, 1987 [orig. pub. 1971]), pp. 97–129.

20. An intriguing example is G. D'Eichtal and I. Urbain, *Lettres sur la race noire et la race blanche* (Paris, 1839).

21. Fredrickson, *Black Image*, pp. 71–96; William S. Stanton, *The Leopard's Spots: Scientific Attitudes toward Race in America, 1815–1859* (Chicago: University of Chicago Press, 1960).

22. Claude Blanckaert, "Of Monstrous Métis? Hybridity, Fear of Miscegenation, and Patriotism," in *The Color of Liberty*, ed. Peabody and Stovall, pp. 61–64.

23. Blanckaert, "Of Monstrous Métis?" pp. 46–47; Fredrickson, *Racism*, pp. 67–68.

24. Fredrickson, *Black Image*, pp. 228–55.

25. Alice L. Conklin, *A Mission to Civilize: The Republican Idea of Empire in France and West Africa* (Stanford, CA: Stanford University Press, 1997), pp. 20–21.

26. Owen White, *Children of the French Empire: Miscegenation and Colonial Society in French West Africa, 1895–1960* (Oxford: Oxford University Press, 1999), pp. 15–16.

27. White, *Children*, p. 51.

28. The extent to which neo-Lamarckism impeded the French acceptance of strict hereditarianism in the early twentieth century is evident in William H. Schneider's account of the French eugenics movement, *Quality and Quantity: The Quest for Biological Regeneration in Twentieth-Century France* (Cambridge: Cambridge University Press, 1990).

29. Matthew Frye Jacobson, *Barbarian Virtues: The United States Encounters Foreign Peoples at Home and Abroad, 1876–1917* (New York: Hill and Wang, 2000).

30. Sollors, *Interracialism*, pp. 30, 55, 480.

31. Hannah Arendt, "Reflections on Little Rock" (1959; reprinted in Sollors, *Interracialism*, pp. 492–501).

32. Joel Perlmann, "Reflecting the Changing Face of America: Multiracials, Racial Classification, and American Intermarriage," in Sollors, *Interracialism*, pp. 506–33.

33. Ibid., p. 514.

34. George M. Fredrickson, "America's Diversity in Comparative Perspective," *Journal of American History* 95, no. 3 (1998), p. 875.

35. Ira Berlin, *Generations of Captivity: A History of African Slaves* (New York: Belknap Press, 2003), p. 42; Debbasch, *Couleur et liberté*, p. 47; N. Schmidt, *Histoire du métissage* (Paris: La Martinière, 2003), pp. 77, 91.

36. Jean-Philippe Mathy, *French Resistance: The French-American Culture Wars* (Minneapolis: University of Minnesota Press, 2000), pp. 114–15.

INDEX

ABOUT THE AUTHOR

The late George M. Fredrickson was Edgar E. Robinson Professor of United States History Emeritus at Stanford University. He was a former president of the Organization of American Historians and was author of several books, including the prize-winning *White Supremacy: A Comparative Study of American and South African History; The Black Image in the White Mind: The Debate on Afro-American Character and Destiny, 1817–1914; The Comparative Imagination: On Racism, Nationalism, and Social Movements;* and *Racism: A Short History*, which has been translated into five languages. He was elected to the American Academy of Arts and Sciences in 1986 and delivered the W. E. B. DuBois lectures at Harvard in 2006, which were published in *Big Enough to Be Inconsistent: Abraham Lincoln Confronts Slavery and Race* (Cambridge, MA: Harvard University Press, 2008).